Three Dead Dogs

A Short Story Collection

by Barry Jacques

Worry over money and your heart will never find ease,
Worry about what others think and a slave is all you'll be to the opinions of others.
Worry not too much in this life;
you'll be dead long enough in the end, and can worry about anything you might have missed worrying about then.

Stories

The Bus to Ballybeg

With her eyes closed, Maisie Brennan mentally ticked off the items on her 'to do' list. Home six weeks, having returned to spend some time with her mother whose cancer had returned, after what the family had believed to be a successful treatment some five years earlier, she assured herself every passing day that she would return to London once everything settled down. Her assurance calmed her mind, but it didn't feel like it would be anytime very soon. Luckily for Maisie, she was between jobs and could just about afford to squeeze a couple of months in for her family's needs.

Having finally managed to get out for a run the previous evening, her first bit of exercise since she got back, Maisie had jogged and trumped her way noisily around the ring road near the rectangular plot of the housing estate on which her mother lived. The soft boiled vegetables of her mother's kitchen had caught up with her, and she resolved on the run to take back control of her own diet; even with her illness returned, her mother retained a firm grip on all happenings in her kitchen, and a row had been needed for Maisie to get her way, just for an evening.

Maisie's mind ticked small boxes that she made in a mock menu in her head; oblivious for a few precious minutes to the world around her, she hummed pleasurably at her own dreaming thoughts.

Looking over at her, and then at the basket of groceries disdainfully, her mother shook her head; still in a strop that her own food was no longer good enough for her own blood, a stubborn streak cut deeply through her veins, and despite her awareness of the short time she had left to live, she wasted much of it sulking about things that didn't matter.

Maisie caught the movement of her mother's sniffy survey, but said nothing.

Sometimes it was best just to keep quiet and leave people have their cranky time. They set off for the bus near the Clock Tower on The Quay shortly after Maisie had grabbed some extra provisions for the week from the independent health shop. Remaining outside, looking in, and not recognising any of the brands or products; other than commenting on how expensive it all was, with a couple of emphasising sniffs and snorts thrown in, her mother had more or less managed to control her disapproval of the whole affair.

Having forgotten how many blind eyes being at home brought with it, the run had helped her sanity; it cleared her mind and allowed her to focus on the bigger picture. Despite the tension, she linked her mother's arm and steered them both along The Quay to the bus stop; poking random, distracting questions about small changes she'd noticed since she got back along the way, Maisie filled the brooding quietness her mother was setting between them.

Rolling up next to them as they reached the stop, they stepped aboard the bus with a couple of others, and were happy and relieved not to have a wait in the changeable weather; more used to the

3

crowded buses of London, Maisie was also pleased to get seats. Oddly, her mother fussed about having to sit on the outside away from the window, and Maisie, lost as to what she was going on about, or when such a thing had become an issue, changed places with her once the bus came to the next stop—she hoped it would keep her happy, or at least quiet. The day felt as though it was darkening, and for Maisie, it wasn't just the weather.

"I don't like them at all, that lot," her mother's mouth curled in distaste to emphasise the depth of her feelings about whatever had come wanting within her scrutiny. "I don't think they should be here," she hesitated briefly as though uncertain before continuing, assertively. "No! They shouldn't be here."

"Who?" Maisie enquired, uncertain who or what her mother was speaking so vehemently of, as there were only six or seven people on the bus that she could see, and most of those were elderly people on their way back home from visiting the city centre.

"Those," her eyes met Maisie's; their shift drifted slowly with a cinematic pan of her head to the newspaper the man in front of them was reading.

"I need me glasses, girl. I can't see anything from this far away. You know my eyes have always been rubbish. God, these days I'm lucky to be able to find me way home. God's sake, mam, I'm always going wrong in London. What does it say? Read it out to me," Maisie suspected the gripe was nonsense and found herself disinclined to make the effort to lean forward and read it.

Maura Brennan, her mother, at thirty would have accepted six score years as a not inconsiderable life-span; she had seen many changes in her world, albeit a world of limited range, or even ranging—Maura's spirit of adventure had been smothered by a more dominant and resolute spirit of timidity and conservatism—and many of the changes she'd witnessed were of the variety Maura would have preferred not to have occurred. She mouthed a word without sound, but Maisie's eyes were no better at reading lips than they were at reading a newspaper three or four feet from her face, which was vibrating in the movement of the bus too; she shook her head, and drew her lips downwards in a sad clownish face to indicate Maura's lack of success in communicating.

"Immigrants," Maura whispered audibly, and shifted her eyes as though the word had leaked from elsewhere.

Nothing wrong with Maisie's hearing, she looked at her mother in surprise.

"Immigrants?" She repeated the word loudly and clearly, to ensure there had been no misunderstanding. "What about 'immigrants'?"

"I don't like them," quivering, and indicating with a downward nod to indicate Maisie should speak lower, Maura leaned closer. "They shouldn't be here."

"How do you know you don't like them?" Not the type to care who heard her, Maisie leaned back and looked more closely into her mother's eyes. "It's not like there's any out our way now, is it?"

Maura said nothing, but her right eye darted a suspicious look at Maisie.

"Which of them don't you like?" With her curiosity piqued, Maisie thought to investigate the hitherto unbroached topic further.

"None of them," Maura ambiguously replied.

"None of them?" Maisie looked at her questioningly, "You don't like 'any' of them—is that what you're telling me?"

Maura nodded; she pursed her lips and lifted one eye as she angled her head forwards and slightly sideways to meet and hold Maisie's gaze. Rubbing her face and nose, she used her hand to further hide her mouth.

"Especially them Nigerian ones," she confided her specific dislike of Nigerians discreetly, lest the man reading the newspaper in the seat in front of them hear, or in case of the unannounced presence of a lip-reader aboard the bus.

"The Nigerians?" Maisie pondered her odd disaffection with a people by and large absent from the island, with perhaps a small exception around parts of Dublin. "What have the Nigerians done to you, that you don't like them, so specifically?"

Raising both of her eyebrows, Maura tilted her head away from Maisie towards the window; it was unlikely in Maisie's mind that Maura had ever even spoken to a Nigerian, male or female, or child for that matter. What they might have done to put her mother out intrigued her.

"Is it because they're black?" Maisie asked.

"Shhh! Of course it's not!" Aghast at Maisie's words, Maura's retort was an unholy combination of defensiveness and mortification. "I'm not a racialist Maisie, no matter what you might think."

"Racist," Maisie moved her head to look at three motorbikes that had pulled up next to the bus as they slowed for the lights.

"What?" Maura queried, "What are you saying? Are you calling me-,"

"The word—it's racist, not racialist, mam. At least that's what I think it is now anyway," holding her patience, but a little irked, Maisie scrutinised the three bikers beyond her mother's window but gave up once she realised that nothing seemed familiar about them. Snippets of her past slipped across her thoughts, causing her to smile before her mother's voice intruded once more.

"Well, I'm not one of them! I'm not a 'racialist' or a 'racist'. I just don't like them Nigerians coming here, that's all," starting louder than she'd anticipated, Maura's voice lowered to a whisper as she sought emphasis for the target of her displeasure.

Quietening for a moment, they held their peace; the man in front of them closed his paper, and the bus slowed, edging its way inwards to the kerbside bus-stop out of the slow-moving city traffic. Tall, slim, and wearing an expensive grey wool coat, beneath his left arm he tucked a small man-brolley, folded the paper he'd been reading, stepped out of the seat and made his way to the doors. Glancing back through the rear window, he noticed both women's eyes following his movements and half-smiled politely before stepping off the bus.

"That fellow should've walked those couple of stops," Maura couldn't help herself, and the comment slipped out before her brain had put a rein on it.

"What?" Maisie counted backwards from twenty-five in her head.

"He's only a young man. At his age, he should've walked rather than getting on the bus—didn't he only get on near the Clock Tower with us, and we've only gone along two stops? Young people today are all so lazy," her eyes followed the direction the young man had headed off in, as though she hoped the wisdom of her words would somehow seek him out.

"Maybe he thought it was going to rain, mam," grimacing as she glanced at the descending gloom outside the bus window, Maisie tried to make light of it.

"Well it hasn't, has it?" Maura was in no mood to have her griping defied.

"No, it hasn't, but maybe he-! Oh, forget it! I don't know why I'm even bothering," losing interest in wherever her mother was trying to take the conversation, Maisie took her thoughts inwards. Not dealing with her news well, it seemed to be setting her mother against the world at large. Trying to forget about it, she gave some more thoughts to her intended pancake; Maisie decided she was going to have two of them to herself, as she suspected that she'd probably have to wrestle her mother to get back in front of the cooker again.

"There you go. Look! Now! That's what I was talking about," elbowing her sharply, Maura nodded towards the window, and took Maisie's thoughts back to the bus.

Annoyed with the sharpness of her mother's poke, Maisie looked out. In the bus shelter an African woman and her small child sat on the plastic bench awaiting another bus; with her focus locked on her phone, the woman's face held no expression other than the slightly mad looking eyes of a person staring at a screen. Chewing on a long, pink flat chewy sweet, with the sticky wrapper pulled down over her fingers, the small child swung her feet beneath the seat and banged them obliviously against the metal wall of the shelter as she watched the bus before her.

Maisie looked back to Maura.

"'What? What am I supposed to be looking at?" She asked.

"You see?" Casting another sideward glance at the woman and child before nodding knowingly at a silent Maisie, as the bus pulled out into the traffic once more Maura sniffed haughtily as though a point had been proven, before speaking once more. "They come here and have their children all over the place. Dozens of them. All of them. 'That's' what I was on about! You saw it for yourself."

"Dozens?" Maisie checked and put her hand firmly on her mother's knee. "There was only 'one' child there that I could see, mam?"

"That's not the point," Maura's eyes glared at Maisie's grip; she could feel how firm her daughter was holding her, and the small shake Maisie pressed was what a grown woman might impose upon a child. "You know it as well as I do. It's been in all the papers as well."

"What has? What is the point?" Maisie shook her head in confusion. "You don't read the papers, mam? Unless you count looking over that fellow's shoulder as reading the papers, or those problem pages in the magazines that you love?"

"They were talking about it on the radio too. On WLR. Did you hear that?" Maura tsked her impatience at Maisie's obstreperous reply.

"When?" Riled by her mother's stubborn behaviour, Maisie no longer felt the inclination to let the matter drop. "I can only listen to WLR when I'm here, and I haven't heard anything or anybody complaining about Nigerians? What did they say?

What programme was it? We can listen to it together on my laptop when we get in."

"Oh, I can't remember all of it now. My head's too full of stuff with everything that's going on," with a slow, sad shake of her head, Maura sighed and allowed her eyes to glass over; her comments had been meant as flippant, off-hand remarks to justify her mood as originating in more than her illness. Maisie had always been like a dog with a bone when arguments stirred, and she'd forgotten how little her daughter left anyone off with—she hadn't realised that 'Nigerians' were another of the things Maisie was defensive about, so Maura sought to move away from specifics to the general. "They were giving out about all them immigrants though, and what I was saying, you know, all the babies and that."

"What were they saying? What were they saying about Nigerians? What exactly was it they were giving out about them?" Maisie pressed her mother on her original comments.

"No no, not just them. The other ones too, you know. The Poles and the other ones from over that way," waving her hand vaguely, Maura dismissed the north-eastern continent of Europe with a few wrist flicks.

"What—the Latvians? Lithuanians? Estonians?" Maisie could tell her mother was floundering, but inside she felt she deserved little quarter, so continued pressing her gently, and Maura nodded, casting her eyes upwards in despair.

"What?" Maisie held her palms out.

"What?" Maura looked at her daughter's hands in confusion.

"The Latvians," waiting until her mother's eyes met hers before she spoke again, when she did, she purposely spoke the words slowly and enunciated clearly. "I said Latvians, and you cast your eyes to heaven? What's up with them? What is up with the Latvians?"

"They shouldn't be here either," Maura's ire was up again. Maisie really should have left this go by now. At this stage, she was just looking for a fight. A daughter wasn't supposed to treat her mother in this way. Maura dry-washed her hands, before brushing imaginary dust from her leg; she could still feel where Maisie had gripped in that vice-grip earlier and thought her daughter should show more consideration of her condition. "I mean … we're only a tiny country, Maisie. We can't be having everybody come living here. We don't have enough houses or jobs for ourselves, and our children too, we don't have enough jobs for them either, Maisie. Look at you! They should stay in their own countries. It's too much to be expecting of everyone these days. Too much!"

Looking out the window, once the bus came into the more open expanse of the Cork Road and began to speed up, Maisie watched as an unmoving lead blanket of cloud hung across the entire sky, and beneath this, a darker cloud layer roiled threateningly, promising imminent heavy rain; Maisie hoped the heavens wouldn't open just as they got off the bus out by the college—it was still a ten-minute walk home from there, and neither of them had taken an umbrella. Maisie hummed a ditty to herself to take her mind off things and tried to find her way back to her imaginary pancake; they'd only popped into the City centre to pay for the bin collections over the coming months, and for Maisie to grab a few ingredients to make her own life easier. Maura hadn't wanted to stop for a coffee, as she thought the prices ridiculous—Maisie found herself unable to disagree about the prices—but unwilling to maintain her cold-turkey caffeine abstinence Maisie had nevertheless grabbed an espresso and downed it in a gulp. A bewildered Maura had watched the transaction scrupulously; her nose had twitched like an irritated dog's tail as her mind replayed it. The size of the espresso had left her flummoxed; feeling out of her depth, and as though she might have missed something, by the time she'd got the whole thing clear in her mind, too much time had passed for her to make a comment. Once the collections were paid for, they'd grabbed the few groceries Maisie wanted and got straight back on the bus.

"How's himself doing at the moment? I haven't seen him much since I got back," Maisie shifted the topic to her father.

"Oh! Don't ask. Same as ever, I suppose," shaking her head with a look of the eternally disappointed, Maura's thin lips tightened and were nearly white at the edges.

"What now?" Maisie recognised the tone.

"Well … he's back on the stout. For starters. Big time again. The bottled stuff too! That's probably why you haven't seen him. You've been in bed early, or out with Joanne and Clare," Maisie nodded agreeably but remained silent, certain there was more to come.

"He had to go back in to see your man over in Ballybricken about a week back," Maura continued, after a pause to gather her thoughts.

"Who—Dr Chowdri? Is he still there?" Maisie checked.

"Oh he swears by that fella now, especially since he helped him with the gout," Maura expanded. "His piles came back worse than ever though, so he thought he'd give your man a go for those too. I told him years ago it was that stout, but you know what he's like."

Maisie nodded and leaned across her mother to look out briefly; her breath fogged the window as she looked up at the grey cloud shroud. 'No problem with Asians then?' she thought to herself. Distantly, she could see rain falling already, and winced a little at her own reflection before sitting back.

"He lassoed them all apparently, and now they're all beginning to fall off," Maura's eyes followed Maisie's, and also showed concern for the imminent squall.

"What?" Maisie's distracted thoughts processed the words. "Did you say, he lassoed them all?"

"Oh, that's what he said," Maura nodded and shrugged her own bemusement. "It's a kind of knot you see, and they put it around the—you know? The things? They lasso them like the cows in the films."

"The grapes? The pile grapes? They lasso the grapes hanging out of his arse?" Maisie snorted, and both of them held themselves as they chuckled at the thought of it.

"That's how they do it apparently?" Maura confirmed the feedback from her husband. "Then, don't they just fall off after a few weeks or so. Or so himself said, anyway."

"Well. That's a new one on me," for a few moments they both chuckled some more and shook their heads in wonder at the medical world.

"Have you heard from Eamonn this week?" Maisie looked forward to the front of the bus where the driver had switched on his intermittent screen wipers—the rain had caught up with them, or they'd caught up with a shower ahead of them. Catching her movement, the driver smiled at her in his magnified internal mirror.

"Oh, I did. I did—he rang me last Saturday. Half-cut as usual, that fella—after twelve here too, so it was, and he said he was only on his way out. He's loving it there, isn't he? Loving it! That fella he knew, what's his name … Aidan Power is it? Yeah, him from up the way, you know him? Or his brother? You knew his brother—he's your age, isn't he? He met up with him and his buddies, and they've sorted a job out for Eamonn in the hotel. Everyone is 'buddy' now. Buddy-this and buddy-that! He's some chancer. Cracks me up, but he thinks he's landed on his feet. There's loads of chefs and under-chefs he says; apparently, the place is huge too, so he's saying he's had a great break and it'll put him on the road. Loves Chicago, doesn't he? I don't think your brother will ever come back from America now. Maybe next year, for my funeral, he'll come over? Who knows though? He mightn't even make that the way things are. They're getting an apartment too he said. Just a small one, you know. I don't know what that Paula is up to though—it was so late, and I didn't want to keep him talking too long. Always been cute, that one, so I think she'll get another job in no time; she'd buy and sell our Eamonn before she's had her breakfast, wouldn't she?"

"Come on, Mam," pressing the bell on the pole, Maisie stood up and sucked her teeth as she looked out. "We might be lucky, and get across to the house before it starts for real."

Inching her frame along the seat before standing up; no longer as strong now, she found it too difficult to stand on a moving bus. Maisie should have waited for the bus to stop, she thought. Fixing herself while Maisie waited, the driver watched her through his internal mirror and smiled again at Maisie as he did so. They shouted their thanks as they stepped off the bus and the doors behind them swooshed closed; the bus eased back out into the sparse traffic of the outskirts.

Looking up to the sky, Maisie yelped and linked their arms to scurry them along the exposed path across the green as fast as Maura's older legs could shuffle.

Watching the two women across the open space, Daniel Bartos was surprised that the girl got off where she had; from her looks, he expected that she'd stay on the bus until it had looped around at the top and had begun moving back towards the town along Paddy Brown's Road. Ballybeg wasn't one of his favoured areas. None of his friends liked it either. It wasn't the kind of place in which you could just wander about at night. It wasn't the kind of place you would wander about at night. 'Rough as rats, that place', his Irish friend Liam always said, and Monika, Liam's wife, backed him up. She always shook her head in distaste. Here longer than he was, and like a local now, Monika had said it was cheap to rent there, but she recommended that

Daniel and his new girlfriend should pay the extra to live on the east side. Too many Tinkers settled there now, Daniel thought, smiling at his own thoughts and his use of the Irish word. Too many Tinkers. Tinkers, Gypsies, Knackers—were they all the same thing? People here made the same face. Maybe when they met up for a beer, he'd ask Liam if there was a difference between the three.

***

Mushroom & Asparagus Pancake

Ingredients
Pancake
100g plain flour
2 large eggs
300ml milk (your choice)
salt plus 1tbsp rapeseed oil (plus frying splash)

Filling
8 asparagus spears, very lightly steamed then sliced
lengthways (otherwise use slim asparagus tip and
just add a few extra to each pancake)
1 leek, topped, tailed, washed and sliced
250g field/chestnut mushrooms - wiped and finely
sliced
(or if you're feeling more adventurous and want to
impress, soak a pack of mixed dried wild
mushrooms for 15 minutes in boiling water before
squeezing them dry and follow the rest as normal)
1 onion, finely chopped
5 cloves of garlic, crushed
100g fresh baby spinach - washed
50g of Cheddar/Parmigiano or hard goat's cheese
(your preference) grated

Prepping the Pancake mix
Put the flour into a decent sized mixing bowl, add
the amount of salt you'd like (a good sprinkling from
a cellar or quarter of a teaspoon), make a well in the
middle and crack both eggs into this. Add a little
milk and the tiny splash of rapeseed oil and begin to
whisk it into a thick batter. Add more milk as you go
along and eventually you'll end up with a nice

aerated batter mix. Set aside, and turn your attention now to the filling. This shouldn't take more than fifteen twenty minutes from prep to finish, which will give the pancake mix plenty of time to allow molecular chemistry to work its wonders.

Making the Filling

Sweat the onion for a few minutes, add the leek and a couple of minutes later add the garlic. Mix them in for a minute, and toss in the mushrooms. Cover and allow the mushrooms to sweat for a few minutes before removing the cover and letting the released moisture to steam off. Once the moisture has reduced, remove from the heat, add the spinach and fold it in, replacing the cover to keep some residual heat and allowing the spinach to sweat and shrink.

Making the Pancake

Put a wide heavy-based frying pan on the heat and make it hot! With a pancake, you're looking to seal everything pretty quickly. Add a splash of oil and a small bit of butter and with a piece of kitchen towel, spread it quickly to all corners of the pan (I know there are no corners in circular pans, but indulge me). Using a ladle, scoop a good dollop into the centre of the pan and tilt it all ways to spread it as far as you can. Add a little more and do the same filling the pan base. Allow to seal for a minute or two, shake the pan and feel it move. The top should also no longer look moist. Have a peep underneath and if it's browning, flip it. Once flipped, gently press with your turner/egg-flip flat utensil and encourage it to flatten and expand. When happy it's as big as you want, flip in once more before placing it on a warm and lightly oiled oven tray. Place a quarter of the filling along its length, near to one end than the other, add just under a quarter of the cheese, roll it, and add a little cheese again to the top to help it stick closed. Cover with foil and put in the bottom of a warm oven. Repeat the process three more times!

Serve with buttery sea salted Anya potatoes, and a side salad, or steamed broad beans.

***

Hole-in-One

Hank tossed a two-bit coin high in the air, and then waited patiently as it bounced and rolled, annoyingly, beneath the angled commercial blinds of his office.

Looking once more to the claim forms before him, Hank reminded himself of the claimant's name before rising to find the coin.

"Heads you get it," he spoke directly to the form, as he pushed off his seat, and made his way towards the window.

A regular game for Hank, bread and butter low-level claims were like that. Hell, some of these people lived near two hundred miles away in rural spots he'd never have found without his satnav. The gas, his time and his feeding, not to mention any contrary contestation that might occur, and also not to mention any potential re-visits—those things alone probably cost the company more than half the claims made. Most people weren't even aware of their own excess charges.

Hank understood numbers.

"Tails you don't," Hank mumbled, as he bent over to shunt the blinds aside. "Heads it is Mrs Coping! Congratulations, you get what you asked for."

On Mrs Coping's side all along, in his own mind, there wasn't really a mean bone in Hank O' Keefe's body. Percentage games he understood— had always understood. Mrs Coping's premium increase would recover some of the monies paid out over the next few years. Her satisfaction and continued loyalty to the scheme would cover it in one most likely. Everybody was happy with everybody else, and that, Hank felt, was the way things should be.

Now that he was standing, Hank couldn't resist picking his Odyssey White two ball putter from where it leaned against the wall. Sending one of his favoured Pro V1's smoothly along the carpet to clip the edge of a small tumbler he kept resident on the floor at the other side of the room, Hank groaned at the near miss. Finding his groove for the season. 'Putt for dough!', that was Hank's motto; rarely a day passed that Hank didn't send thirty or forty balls towards that tumbler. For Hank, it was all about the rhythm and feel.

As a young man, Hank would have read and re-read Mrs. Coping's claim form, and any comments she might have made—multiple times too. After those readings, Hank would've sat, closed his eyes to allow his mind to form an image of whomever his company's customer happened to be, knowing full well he'd most likely met her, or him, at some stage, and Hank would've imagined the words they might have used, against those they actually used on the company claim form. This wasn't near as onerous a task as you might imagine. Hank, his sister Arla, and Hank's brother-in-law, Arla's husband, Nathan Bodamer, these three were the company's sole senior regional employees, and they covered pretty much a quarter of the Wisconsin district west of Madison. All three had agreed to use the same method over the years, and in the early days shared pretty much everything they knew, about everybody they'd met, and specifically those they happened to sell a policy to. Bodamer had come out of Milwaukee, so he wasn't Madison born, but he still caught on quick, and Hank knew, that in truth, he didn't have a better friend than his Milwaukee-born brother-in-law. Bodamer brought their client base from the hundreds well into the thousands now, and Hank felt that when the numbers got bigger, the percentages were ever more predictable, and stable too. Nothing had shown him to be wrong about this in the seven years Bodamer had been married to his sister.

May kicked in, and once May came little occupied either man's mind for eight weeks other than trout fishing in Copper Creek. They sneaked an odd golf game on the way up or down. Nobody got hurt in them doing that. That was another thing Hank liked about his brother-in-law. Bodamer saw the world in the same way as Hank.

Copper Creek was a short forty-minute drive from Madison.

Both men carried cell phones with enough capacity to access every file their office kept, should the need ever arise, when they were out. It never did. Hank's sister, and Nathan's wife, Arla, well, she ran a tight office and nothing really got by her. 'Nothing gets by Arla!', that was Nathan's motto, and normally Nathan followed that with, 'Nothing 'ever' gets by Arla!'.

'Happy days for all', was the toast that Hank, Nathan, and Arla touched glasses to once a month when they 'final-checked' their 'spread' figures, and then electronically posted their agreed accounts to head office—less their commission of course. In summer, they did this on Hank's patio, and ate a spread too afterwards, before Nathan and Arla staggered back across the lawns to their own house. In winter, they did it indoors, but everything else was much the same.

Gerty O' Keefe didn't really share the Madison consensus on her husband's loveliness. In fact, that consensus alone made Gerty very wary of any kind of consensus. Gerty was quiet and kept most of her thoughts to herself. Brown trout fishing season was Gerty's favourite time of the year. This wasn't an official season you understand. That runs from May right through to September for the brown trout in Wisconsin, well, near Madison anyway. For Gerty, the brown trout season ran from early May 'til the end of June. During that time, her husband who people knew as Hank, or even on occasion as Beefy—for Hank was a big boy, then a big man, and his named rhymed with beef, and kids being kids, the rest is familiar to anyone with a nickname—well, let's just say that he was absent, and Gerty could get on with her life, without fear or dread of her bullying man.

She still had to do their monthly food spreads, though.

When they fished, Hank O Keefe and Nathan Bodamer both liked to eat. A lot of trout fishing is about waiting … waiting for the right time of the day; waiting for shade to be just so from the river bank; waiting for the sun to come out; waiting for the clouds to come over; waiting for the fish to feed so they were biting whatever was in the water, and sometimes just plain waiting while the fisherman gathered his own thoughts, patiently put his equipment together, and planned the day ahead. Picking the fly a man might choose on a given day, well, that might even take an hour of deliberating and talking over.

Nothing makes a man hungry like waiting.

Arla ran the office when Hank and Nathan fished; she answered all the calls, dealt with any queries, or quotations that needed posting and she saw to any walk-ins with or without appointments; she organised the stationery too, the cleaners, the vending machine, and the various maintenance complications that somehow always popped up. An organised lady, she still had time to meet Jerry Fisher at the Kings Inn Motel, on the Highway going south, at two o clock most days Nathan was away for a dalliance that had been going on since before she met her husband. Fisher was married when she met him. Getting married only balanced her side of the ledger, Arla reckoned. Fisher was a cost accountant out in Hinchley's Dairy, so he understood Arla's thinking. Like Arla's, his job was often out and about. Nine years of occasional fun, with a bit of extra in May and June, well, that suited Jerry Fisher right down to his plastic-covered boots.

Only common sense then that Gerty should make the food for Hank and Nathan. After all, the business was about the two families, and if Arla was pulling her weight in the office, then the least Gerty could do was pick up some of the background slack and look after the men, like any good woman was supposed to. That was how Hank had put it. It wasn't how Gerty saw it, but Hank had loomed a little some years back, and been a bit free with one of his fists too, and Gerty had succumbed. A few years had gone by and Gerty's contributions, amongst other things Hank made her do against her will, had now become a given.

Today, Gerty decided she was going to bake some pies Hank would never forget. Hank and Nathan just loved pies. Not just any old pies now, no. Gerty's pies were the best either man ever encountered. Might have been the fresh air, and the appetite that gave them, but sitting on a river bank, with a cold beer and a floppy hat to keep the warm sun off your face, with a pie from Gerty in your lap, well, that was as near to heaven as either man thought you could get whilst still on this earth.

Looking over her list, and at the scattering of ingredients she spread on the table, Gerty felt her knees go a little weak. She steeled herself to push on. Sometimes there's only one chance in this life. Her plan, some years now in the making, or hatching, for Gerty never really sat down and plotted it specifically, whatever, it was too darn late to back out now, she thought; Gerty knew, this was her now or never moment.

Chewing the end of her pen, she ticked along the list. One box of field mushrooms, one small box of shiitake mushrooms, one diamant celeriac, four garlic cloves—the whole way along until she came to pastry. Gerty used to make her own pastry, but now she bought it from the store.

With a large heavy bottomed pot on the heat, she began to cook her pie fillings. Feeling her legs weaken again, trembling a little as they did, she went to her fridge to seek some fortification of the spirit. As a rule—Hank's rule—Gerty didn't drink alcohol, but if she'd had some available then, Gerty was sure she'd have knocked a stiff one back. Sipping a glass of milk instead, she put the empty glass in the sink and spat to one side of it.

From the pocket of her apron Gerty removed a small plastic zip bag that had been causing her to tremble. Stashed within the bag were five dried and chopped brown mushrooms she'd picked previous fall, with the assistance of a small picture book from the 'bring and buy'. Having turned the book to ashes since on a barbecue she had to put on earlier in the summer, they were burned on Gerty's mind as being of the Amanitin family; she Intended to put them in a man to. Destroying Angels, they had little or no taste if cooked. Added to the small pot, after a few moments, she also added a small amount of the onion, leek and mushroom mix. Piling everything else to the big pot, a small amount of everything also went to the small pot. Lidding both, Gerty left them to simmer and prepared her pastry. Once the filling was cooked, she set about completing her task; her special pie she forked the letter 'H' into.

Gerty had an eight-stack of tin pie dishes, similar to the camping mugs both Hank and Nathan drank their morning coffees from when they arrived at the river. Six of those pies went aside to go into the freezer for the coming weeks once they'd cooled. Hank's day bag was packed with his breakfast, morning snack, his lunch pie, and his afternoon's snacks. Back home around nine, he'd eat a proper meal then. Nathan's was packed in a separate Tupperware container Nathan dropped in each evening with Hank when they returned. It contained pretty much the same stuff.

Just before seven-thirty the next morning, both men set off for their day of fishing. Collapsed in a heap when they finally left, for most of the day Gerty found herself unable to think or concentrate on anything at all. Defrosting a meatloaf that afternoon, she put it in the oven and timed it for later for when Hank came home.

Both men arrived back just before nine-thirty. With more than a few drinks imbibed each: they were rat-arsed drunk. Nathan had fluked a hole-in-one on the par three eight at Hawk's Landing on the way back. They came off the course after the ninth to celebrate. Hell, who wouldn't? Cost Nathan over five hundred dollars in drinks, but a man couldn't be caring about things like that when a once in a lifetime event struck. Hank ate the meatloaf talking non-stop about Nathan's hole-in-one, and finally talked himself to sleep on the couch. Nathan did something similar, and when Arla woke him the following morning he rose reluctantly before proceeding to throw up all over the bathroom floor. Eventually he managed to get his spinning head to the toilet, but by that time he'd slipped all over the place and was not in a happy shape. A ding-dong doorbell echoed around the house and stepping in, Hank boomed from the doorway. Looking into the bathroom, seeing Nathan all sprawled the way he was, well, Hank just broke his ass laughing and left to go fishing. Hank was no fool. He knew if he stayed Arla would make him work in the office, so hiding his own hangover and gut-ache Hank climbed into his RV to head south to Copper Creek—he could sleep the day away on the bank and nobody'd be any-the-wiser.

From her window, looking across, Gerty could see the concerned and annoyed looks on Arla's face; she also saw that Nathan wasn't going with Hank, so, with a heavy feeling of dread, and after much deliberating, Gerty eventually opened her front door and trudged across the grass.

Arla opened the door to leave for work, having decided that Nathan had made his bed of mess and he could very well get on and deal with it once he'd come 'round. Slamming the door, she swivelled on her heel and nearly sent Gerty flying.

"My God Gerty!" Arla declared, fanning herself with her work folder. "What on earth are you thinking of? Creeping up on a girl like that … damn near had a heart attack."

"Really sorry Arla … d-didn't mean to make you jump like that," Gerty apologised meekly. "It's just-? I couldn't help noticing that my Hank went off on his own like? Is everything okay with Nathan?"

"Oh he's fine, Gerty," Arla assured her. "Thrown up puke all over my new bathroom, but luckily on nothing that's fabric-like, so ain't nothin' he can't clean up once his head stops pounding. S'pose Hank told you all about his 'hole-in-one'?"

Gerty nodded, and both threw their eyes to the heavens.

"And told you they suspended their game too, I s'pose?" Arla asked again.

Gerty nodded again, and both threw their eyes to the heavens once more.

"Well, heavens above, did he tell you they then proceeded to guzzle two bottles of champagne each. Each! Champagne! I ask you, Gerty. As well as a gut full of beers and whiskeys, and half a dozen-a-those stinkin' Cuban cigars between them too? Bought drinks for the whole clubhouse, Nathan did! And then drove home! Hank tell you that, Gerty?" Arla asked.

Gerty shook her head and sighed, and both nodded to the other knowingly.

"Well, I for one ain't showin' no sympathy, Gerty. Not a bit of it. Mark my words, girl. You mark my words," Arla declared. "A man only ever gets what he deserves - that's my motto, Gerty! A man only ever gets what he deserves! Today Gerty, both of those men will get punishment! Mark my words, Gerty! Both of them! Lord give me strength. I mean give me the strength to cope with grown men still acting like they're still frat boys!"

Gerty nodded and retreated back across the lawn to her own kitchen. Her nerves still unsettled, Gerty looked in her fridge once more and poured herself a small glass of milk. In her soft-top Mercedes two-seater, Arla eased out of her parking bay with barely a sound, leaving Gerty sipping her milk and watching at the window. It looked like a nice car to Gerty, and she wondered what it'd be like on the freeway with her hair blowing in the wind.

Chuckling to himself, Hank O Keefe pulled into his usual parking spot near Copper Creek; he waved his hand frantically above his steering wheel and tried to drop the window at the same time—he'd been dropping them like that the whole way down and some of them had been knock-outs. Grabbing his gear from the trunk, making sure it was his Snowbee single-hander, and not Nathan's, he traipsed over the two hills to the creek and meandered along a flattened-grass path to find their favourite patch of meadow on the bank. This wasn't where Hank or Nathan generally fished from but was more their den for the days. With all his gear down, Hank slumped flat on the ground and groaned with relief. Sweating like a track-horse from the small exertions, he clucked to himself that his body was just leaking some of yesterday's fun back out through his skin. Hank closed his eyes, thinking to give himself an hour or two of recovery sleep. Dropping another one, even in the outdoors and the small breeze off the river, his gut-stink crept its way up to his nostrils.

Hank slept.

Two hours later, still on his back, Hank woke in a dreadful hurry; with his gut cramping something rotten, Hank projectile vomited straight into the air— the sheer force of it causing him to come upright— and felt it all splat back on him. At the same time, Hank's sphincter muscles let loose and released whatever his larger colon had been harbouring and causing his fart-stink. Trying to move away from it all, towards the creek, desperately trying to retain a little dignity, the gut pains were so severe he passed out. Waking moments later and vomiting severely once more, once more his ass echoed his mouth. In the few seconds of relief, Hank kicked off his shoes and tore off his puke-covered shirt; he tried to roll nearer the creek and pulled off his pants and shorts as he did so. Hank puked and shat himself, passing out intermittently for the next two hours, until another fisherman happened by and recognised him— despite the mess and nakedness. Seeing something was badly wrong, he called 911. Within thirty minutes an ambulance came and took Hank to the Emergency Unit at St. Mary's. Managing to get him on to a drip pretty much straight away, they probably saved his life, according to the driver. In the hospital they suspected a severe case of gastroenteritis, or some kind of severe poisoning, and they managed to get Arla's details from Hank's wallet in his trousers—which the driver had bravely picked up. Arla confirmed their suspicions by telling them of her husband Nathan going down earlier, and also advised that he'd rung her to say he was feeling better and had finally stopped puking. Bodamer was now back in bed and sleeping like a baby. Hank slept for twelve hours. Arla came to visit with Gerty after she'd been home and realised Hank had been kept in for the day. Nobody told Arla how he'd been found, or Gerty at all about anything until Arla got back. The hospital decided to keep him in overnight—just in case—but they anticipated Hank being released the following morning.

Arla and Gerty returned then and brought Hank home; he seemed more embarrassed by the incident than anything else. Appearing to be fine, he even declared that he 'didn't feel too bad at all, considering'. The hospital issued some medication; he just needed some rest, they advised. Nathan could drive the next day and Hank would rest up on the way; they'd have to find somewhere new to set up, at least until the rains came, Hank told him, and chuckled himself into a coughing fit.

Laid back on the grass on their new patch the following morning, Hank closed his eyes; his guts still didn't feel right, but he reckoned it'd pass. Unaware that he'd now absorbed the Destroying Angel toxin completely, and would shortly pass into a coma from which he'd never recover, Hank O Keefe would ultimately pass away in a matter of weeks. That was one of the peculiarities of the Destroying Angel; a seeming miraculous recovery for a day or so, and the hospital if they haven't pinned it will send you on your merry way to an almost certain death. Hank laid his head back into the tickling grass and closed his eyes, enjoying the warmth of the May, Wisconsin sunshine for one of the last times in his relatively short life.

The mystery of his death flummoxed everyone, including the coroner who found some minute traces of the Amanita Virosa poison in his blood stream. Analysing what Hank had eaten had been near impossible as he'd ejected so much of it over the past days. Gerty listed the things she'd made for both Hank and Nathan, and suspecting some rogue mushrooms amongst the shiitakes, which none of the team had been particularly familiar with, Gerty's pies were put under the microscope at the lab. All came up clean. Buried six days after he'd died in the local cemetery, where Hank himself booked a small family plot in one of his frenzied planning moments some years earlier, Gerty didn't plan to join him there.

Ever.

For Gerty it took another six weeks, once all the investigations were over, for Hank's Life Cover to pay up. She didn't chase it; she let it come in its own time, knowing it would. Having been in the industry for some years and not been one to lie to his customers about recommendations he wouldn't take himself, the cheque Gerty received was just a little short of two and a half million dollars. Gerty lamented to Arla that there was now too much sadness in her family house for her, so she sold it, and all the land Hank had bought over the years too. On a whim, she suggested that Arla buy her family's share of the business, which Arla did, for a knockdown price of seven hundred thousand dollars, and then, following that, she transferred all her and Hank's life savings to a new account.

Gerty moved.

Gerty moved away.

Gerty moved far away from Wisconsin and Madison.

Three miles south of Laguna beach in California, where she could see the ocean from her kitchen was her choice of move, and after a month of living there, Gerty joined the Aliso Viejo Country Club; she came to like Long Island Iced Teas. It still felt like she didn't drink alcohol when she ordered it, and that made her smile. Gerty decided she might like to play golf, and see what all the fuss was about; she didn't think she'd ever get a hole in one at the club, though.

Hank had assured her that was something the ordinary person only ever got once in their lifetime.

***

Mushroom Boomer Pie Recipe

(No Destroying Angels)

Ingredients
Pastry
300g sieved spelt white flour (or plain)
100g wholemeal brown flour
2 teaspoons of salt
100g of butter
Several splashes of very cold water

Filling
250g of field mushrooms
200g of shiitake mushrooms
2 onions fine chopped
2 leeks fine chopped
6 garlic cloves crushed
1 celeriac peeled and cubed
2 carrots peeled and cubed
4 potatoes washed and cubed small
1 cup of butter beans
4 sage leaves
3 stalks of thyme…leaves only
2 stalks of Rosemary, leaves only
salt & pepper
1/2 pint of vegetable or mushroom stock

Making Mushroom Boomer Pie
The Pastry
Add the flours, salt and butter to a mixing bowl and rub it through the fingers until it resembles breadcrumbs. Once done, add a few splashes of

very cold water and using a butter-knife caress the mixture and bring it together. Continue to do this and add small splashes of water until it comes to a coherent pastry ball. Wrap in cling film and put in the fridge. A couple of hours is always best, but it can be used pretty quickly.

When you remove it from the fridge flatten it into a rectangle and cut a third off to use as the lid. Roll out the two-thirds to double its size on a non-floured surface. Butter it lightly and fold it over. Roll it out on a floured surface to over-hang a lightly oiled 10" x 7" deep pie dish. Roll the lid using the same technique and leave it on the rolling pin until ready.

The Filling
Using a chef's knife, fine chop the herbs and salt and pepper together.

Sweat the onions and leeks in a deep heavy bottomed pot. Once lightly browning at the edges add the mushrooms and cover to allow heat and moisture to build. Once the mushrooms have sweated to soft, add the celeriac, carrots, potatoes and butter beans and stir it together. Add the herbs and the stock. Cover and reduce the heat and leave to reduce for about thirty minutes.

Pour into the pie dish and add the lid. Fold the overlay together to create a nice crust edge. Prick with a fork in four places. Serve with a side of lightly steamed spinach and asparagus.

***

Leftover Boxty

Seamus Browne was an arrogant arse. All his life he'd bullied, bossed, bothered, and bollocked whatever peer group he happened to occupy—right from junior infants.

At sixteen he was already a near-hardened drinker, smoked twenty to thirty strong filter-tipped fags a day, and had a broken nose through which his breathing sounded laboured. It irritated like hell if you sat next to him on a bus, but it lent him the look of a seasoned boxer, which Seamus liked.

When the career guidance teacher sat his class down and forced them all to select a path for their future, with a distant hope of getting some of them to focus on something, or anything – it was that kind of class – Seamus only applied for one thing. Chastised for not making the obligatory three choices, but being who he was, he didn't give a fuck about chastisement, Seamus—or the Career Guidance teacher's opinion. Or many other things for that matter.

Seamus Browne was an arrogant arse, but an arrogant arse who knew what he wanted to be.

Glaring at the discoloured water twenty inches from his face in the toilet bowl—he'd already pissed twice, and less than fifteen minutes earlier had shifted an enormous crap that needed three flushes to move fully—hunched over, with his gut contracting, cold sweat condensed on his now balding head; sour reflux bile leaked into the back corners of his mouth and he spat agressively into the bowl at the drying skids. They weren't helping his current condition.

Dry retching a few more times, he sat on the floor with his arm across the toilet seat.

"I need to soak this up with something," he muttered to the air about him. Bracing himself to rise, he anticipated a wave of nausea would flood through him in the movement. Hoping it would help, he closed his eyes.

§

The earlier sunshine, dazzling the world with bright sparkle, abruptly stopped and Freda Bresnan watched the heavy clouds scuttling in from the coast as she drove towards it, and away from the town hospital. Her sunglasses redundant, she tossed them onto the passenger seat with her mind still circling her night shift in the emergency ward.

A quiet but gritty night—she now just worked on Tuesday and Wednesday, so the occasional mayhem of the weekend shifts was behind her— only three people had been admitted over the eight hours of her shift. The first was a familiar old man whose chest rattled louder with every breath, and for whom Freda could do little other than comfort and reassure with platitudes; death wasn't far away for him, but neither he nor his family were yet ready for it. Freda suspected the family took him regularly to the hospital on the quiet shifts in case of his passing, thereby removing the difficult decision making they might have to undertake at home without any guidance. Most of the family Freda met were in tracksuits; none ever looked to be a sporting type, and like the old man, all honked of fags and sour milky tea.

The second admittance was a student from the local college who'd been in a fight and taken a bit of a beating. Wearing a blood-splattered rugby shirt, with black and red hoops, Freda remembered thinking how much more the blood contrasted on the red than on the black. Apparently he'd been out drinking, and Freda pursed her lips as she winced a little; looking at his once nicely shaped face she could see that it was swollen and would be forever blemished from hereon with a skewed nose, which would be accompanied with a likely scar too beneath his right eye, where something had gouged a lump of flesh. The boy's main concern was his ribs, as this was where most pain was emanating; they were bruised badly from what must have been a merciless and prolonged kicking.

On her break Freda struggled with a difficult sudoku, frustratingly not getting beyond a scattering of numbers; annoyed, and irked at her distracted mind, she'd switched to a crossword to pass the rest of her break while she munched a breakfast biscuit and sipped the odd tasting vending machine tea from a thin plastic cup.

The third admittance for Freda was what caused her melancholic mood to stay with her. With her wipers flicked on, she leaned forward and looked upwards; the squalls raged over her in the November breeze and scattered random hail spray along the road on their way to the town. Screeching in their dry rubber protest, she flicked the wipers off again; catching her own eyes in the rearview mirror as she checked and then indicated for the upcoming left for the road to Passage East, Freda knew that some nights surely aged you more than others.

"Fucking men and fucking fucking drink!" Swearing grittily at the sky, she manoeuvred her way into the turn.

§

Thoughts absconded, staring into his fridge Seamus struggled to remember why he was standing where he was; he belched, rubbed worryingly at his chest, and began removing what he could find.

Some milk in the bottom of a bottle without a lid came out. A metal pan too, in which sat about six half-mashed potatoes. Two greening potatoes, two old leeks, and half an oversized onion tumbled noisily in the vegetable tray as Seamus yanked that outwards. A fridge hardened lump of cheddar had survived, overlooked in a small Tupperware bowl, and Seamus added this to his sorry pile. Catching sight of his reflection in the kitchen window he grimaced; never a handsome man he had to admit, he knew he was now verging on downright ugly, and no matter what he hoped, he'd have to expect more comments to come his way if he persisted drinking in younger bars. He needed to get a handle on his temper. Hot-headed, and quick to rise, no matter how much he disciplined himself, or what resolution he made, nothing ever changed. Grimacing at his thoughts, he sucked his upper lip upon seeing the dark line against the white of his skin and tasted the sour, stale stout from the previous evening.

"The world is full of arseholes!" Seamus growled at his reflection.

From the cupboard, he removed a large plate, picked a knife from the block, chopped the ends off the leeks, and cut them about three-quarters length where he felt the decay might have stopped, before slicing them along their length without cutting through; he removed a few layers until what remained looked fresh as he rinsed them.

"The world is full of arseholes!" Repeating the words, he ground his teeth in anger as he did so.

Doing that more and more, he wondered why. Age? A bitterness and misery at his own life? His ex-wife? Lowering himself to look upwards he checked the sky out the kitchen window; lead clouds sat low and darkened the morning and Seamus felt the sudden quiet of the birds; rain was imminent: even when the sun shone, rain was always bloody impending, that Seamus could remember.

Picking a cup from the sink, he ran it beneath the tap coughing and gobbing bile-spittle beneath it at the plug hole. Set to drain, he turned back to the pan which was now hot enough. He added the chopped onions.

Rain began to fall. First, a few gentle taps caressed the window panes, followed by gusts as the squalls slipped directly overhead, until finally the heavens opened and hail rattled off the sills, the shed roof, and the metal ashbin, and drummed loudly on the plastic wheelie bins in the yard. It was heavy enough to stop him for a moment, just to witness it.

The onions were just browning at the edges when Seamus added the leeks, and he shook the pan to stir them all together. Checking the cupboard to see if there was any other food to be had from there he found next to nothing: a Mother Hubbard day, but a misplaced vine in the fruit bowl with five over-ripe tomatoes still attached got thrown in beneath the grill.

§

Skipping to the porch from the car through the now steady rainfall with her bag above her head and her key ready in hand, the door opened slowly as Freda neared; her older daughter Molly tip-toed backwards with her finger hook-stuck to the latch at the top of her reach.

"Oh thank you, sweetie," Freda slipped in the gap, grabbing her little girl for a quick hug as she did so.

"Oh, Mam, you're all wet!" Molly protested.

A man's head angled around the door at the end of the hallway.

"You brought the rain," he smiled as he watched Molly trying to close the door—her new height access was still a novelty.

Squeezing her eyes shut and opening them as though to waken properly, Freda rubbed Molly's head as she did so and released a sigh of relief.

"Rough night?"

"Go get your school things, Molly, and don't forget to pick out your gym things for today," Freda released Molly up the stairs as she made her way to the kitchen.

"Sometimes I really hate this place, Jim," she stopped and stood at the kitchen door.

"That bad, huh?" Jim checked.

"Four o clock in the morning," Freda paused and forced herself to walk towards the draining board for the kettle.

"Fresh tea in the pot," Jim anticipated her need and Freda nodded her gratitude.

"Four o clock! I mean? A young mother too! I mean, who the-? Who is up at four in the morning? Let alone! Jesus, Jim! Like a bloody animal, he battered her to a pulp! What kind of husband? What kind of man? Ach ... I give up with people sometimes, love."

Eased to her chair, he poured tea for them both; his hand remained on her shoulder once he'd put her cup before her, and he sipped on his own as he listened, knowing that she wouldn't say much more; sometimes a day, sometimes a week, but it would pass. Hers was not a job he envied; he felt her calm beneath his touch and squeezed her shoulder reassuringly. A gust of wind threw a loud splattering spray of rain against the kitchen window, and he looked up at it.

"I'd better check her," he flicked his head to indicate Molly upstairs and watched Freda's responses as he spoke. "I've done you some boxty and tomatoes. It's on a hot plate in the oven. I'll bring her over to the school, and go on to Sheridan's from there. The meeting is at ten, so I can't hang about, girl. You're okay, yeah? Are you sure?"

§

With his mix ready, Seamus set about it; he would have floured his hands, and even added a spoon to the mix, but knew he had none; he would have added a quarter teaspoon of baking soda to the mix also, but he had none of that either. Tomatoes checked, he put two teabags in the pot. The patties he turned a couple of times, over seven or eight minutes, browning them all over. The tomatoes were spitting juice on top, and the skin was beginning to split, so he turned the grill off. Not a crust of bread in the bin—Seamus regretted not having grabbed a soda loaf when he and his 'boss', Superintendent-bloody-Cuddihey, as he thought of her, picked up some bits at the baker's the previous day. Now the driver, he could have quickly put it in the boot and Cuddihey would have been none-the-wiser—surely she wouldn't have had a problem with that like she had with everything else he did. Bossy bitch! With the bread and a few more vine tomatoes this would have been good enough for four, Seamus thought to himself. All four patties removed, arranging them at a tilt, one by one along the plate, he picked the vine out from the grill and lay it beside them before grabbing a small fist of sea salt from his salt bowl which he scattered across the lot. There wasn't a jot of pepper left in the mill, so he didn't bother picking it up.

Slumping into the chair, he groaned loudly and rubbed the sore, drying scab from his knuckle; he flexed his fingers as he spun his signet ring to ease the pain, before picking up the fork and tucking in.

"Fuck!" He thought and swore aloud, before throwing his head back in annoyance.

"Forgot to make the bloody tea!"

***

Leftover Boxty Recipe

Ingredients

4 large potatoes, 2 grated raw, 2 boiled and
mashed)
3 tablespoons of plain flour
1 teaspoon of baking powder
2 free-range eggs
1 teaspoon of fine sea salt
1 onion (large, finely chopped and fried to browning)
optional
140 mls of milk (your preference)

Boxty is particularly easy, and if you fancy it, you
can add things like wilting leeks or spring onions to it
also, if you don't think you'll get around to using
them. You can always throw in a bit of hard cheese
if that's on the way out too. Like Colcannon, it was
often popular to make on Mondays when the excess
from Sunday roasts could be used up and a 'waste-
not-want-not' ethos prevailed. If served on a bed of
salad with a bit of lime and chilli dressing, 'boxty'
moves upmarket with ease and can hold its own on
any gastro-pub menu, or any guest house breakfast
menu.

Making Boxty

Run the grated raw potatoes under a cold tap to remove excess starch and dry with a tea towel before putting them in the mixing bowl.

Add everything else to the mixing bowl and stir well to get it all together.

Put a large flat pan on the heat with some groundnut oil and a good dollop of butter. If your mix is moist and feels more like very thick batter, spoon four large measures of the mix into the hot pan and allow the heat to seal the bottom and cook off the moisture a bit before turning them. If the mix is drier, shape with your hands into patties and add to the pan allowing the heat to seal them before turning them. Turn a few times and brown the patties nicely.

Boxty is often made as part of a large breakfast, but it can just as easily be presented with tomatoes on the vine as accompaniment, or on a bed of salad with a bit of tomato chutney and pickles to tart it up, which effectively turns it into a light lunch, or as said earlier, on a bed of salad with some chilli and lime, a workman's breakfast, boxty transforms well into a gastro pub starter.

***

Matty Monroe in Paradise

Matty Monroe's eyeballs felt sore, tired, and very, very dry. Almost dusty, Matty suspected they were also bloodshot; he blinked slowly and hoped it would help as he steadied himself before turning in his seat.

"I need a cup of tea and a biscuit, sweetheart," Matty looked up at the young lady hovering by his side.

Unused to looking at a computer screen like he had earlier, it had made him dizzy and afterwards he'd needed to sit and gather his strength. With the help of the young girl in the library he had managed to book the hotel he wanted for four nights; he'd also ordered the flowers his wife had loved and for those to be delivered beforehand directly to the room. Arranging then for a seat on a bus to the town nearest the hotel, and even a taxi to meet him when the bus arrived—despite the girl having done pretty much all the work—Matty was impressed with himself, and his input. After a small rest, Matty thanked the girl once more and shuffled off on his way home with several bits of paper that the girl gave him tucked into different pockets of his overcoat to help him remember his various needs.

Slowly meandering back to his small bungalow, once home, he set about getting himself ready for the following day when he planned to leave. Laying out his black shirt, black trousers, and black jacket, he then tucked some tissue into the front of his black boots as his feet seemed to have shrunk or lost a little of their fat, and he did so want to look his best, so the boots were a must. He also put aside his yellow neckerchief, his black socks, and a clean pair of black underpants, in the boxer style, before finally settling his black hat on top of them. Matty deemed himself ready to depart. Then, Matty went to bed where he slept for two periods of four hours; his sleep was always broken by his toilet needs these days. Up at three in the morning, he ate a substantial breakfast comprising of two cold sausages with four slices of toast; he washed, dressed, and then sat on the toilet reading his book until his thighs tingled with pins and needles, which forced him to rise and finish. The whole routine took him just under two hours.

Matty moved slowly.

Walking out his front door he made his way to the bus-stop—too short a distance for a taxi, but for Matty, it was still some twenty minutes' walk from his residence. Arriving early for the bus, which he didn't mind as Matty knew the days of hurrying to catch up with lost time were gone, he then watched the quiet emptiness of the bus station slowly emerge from the depths of its slumber. The yawning and farting street sweepers began the early shift at six to clear up the detritus of the night owls; their yawns were infectious, and Matty rose to circle the bench

he'd chosen to wait at, just to prevent himself
falling back to sleep before the bus arrived.

   Pulling in shortly after six, Matty found
himself a seat and promptly fell asleep; he left it
to the driver to decide whether or not to wake him
for his ticket check, which Matty didn't have, as
the young girl explained that he'd only now need
to show the driver a reference number he kept in
his pencil pocket. The driver looked at Matty
sleeping and chose not to bother him, and for
most of the day the gentle rocking movement of
the bus kept Matty blissfully asleep, except for a
single stop for the driver's lunch where Matty
bought an egg sandwich and went to the toilet.
Once the movement began again, Matty fell
promptly back to sleep. When he finally awoke
later, the bus was in darkness, the door was still
open, and he found himself to be in a deserted
bus depot. Lights emanated from one end; the
rest was in utter darkness, and Matty edged his
way tentatively towards the light.

§

High above Hotel Paradise a full summer moon
reached its zenith; Agnes watched the village
square from behind the tall hotel lounge windows,
and it felt as though the earth and heavens had
come to a stop. Nothing moved. No sound
disturbed the air. Her tired eyes gazed at the
bright moon's halo and without thought Agnes
absorbed and felt the beauty and wonder of it all.

   A small light came on directly across the
square, and after some moments, even through
the windows, and at a distance, in the quiet of the

night, Agnes felt she could hear the sound of the flushing toilet just before the light went out once more and returned the square to darkness.

With her mood broken, she returned to her desk to sit once more at reception. Beneath the desk she shifted her fidgeting knees from side to side; the socks weren't helping her restless legs, and Agnes felt that if she drank any more water she'd never leave the toilet.

Agnes hated the graveyard shift. Her turn came but three nights a month, and these three nights she felt somehow marked the twilight of her life drifting away from her in utter futility and empty loneliness. Picking her handbag from the floor beneath the desk, she removed her small pocket mirror, checked her eyes, teeth, and finally, picked at the canals of her nose. Removing some floss, Agnes worked her front teeth for a few minutes before puckering her lips and doing a series of odd facial exercises at her reflection in the small mirror frame. The desktop screen before her beeped, and a message received notice appeared. Returning the mirror to her bag, she shunted it beneath the desk with her feet. At the same moment the revolving entrance door spun and Agnes looked up in surprise before scowling in disapproval. It was Tomas, the under-chef, arriving. Remembering he'd told her previously he'd be working through the night, her eyes narrowed as she watched him saunter in; she was unsure still about Tomas, but the owners Peter and Gertrude thought he was wonderful, and there was little she could do about that. Tall, and a would-be-handsome young man, with deep-set, watery-blue Slavic eyes, he had pronounced bony cheekbones, blond cropped hair, and sallow, freckle-free skin; somehow to Agnes, it just didn't all come together to make a handsome young man she might enjoy looking at—he never smiled for a start. Oh, he did laugh. He guffawed loudly when amused, and even snorted along with it, but once the moment passed his face returned to a stony blankness that reminded her of pictures she'd seen of gaunt men in pyjama outfits when the Allied troops liberated the concentration camps. Agnes had read once, or heard, more likely heard, she thought, that Slavs and Russian people were averse to smiling, apparently deeming it somewhat idiotic, clown-like, and even foolish. Bloody daft notion, Agnes thought, smiling to herself; they never looked happy either, when she saw them on the telly and always had a put-upon look about them, as though the world was out to get them. The world had better things to be doing trying to keep its head above water, Agnes thought, and she nodded at her own reflective wisdom.

"Misery begets misery after all," forgetting for a moment about Tomas, she uttered the words aloud.

"What?" Tomas lifted an eyebrow questioningly as he walked towards her.

"Nothing—it was just-! Why didn't you use the kitchen entrance? You know we don't like backroom staff out front," Agnes instinctively retaliated with her own question.

"Kitchen is locked," Tomas walked on past her, but his eyes remained fixed on hers. "Peter has key, so I need to go this way tonight. It's okay?" He stopped briefly and glanced at her, waiting for her response.

"I suppose," Agnes conceded and glanced at the lobby clock. "It's late, so there shouldn't be anybody around."

With Tomas dismissed from her mind, she scraped gently at the corners of her eyes with the painted nails of her smallest fingers, yawned, and looked once more to her desktop monitor, tapping her space bar to re-activate the sleeping screen. The whooshing sweep of the revolving door sounded once more and Agnes raised her gaze in surprised curiosity. A man stood inside the lobby, reluctant to move further; wearing a dirty yellow oilskin bottom, with a thick black jumper, in his hand he held a bright orange bucket with a cling film cover.

"I was trying to deliver this to your kitchen, but there's nobody there," he spoke the words in French.

"At this hour?" Agnes queried the man in Flemish.

"Apparently there wouldn't be anyone there 'until' this hour," the man replied, shrugging, and stubbornly sticking to French.

"Aaah!" Agnes smiled, but stuck to her own guns, "Tomas has just arrived. What is it? What's in there?"

She held both of her hands out in query.

"I don't know," he looked down at the bucket. "It stinks, though—like it's gone off. Can I leave it with you? It's from Marie—the boulangerie in-." he waved his hand above the bucket as he spoke.

"Marie's? I suppose that's okay. Come on over," Agnes tilted her nose slightly despite the distance between them.

Gesturing to his clothing and shoes, he indicated that it was probably best he didn't come in any further and soil the area. Agnes rose from her seat and went to him instead; reeking of cold sweat, earth, pitch, and creosote, like someone who rarely came indoors, she suspected he worked on the roads or highways.

"Is there any paperwork?" She felt she had to say something.

"For a bucket of stinky goo? I don't think so," the man shrugged and grinned. "I'm just glad to get it out of my van, and that's saying something for it." Pulling a face, he quivered, before softening his eyes and looking back at Agnes.

"I'd thank you, but in honesty I'm not sure if I should," Agnes took the bucket, and they exchanged a friendly smile and wink. The handle was greasy and unpleasantly cold. The man nodded, bade her a good-night, and left. Agnes watched him go and wondered why such a strong looking man left himself stink and run to fat; he either lived alone and drank too much, or had a wife who overfed him, and drank too much with him, she mused. Looking about again, thinking to return to her reception desk and call Tomas, she decided it might be best to get rid of the stinky bucket and take it straight to the kitchen.

Tomas looked up in shock when Agnes came through the door. Working at a bench, stirring what looked like a large pot of berries and bay leaves, Agnes looked about him approvingly—he'd only switched the lights on where he was working. Tomas was naturally frugal; it seemed East-European parents had nagged their kids about leaving lights on too.

"Come," Tomas gestured to Agnes and beckoned her closer while he held the large pot. "Smell."

"Speaking of smells," Agnes held up the bucket.

"Aaah!" Tomas exclaimed, taking the bucket from her; he looked truly joyful for the first time Agnes had ever witnessed, and like an excited boy, he began to peel back the flimsy cling-film lid. "My starter!"

"Your—starter?" Her surprise was apparent, even as she bent and smelt the blood red mixture Tomas had been stirring. "Wow! This smells wonderful. What is it? What do you mean 'starter' Tomas?"

She gestured to the stink-bucket.

"Bread starter," Tomas explained, gesturing to the bucket with both of his hands. "You have name for it. Leaven I believe. But this! This is leaven from heaven. You know why? Because it's rye!"

Clapping his hands, he laughed loudly at his own comment.

"If you say so, Tomas." Agnes shook her head and lifted an eyebrow at him, only to be greeted with more laughter from Tomas, who was obviously proud of having pulled off a joke of sorts in English with her. "What is this stuff? This smells more like something I might enjoy," she looked into the berry coloured liquid and took a deep waft of the draught once more.

"That is my witches brew! It is currants, cassis, and bay leaves, but it looks magical, no? I make it yesterday, but I like it warm. It helps the yeast—it is like—like a trigger. I use it for bread. It is very beautiful. Yes? You will see at lunch special in bar tomorrow," Tomas's enthusiasm for the starter was infectious.

Agnes was no fool. If the under-chef was this excited about making bread and was doing it for the business, this was not a time to discourage. Looking back into the currants and cassis mix, she inhaled once more before looking back at him.

"I can't wait! If I'm gone home, stick me some aside please," she smiled at his rare exuberance before leaving the kitchen and making her way back to reception.

As Agnes pushed opened the left side of the double doors to her lobby she looked up in time to see a man's shaking hand tapping the butler's bell she kept on her counter; he whispered to his side that the hotel seemed abandoned.

"Good evening, sir," Agnes greeted him quietly and was pleased to see the man spooked at her materialisation behind him.

"Shooo! Evening Miss," the stranger tapped his chest, released a sigh, and tilted his head to look behind her; the door through which she'd slid gently slotted back quietly and no trace of where she'd come from was evident to him.

"I believe I have a 'computer' booking," the man suggested, a little nervously; he patted his pocket before removing a piece of paper with a number on it. "I might be a little bit late?"

Dressed entirely in black, with the exception of a small yellow neckerchief inside his shirt, and wearing black skinny jeans, a black working style shirt, black boots with a good heel despite already looking tall, if a little stooped; a black leather jacket hung over his arm, and in his hand was what looked like a black felt hat that finished the look.

Agnes found her interest piqued.

"You have?" Generally aware of her bookings, she wasn't anticipating checking anybody in at this late hour. Not having looked earlier, as the manager Peter didn't mention anything to her about late arrivals when she began the shift, she opened her booking system and heard a small cough. Looking up from her screen, she took the piece of paper he held out to her with his trembling fingers.

"Your name, sir?" Her automated questioning kicked in as she seated herself more comfortably and checked the bookings menu.

"Matty, Miss," the man answered.

"Mr Matty, I don't seem-," her fingers typed the first letters of his name, and the computer didn't return anything.

"Matty Monroe, Miss. My apologies-," Matty interjected and suppressed a small rise of panic; his trust in the computer had been limited.

"Monroe—M. Oh! I see. Yes. You booked it just yesterday," Agnes spoke her thoughts aloud as her fingers worked, and she searched to see if Matty had reserved a specific room.

"Yes, Miss," Matty's relief was palpable, and he pulled on his nose uncertainly before offering his explanation. "With a computer."

Leaning forward a little to see if he could get a glimpse of Agnes's computer screen, his mind was still a little reluctant to believe that she might have his details.

"Mister Matty, sorry, Mr Monroe," Agnes began.

"Just Matty, Miss. I'm as likely not to hear or answer if someone comes-a-looking for a Mr Monroe."

Straightening once more, he realised that he couldn't read or figure anything from where he stood; his eyes were long past that.

"Ah, here we are," Agnes's mind juggled several questions before she spoke and she checked down the booking form to see if anyone else was expected with Matty. "I see you already have our 'Honeymoon Suite'? That will be nice for you. Okay, Mr Monroe, now, I just need a swipe of a credit card, unless you want to pay cash as you go along?"

Agnes disappeared from his view as she fidgeted for a moment beneath the counter before picking out an electronic contraption, unfamiliar to Matty.

"Cash will be just fine, Miss," Matty nodded, and eyed the machine with distrust.

"If you would sign here," Agnes passed Matty a form with a box marked by her, which he signed.

"And here," she began arranging items on top of the counter for him to take to his suite.

Matty watched the bundle grow as he looked for the second box to sign, and his curiosity and confusion with the turn of events grew; consisting already of a towelling dressing gown, slippers, a bath and hand towel, a face cloth with two small bottles of shampoo wrapped in it, and a bottle of body wash, Matty raised his eyes in query as Agnes finally placed a block of wood with a small key attached to it on top of everything, and her body language indicated their transaction was somehow complete.

Picking the awkward pile up, Matty put his hat on, touched it, nodded to Agnes, and looked about, before looking once more back to Agnes for some direction through the doors.

"Through the left double doors and right to the top. The lift stops at ten I'm afraid, so you'll have to climb the stairs," her toes curled in her shoes as she said the words.

Matty weighed her instructions in his mind for a moment, turned, and crossed the shiny tiled lobby carefully.

"I thought they'd have all this ready for us in the room, didn't you?" He spoke quietly to his side as he went through the doors, and nodded in agreement with himself.

§

Few things animated Tomas Wozniski more than making bread. A gift passed from his babička, on his mother's side, if Tomas encountered a bread new to his palate, he sat and slowly chewed small pieces until he felt he'd identified all the ingredients, and how they might have been put together. Stored away in his patient mind, it would remain untouched until the opportunity arose for him to set about making his interpretation of what he'd eaten. Tonight was such an instance for Tomas. Tonight he was making a cassis currant loaf with a combination of rye and whole-wheat flours, and his newly sourced leaven; in his dream, the sweetly caramelised currants combined with the sharp cassis and sat alongside the sour rye and leaven, the combination of flavours were perfect to accompany a good beer cheese.

Stretching his back, he yawned loudly and idly wondered if Yvette would be on the morning shift. Tomas hadn't seen her now for three days, and he knew that Joseph in the bar fancied her too; he was unsure about Joseph and the way he was always so slick and groomed and had concluded that he was either very vain or very insecure. Neither of these was traits that a girl like Yvette could admire for long. Or shouldn't, Tomas thought; Tomas also knew he didn't know his way around a woman's mind, and most of his assumptions went awry at some stage resulting in him admonishing himself in the privacy of the kitchen shortly after that. Banging one of his pots in frustration at his own thoughts, he looked at what he was doing.

"He can't even have a conversation in English yet, and he speaks no Flemish or French either!" Tomas protested Joseph's limitations loudly to the white tiled wall and pointed his spoon at it, and his ghostly reflection. "I know more—I knew more, knew more! I knew more when I came here a year ago than he does now!"

Feeling that he was winning his battle with Joseph, Tomas removed the cling film completely from the bucket of leaven and took a scoop, which he added to the cassis-currant combination; this was the messy bit his baker's blood loved, and for ten minutes he squeezed, stirred, and mixed until it came together, and after which, Tomas put the kettle on to boil; he liked this habit of the English that the hotel boasted of as one of its oddities. This tea-making was a good way to step back from things and allow your head to clear; he could take stock of things, that was the phrase they used. He couldn't think of the words in Flemish but knew it was something about balance—it didn't seem to quite capture the standing back—but that might have been just his language. Another year, perhaps, and he'd be nearly fluent.

"Sugar, Sir?" Tomas offered himself the option.

"No, thank you very much, but just a little milk, if I may?" Smirking at his antics, he spoke directly to himself in the reflection once more.

"I forget all these 'thank you' and 'please' things all the time," he poured some milk into the tea, thanked, and then welcomed himself.

Thomas liked it when he worked alone; there were no unpredictable variables and nobody to annoy him, or grate on his nerves. Scanning the worktop, he nodded in satisfaction with how things looked.

§

Half an hour passed and Agnes looked up in surprise to see Matty Monroe come through the double doors once more, looking slightly troubled.

"Mr Monroe?"

"The key," Matty held it up almost apologetically. "It's a—it's a bit tricky."

Agnes took it from him and compared it with her copy; she lifted her glasses to her nose to bring it into focus and could see no discernible difference, but switched them nonetheless; she removed Matty's key from its block of wood and attached the hotel master key, offering to go to his room to make sure. Given the long climb up the stairs, Matty gratefully accepted her offer; it had taken him near fifteen minutes to go up the few flights. Getting down was tricky too, and a mite sore on the knees for him, so he didn't fancy another wasted trip.

"You go on up and open it," he handed her back the block of wood, holding it with both of his hands. "I'll make my way up behind you and take that thing from you when we meet on the stairs, if that's okay."

Opening the room door without any problem, and trying Matty's original key once more, Agnes realised it was a lot stiffer, and she could see how he might have struggled with it after the climb. Picking all the bits Matty had received at reception from the floor, she went in to set them out in his room. On both sides of the bed, next to the lamps, a large vase of scented lilies sat in prominence and filled the room with their fragrance. The white sheets of the bed were offset with black pillows and a black throw cover. Agnes raised an eyebrow, muttering to herself about people's foibles. This would have been arranged with the day-shift, and nobody had even left her a note about the peculiar request. Oddities were the bread and butter of hotel gossip. Stopping the outer door with a rubber door-jam the cleaners usually used, she made her way back down the stairs. Matty had just passed the first floor. Agnes passed him the block of wood once more, apologising for the inconvenience; she wondered why, if he'd booked the Honeymoon Suite himself, and had such particular and odd requirements, why on earth he chose the top floor, given his frailty and age. Her wonder she kept to herself, but she found she had to say something; she suggested perhaps changing his room the following day.

"No! Please? I don't want to move," Matty's response was surprisingly anxious. "It was where my wife and me ... it was forty-five years ago today-."

The fear upon his face took Agnes by surprise.

"Aaaah!" Perceiving the significance of the room for him, Agnes suggested her understanding with a deliberately slow blink of her eyes. "Of course Mr Monroe. I hope you enjoy your stay with us in Paradise, as we like to say."

Matty smiled broadly and nodded to her as he continued his way. "That's just what they used to say, dear. Did you hear that, just what they used to say," holding firmly to the handrail, he began to negotiate the next flight of stairs.

Returned to reception, Agnes passed an uneventful night thereafter. The morning staff drifted in from six-o-clock onwards; she wasn't due for relief herself until around ten as the owner Peter had been double-shifting and had asked a favour of her, which she'd happily obliged. As people came down to breakfast, Agnes greeted them all and directed each of them on to the floor girl Anna, who in turn guided them to their allotted table in the breakfast room. Nine-o-clock came and went, and Agnes noticed that Matty hadn't made a showing. By nine-thirty, the breakfast room was empty; a single table remained set, and a no-show was normal, especially on the weekends, so nobody but Agnes paid it any mind.

Something nagged at her and stayed with her until the time came when her shift was ending. Leaving reception in the hands of her colleague Yvette, who always arrived early, and could have run the place herself, but hadn't yet found full favour with Peter, Agnes set off to the kitchen to see Tomas; finding him still in the kitchen, she explained her concern about the elderly gentleman in the Honeymoon Suite and described the room to him as she did so. Agnes was unsure why she went to him, but something about him conscientiously working away through the early hours had touched her, and she knew he'd be about until later in the day, as his real shift only began at six. Yvette had also asked about him, so Agnes thought perhaps there was more to the young man than she'd given him credit for. Tomas was bemused as to why Agnes came to him, but seeing her concern, he duly promised to look in on the guest if he didn't show himself later that morning.

The morning ran away, as mornings in small busy hotels can, and Tomas forgot Agnes, and her concerns until he began slicing his cassis-currant bread and preparing his Beer-

Cheese plates for the day's lunch menu. In the cupboard, Tomas had stashed a large baking bowl of cream cheese to which he'd added salt, pepper, and some crushed caraway seeds; he'd left it there from the previous Wednesday, so four days later, when he removed the cover, it was pungent, and for a brief moment, Tomas was transported back to Bratislava, and closed his eyes to fully enjoy the hit. Scooping a large tablespoon onto the side of a wooden breadboard next to three slices of his bread, he resisted the temptation to try it. Tomas had faith in his nose. Next to this, he sat some very finely chopped spring onions with a thinly chopped radish and a large dollop of mustard. Picking a stem glass for a Chimay, he selected a couple of hotel branded serviettes and put them all on a tray with a bottle of the Belgian berry beer. At reception, he picked up a spare key for the Honeymoon Suite. Agnes had told Yvette he'd probably be along at some stage, and for some moments they asked about each other before Tomas explained what he was doing. Yvette raised an eyebrow, impressed that a guest's wellbeing and a potentially awkward situation had been left to him. Tomas nodded his agreement, admitting his own surprise, as he wrote a small note, folded it, and put it on the plate. Promising to pop back and see her once it was over, he left the reception lobby and took the lift to the top floor.

Removing the crooked 'Do Not Disturb' notice, Tomas placed it on the cupboard door further down the hallway before returning to the door. He knocked. There was no answer, so he knocked again.

"Mr Monroe," Tomas called, not too loudly, but directly at the door. There was no sound. Picking the spare key from the tray, and with one hand, he struggled to get the stiff key to turn, before pushing in the door and entering the small dark lobby area. Opening the main door to the suite and bedroom area, he was surprised to find Matty sitting upright in the bed, with his eyes closed and a Bible held to his chest.

"Mr Monroe?" Tomas greeted him as though his intrusion was a perfectly run-of-the-mill event.

Matty's eyes shot open, and he looked straight at Tomas with fright, shock, and then annoyance in his face.

"I left the 'Do Not Disturb' sign on the door!" he visibly clenched a fist around the Bible he held.

"I'm sorry, sir," Tomas looked behind as though seeing through the doors. "Cleaner must have knocked it."

Gesturing to the tray he was holding, he bowed his head in a gentle servile fashion before speaking. "This is complimentary from Hotel," he took in the room as he spoke, and paused for a moment. "It is to celebrate your welcome return after all the years, Mr Monroe."

Scanning for a surface to place the tray upon safely, Tomas moved closer to the bed.

"I don't want to be disturbed," still somewhat peeved, Matty was reluctant to meet his eyes; he was reluctant to be angry these days, and didn't want to speak harshly again.

"I understand, sir," Tomas looked about as he spoke. "You wish to die on your own."

With the tray held in one hand, he moved the telephone on the table and set the tray down.

"Yes," Matty admitted and paused in surprise at his own words.

"But, you like somebody notices. No?" Tomas continued avoiding direct eye contact with Matty.

"Yes! What? No! I don't care. It makes no difference," Matty replied, and straightened himself a little in the bed.

"No?" Tomas gestured at the room questioningly. "All this? The death flowers? What are they called here? The black and white? The bible you are holding?" For a moment their eyes met, and Matty just looked at Tomas without speaking.

"They're called Lilies, and they're scented— my wife always liked them? I don't know why I asked for black and white sheets, the girl asked if I wanted anything special, and I thought, or felt, I had to say something? It was her idea really, and not something I would have ever asked for," Matty confessed and gestured his own indifference to the dark bedding.

"How long you think it takes?" Tomas folded some serviettes and placed them on the bedside table next to the lamp.

"What takes?" Matty's eyes shifted uncertainly as he followed Tomas's movements.

"To die. How long? Are you going to just lie here and die, or have you bigger backup plan?" Tomas expanded and clarified his question.

"I have tablets—pills," Matty tried not to look at his jacket where he kept them. "When I'm ready. It won't take long after that, I would imagine," he fussed at the blankets as though to suggest the conversation was over.

"Why?" Tomas asked, "only if you don't mind telling, of course," he began pouring the Chimay slowly into the speciality glass as he spoke.

"Why die?" Matty asked, and Tomas nodded maintaining his concentration on the glass.

"We all die in the end-," Tomas shook his head, grunting loudly, not accepting the answer, and Matty paused for a moment before starting again.

"My wife died seven months ago," he said quietly. "With her my life-," he paused as though lost for a moment.

"Your wife was your life?" Tomas interrupted his thoughts. Matty nodded, and Tomas gestured for him to continue.

"Everywhere I look or go. Anything I do. Everything I look at, I remember her here. I remember her there. Everywhere I look. Everywhere I miss her. You understand? I miss her so much. I can't bear it. My chest feels like I'm being squashed all day," Matty's eyes glassed over as he spoke. "I've had enough! I'm fed up with it," he straightened the covers once more before looking up with annoyance at Tomas and his intrusion.

"You love her very much," Tomas spoke slowly, reflecting on Matty's words; he nodded his understanding as he spoke.

"I loved her completely," Matty cut in.

"No no, you love her completely: you still love your wife Mr Monroe—if you only 'loved' her, you wouldn't feel this way, so bad," Tomas contradicted him, and cut back.

"What?" Matty was thrown a little by Tomas's response.

"Your wife. She was your life. Yes?" Tomas held Matty's gaze, and Matty nodded his agreement with the young man's simple statement. "Now your wife, she is gone. You think, now my life is gone too, but it is not, so you have pain. A big pain. Yes? Pain is normal, Mr Monroe. Some people. I'm not one. Some people believe all life is pain. You know? Suffering. Some people see only problems. Other people see beauty. Even problem can be beauty. You understand?"

Placing the beer glass on a circular paper drip-mat next to the serviettes, Tomas moved one of the lily vases onto the windowsill, before sitting in the chair near the bed. Matty watched him closely as he decisively moved things to where he wanted, and seated himself. Other than the girl at the library, this was the most anybody had spoken to Matty in a long time; with an eyebrow raised at the serious young man, he sat slightly more upright by pushing back into his pillows and looked across at him as he spoke once more.

"Life is all things, Mr Monroe. All things. Everything. Yes? Not just good things. You must be more like vinegar taster—you know smiling one. Not the two with faces."

"What?" Matty queried the words and the face Tomas was pulling.

"You know vinegar-tasters?" Tomas mimed a spooning action and a wincing after tasting something, and after a moment's reflection, and realising he probably had heard something of them over his life, but now didn't remember, Matty shook his head.

"Life is like vinegar, Mr Monroe," seeing Matty's eyes widen in confusion Tomas gestured to let him continue.

"You see … in picture? Let me explain. There is picture, old, old picture, yes? In picture, three men stand above a big—a big pot. This pot we know is full of vinegar. We know this, I believe, because of what the men are using to taste it—the big spoons, yes? One of the men has sour, grimace face—you know that look, that's how you say it? Grimace? Yes? Another of the men, he has no expression—this one, he is blank. I think you would say blank. The story says to us, anyway, this is how I know it, the story says that one of the men is Buddha, and one of the other men is Confucius. You have heard of them, yes? Buddha, Mr Monroe, believed all life to be suffering struggle, and so we get confused by our attachments, our feelings, and our reactions to all these things: he is the blank one, you know, with strange empty face. Not attached, you understand? Confucius, the other one I said, he believed life to be without order. Chaos. Anarchy! Always in need of rules and laws, and all kinds of orders—he liked to make lots of laws and rules. Lots. Confucius, he has a sour face and wants vinegar to taste like wine. Not happy with things. Never happy with things. Makes new rules to change everything to the way he wants. Yes? The last man? The third man. He is not so well known to many but is believed to be a man called Lao Tzu. A Taoist sage, you know sort—no head-hair, long wispy face-hair, wearing dressing gown all the time. Yes? He, Mr Monroe, is smiling. You understand?" He reached for the tray and taking the plate of food from it, put it on the bedside table next to the glass of beer, before standing up once more.

Matty shook his head.

"They taste vinegar, Mr Monroe. Vinegar is very sour. Good vinegar is very very sour, maybe - I'm not so sure. But vinegar is—what vinegar is! No? Yes? If it is vinegar, and you are vinegar taster, then sour taste of vinegar must be good? Not problem, no. Beautiful maybe. See? Lao Tzu accepts vinegar as vinegar. Life, Mister Monroe, must be seen same way. You love your wife very, very much, and pain you feel tells you that this is true: this is beauty—not problem. Maybe it will be true always, as long as you live. Pain hurts. But this is not bad pain, Mr Monroe. If you have no pain, maybe you think you hadn't, and don't love your wife. You understand? Maybe I'm not so clear. It is difficult. This pain Mr Monroe, this pain, I think is good pain."

Matty looked up at the sincere young man from his upright position in the bed. Tomas nodded to confirm that he'd said his bit.

"How did you become wise so young-?" Matty lifted one eyebrow higher than the other.

"Tomas," Tomas answered the unasked question. "Age does not make a sage, I once read. I like rhyme I think. I am not thinking that I am wise Mr Monroe. Sometimes other people's words are better at showing us the world than our own. That's all. I don't think you should die, though. No man should die before he has tasted Beer-Cheese I think. No! This I know! I know this for sure!"

Matty looked up at Tomas and scrunched his nose in slight confusion. Tomas took his leave, smiling at Matty's confused look, and went out the doors to make his way back towards the lift—he put the 'Do Not Disturb' sign back on the door handle.

Matty Monroe allowed his head to sink back into the pillow, and his mind to toy over the young man's odd words. Head tilted to one side, a pungent aroma that decimated any lily fragrance came to him from the plate Tomas set there. In its own way, it was a smell of death; Matty looked at it for a few minutes and found himself tentatively reaching out to scrape a taste onto the tip of his finger. He tasted it. It tingled on his tongue. His stomach, not having eaten anything since the egg sandwich the previous day, rumbled agreeably. Matty straightened himself in the bed and picked the glass off the paper mat before putting the plate of food on his lap. Looking at it, he figured out he should mix the cheese with the onions and radish; a note sat folded in the middle of the plate, and he opened it: 'Add splash of beer to cheese. Mash together. Scoop on bread. Enjoy.' was all it said. Matty complied, and after his first bite sipped the Chimay to wash it down.

It really was very, very good, Matty thought.

What was the vinegar thing that young man was talking about, he wondered? Chewing on the bread, relishing the sweet berry flavour from the cassis contrasting with the cheese, he spoke to the air about him.

"You really would like this. sweetheart," Matty whispered and smiled.

"You really would."

***

Beer Cheese Recipe
(Pivni Syr)

This is a must for anyone visiting Prague or
Bratislava. It used to be available all over the city in
Prague but many of the places that used to be
'tavernas' seemed to have turned into 'bars' with the
usual 'anywhere in the world mall food' now being
served instead. Okay, so the dumplings and
goulash weren't to most people's liking—especially if
you'd planned to cover six or seven miles walking
around the city after them, but the beer cheese was
pure sustenance, and something that stays with you
long after you leave the city. There are two
approaches to Beer Cheese. You can either buy a
Romadur Cheese (salty-rind soft
German/Czech/Slovak cheese), which is by far the
most popular option available in Prague, and you
mix the extra ingredients into that, and that's lovely.
But if you're in some other country, and Romadur is
as alien as a Romulan, then you have no choice but
to have a go yourself at a home-made variety.

Home-made Beer Cheese
A tub of quark (soft white cream cheese) or tvaroh
from a Polski Sklep
A sprinkling of pepper and salt
A teaspoon of ground caraway seeds

Mix it all together in a bowl, cover it with a tea-towel, and put it in a cupboard for three days (some people say hot-press (airing cupboard), but any cupboard will normally do).

Serving Beer Cheese
This applies to both the home-made and bought in Romadur cheese

Scoop or cut about 100g onto each plate
1/4 of a very fine chopped red onion
2 Very finely chopped spring onions
2 heaped teaspoons of strong mustard (Dijon style)
1 radish, thinly sliced
1/2 teaspoon of sweet paprika powder
1 Very nice beer of your choosing.

Personally I find that a dark beer goes extremely well with it, so anything from a dark Budvar, Leffe Bruin, or Chimay, or even English ales or Guinness hit the spot. Try them all at different times and find your own favourite.

Keep the radish aside, but add all the ingredients together on you plate with a fork. Splash a dollop of beer on top and mash them further together. Add another dollop—aim for a texture that's firm, not runny, and sits well on bread. Scoop a lump onto a piece of bread and add a slice or two of radish. Eat with a good rye bread, or a mixture of breads. Sharp flavours work well with it, and the sips of beer as you work your way through it ensure a ridiculously satisfying and easy lunch

***

Varanasi Frittata

With her knees together, and her sarong tucked carefully beneath them to guard her modesty, Vicky Stack stifled another yawn with her fist; the sun was still a pink-red ball this early in the morning haze—it was only twenty-past-five—and already risen above distant trees on the opposite side of the Ganges, it caressed her cheeks with a soft morning kiss of warm earthy breath.

Already, rickshaws jockeyed for space on the distant bridge; their incessant bells triggered a tinnitus muscle-memory within her, despite the distance. Noise. Racket. Bedlam and utter human chaos bubbled, burped, and hacked to life. Trekking in Nepal the previous weeks, a tranquillity of quiet emptiness had somehow encapsulated the spirit of the mountains and the Nepali people, and something of it had locked itself in her heart. An illogical tortuously tragic scar in the tapestry of humanity characterised her sense of India; a constant cacophony of chaos—the country was a riot of honking horns, a hazardous, haphazard, hammering of metal-on-metal, and jam-packed with gobbing, hollering, and excreting humans; her senses were assaulted by endless wafts of defecations, the bellowing of bovines, and goats bleating protests amid the endless demands made on the barely touchable weaving wallahs—yet all of it, almost impossibly, all of it and all of them were drowned by the all-consuming racket of gonging temples bleeding wince-inducing feedback mantras from crap speakers amidst a sea of tinkling rickshaw bells. Varanasi. A heinous human headache on the very thought of life; happening live, it was in her face every waking step, every motion, and for every second of it Vicky knew, more than she'd ever known in her life, that she was truly alive and in a vibrant world that was also full of life.

The ghats gently buzzed with people; with the usual sense of urgent chaos subdued by the early hour, Vicky knew that beneath the early mirage, the cauldron of life merely simmered. Three dhobi-wallahs bashed and pushed at laundry on rocks near the river's edge; their skinny naked kids jumped in and out of the sudsy river water—half washing, half-playing, full of energy and full of life, they were inured to any further waterborne disease their holy river of sewage could transmute to them, and they gulped and spit-sprayed each other with abandon.

Loud and a-rhythmical clangs resonated from the Shiva temple; its pink onion dome dominated the jostling buildings near the water's edge. Over-excited visiting pilgrims clad in ninja-black outfits—some with their arms around each other like schoolboys, all wearing bright orange flower garlands—ambled and danced in groups across the expanse of the giant steps; trying to take everything in, and knowing the trip was the only one they'd ever take, they jabbered nineteen to the dozen, laughing in delight at everything they looked at. Only ever staying for a few hours, or a night at most, they speed-visited the temples of Shiva and Ganesh before seeking out Hanuman's Sankat Sochan, and each one of them announced their arrivals to the Gods in every residence with a loud clanging of the temple bells. Everything happened with a loud clanging of bells, Vicky decided. Following the clanging of the bells, they performed puja, and left soon after. Their stream was constant; the city was permanently crowded and even overcrowded with them, despite their individual transience.

Lapping the circuit of obligatory sacred sites, the pilgrims stopped for phone photos after puja, before piling into the cycle rickshaws; maximising capacity and minimising costs, their excitement kept them oblivious to the skinny rickshaw-wallahs straining their veiny calf-muscles to return them to exit points from the city of sacred exits. Delivered to their vehicles for a pittance too paltry to ponder, nonetheless, they argued over paises—coins deemed of too little value for tourists to be provided with. Directed on their way by the ever-present traffic police lathi, they clambered and crowded back into whatever ram-packed vehicle they'd arrived in, and sped off once more with tinny music blaring full blast from vibrating plastic car speakers, as though in some unknown wacky races event, never to be seen in the city again without aid of an auspicious death or dowry.

Hearing the familiar scrape of a cow's footsteps, Vicky turned to watch it cagily. Already having had a near miss, she was sure after a second take that it was the same unfortunate beast. Locals rumoured that it was lucky if a cow dumped on you, but it wasn't the kind of 'lucky' Vicky wished for. In search of food the animals often found their way onto odd levels of the ghats, as the giant flood steps that led down to the river were named; then, as though their memory of getting there was wiped clean, the cows and bulls meandered forwards and backwards for days along whatever level they'd strolled onto and got more and more annoyed with eating nothing but the discarded bits of paper and cardboard strewn about. Eventually, someone came looking for them, or someone thought to lead them back up to the narrow city streets. Vicky realised that the sacred benefits of the Nandi relatives were more about non-interference, than any visible system of care for them; cows were more perceptive than she'd credited and clearly distinguished between locals and western tourists. Her attempts to move the creature by waving her hands were completely ignored, and it was done in a manner she could only describe as disdainful.

In the quiet of the early morning the first melodic mantras drifted from the Krishna temple near the Yogi Lodge; it wasn't the 'Hare-Krishna' chant familiar to the western world, but the traditional Vaishnavists, or worshippers of Vishnu, the God in whose dream we all live, and whose avatars include Krishna, Rama, and even the more familiar Buddha. From the distance, Vicky could hear the litany of avatar names following the familiar 'Om Namo' chant, as the ritual incantation of names and praise began.

With fond memories of Puri in Orissa, her eyes panned across to the building, and she immediately regretted it; above her, beyond the ghats, four black-clad pilgrims chose that same moment to push forth from their freshly exposed behinds the watery dahl-like defecations a morning movement in this part of the world so often constitutes. Turning quickly in a grimace of distaste in an attempt to abort the memory, her peace with the world for a moment was shattered. Brushing the dust from the arse of her sarong, Vicky rose to go.

Time to make her way back to the guest house, and wake Drew for breakfast.

On this visit, they didn't have a room in the Yogi Lodge where they'd previously stayed before they went north to Kathmandu. An Italian hippy they'd met walking in Nepal told Drew of the 'guesthouse' they were now staying in; it was cheaper, with no café, but it was much cheaper, and Drew had argued that they could always go out to any of the other guesthouses. The budget-conscious Italian irked Vicky with his superior 'much cheaper' recommendation, and she didn't hang with him; she left them both to their endless travel auditing. It was half the price, she acknowledged to Drew, but the place was filthy, and they were sleeping on top of their sleeping bags to keep away from the bedding and had no mosquito net to boot. They washed the manky bed sheet and hung the nasty stained thing out to dry shortly after taking the room. Returning from their venture out to get some provisions the sheet had disappeared. The owner, or the man who allowed the access up to the roof, and who lived on the floor directly beneath the terrace, gave them an ambiguous head shake—he said some words in English that made no sense before he closed the door.

Sure, the roof-top terrace was lovely to sit out on in the evenings, and there was no chance of some random person in his brother's police uniform wandering up and hassling anyone. It did mean the hassle of the monkeys stealing everything that wasn't locked away during the day though. Once

the Italian guy said cheaper, Drew had ignored
everything else—he seemed willing to sleep in a
toilet if it saved him money. Vicky couldn't help but
wonder why all the people she was meeting seemed
so obsessed with saving what was tantamount to
pennies on accommodation and travel costs. Did
everything have to be a poverty endurance test?
Why did they look at her strangely because she
demanded a sheet that didn't stink of a thousand
other people? She wasn't asking for the moon on a
spoon, she thought. With dhobi-wallahs everywhere
they went, every window she looked out of skinny
weathered women bashed laundry off any and every
rock in sight—endless washing, but not a single
hotel or hostel—hotels were what she dreamt of—
none of the hostels ever had a clean sheet on the
bed they offered you. Thoughts on the mattresses
beneath were stored in a part of her mind to which
she'd somehow blocked access.

Everywhere they went, opulent palaces and
Maharaja extravagances screamed at her to visit
and experience. The kind of places back home that
any sane person would near kill to go for a
weekend, they put the spa-breaks she'd paid an
arm-and-a-leg for to shame. But, no! Not here!
That wasn't the type of experience 'they' were after.
'They' were on a tight budget, and every beautiful
place they saw, they trundled by in some shit-heap
crowded bus, or wriggling for comfort in a beedi-
stinky rickshaw.

Picking at the sleep in the corner of her eyes,
Vicky sighed to herself—even that wasn't the
fullness of things bothering her this morning. A
young French man in the corner room of the roof
terrace with malaria had made her uncomfortable;

mostly stoned, nobody else seemed bothered. With talking bollocks about spirituality, or exchanging stories about how off-their-faces they'd been elsewhere in the evenings, and the day-long palaver of getting tickets to Kathmandu while finding chemists who stocked Flagyl to alleviate their giardia kept most of them busy, and away from the rooftop during the days, the young Frenchman hardly got a look in. An Austrian couple managed to stay straight long enough to get him a ticket on the train to Delhi—they also brought forward his return flight booking to France, but the train he was to travel on was still three days away. They hadn't been able to do it themselves online. Stuck in a travel agency for four hours, they paid the agent to do it for them; no mention was ever made of the Frenchman's illness to the airline for fear that he'd be stuck in some hellish Delhi hospital where his general care, outside of the medication, was expected to be undertaken by 'family'.

It seemed harsh, but Vicky just wanted him gone. Or herself. Not from India really, only from this. Whatever this was that Drew decided they were now doing. Knowing that malaria was transmitted by mosquitoes biting already infected people before biting others, it had stopped her sleeping for two nights and was why she'd found herself at the ghats on the riverbank near sunrise on both mornings. It was also contributing to her underlying mood, and that wasn't her happy-clappy self.

§

On the crumbling wall, defining the central shaft in the middle of the roof terrace atop Bindi Lodge, a small macaque picked its nose. The railings, gone on two sides now, lay semi-fused in a crumpled rusting urine soaked heap on the ground floor at the bottom of the shaft. The outer railings were still in their slots, but the plaster and crumbled brickwork suggested their ultimate demise was only a short matter of time. The monkey pissed into the shaft without changing posture; watching the tall blond man who'd come out of one of the rooms, behind him his beady eyes took in the oranges visible on the table.

Glaring at the monkey, Drew removed the small hard wire catapult he bought from a small boy living on the floor beneath. Tucked into the top of his boxer shorts, as he moved about the roof terrace, it somehow assured him. Hacking his throat clear, mimicking a gross local habit, he watched the unflinching monkey eyeballing him back. Folding a small piece of copper cable wire with his thumb and forefinger, and slotting it into the slack elastic, he raised it at the monkey and drew it back in the same motion. Pulling its head back in a manner that Drew thought indignant, aware, and angry, it leapt to one side and dived for the building's edge. Drew released and his copper wire bullet flew and stung the monkey's shoulder before it disappeared, screaming and protesting its pain, over the side. Grabbing the power lines, it swung its way noisily across the street before posting itself anew atop the railings of the grander house opposite; rubbing its shoulder, it vocalised angrily and glared over at him.

At the improvised kitchen two German men had set up some years earlier, he unlocked the shaded cupboard with the 1-2-3 combination written on the door. The monkeys couldn't read. That was the only thing he could say about them for sure. The weedy bhang had inflamed his appetite, and he knew Vicky would be on her way back so decided to sort some breakfast. Vicky wasn't getting the same kick living on a pound a day; this, his third winter in India, each year he'd purposely tightened his budget. It meant he could stay longer, and when he did get back to England it was nearer April; the gardens would be ready for him to begin work once more, and the expensive costs of idle time could thus be avoided. This was the first time he'd taken someone with him, or someone came with him, he thought, correcting his mistake with Vicky's voice in his head.

Four sealed ant-proof Tupperware boxes sat in the simple cupboard, with eggs and vegetables. There were only two pots—one for boiling, and one for frying; he took them both out and wiped them with his tee-shirt end before he set about prepping breakfast. Except for a little salt, Drew was spiced out and wanted the food to be as plain as he could get it; mainly he wanted it to taste of what it was, rather than spices, and the eggs too he hoped would bung himself and Vicky a little. Heading south, they'd planned some long bus and train journeys for the coming weeks—getting caught short was never much fun, and in India it was never too far from Drew's mind.

§

"Chai chai chai, lady? You like chai?" The chai-wallah smiled at Vicky mischievously; his eyes took in her bare shoulders in the way she recognised a western man might take in an exposed breast.

Smiling back, she shook her head softly. Warned off the chai, especially in areas like this, and railway stations, Vicky didn't quite get it. Thousands of people seemed to be drinking the stuff in both of those places, but Drew had been out here a few times, and so far her system had held together following his small tips. Slipping around the stall, she made her way back up the main thoroughfare where the small market stalls were beginning to set up.

Rakhi week, which Vicky had never heard of back in England: everybody not selling fruit vegetables or sweets seemed to be selling bracelets—the 'symbolic item of exchange between brothers and sisters celebrating their love and duties of and to each other'. This, Vicky, found out from an intense Swiss man called Fabian. Fabian spent most of his time trying to smoke clay pipe chillums with saddhus, the saffron-clad and face-painted holy-men, or Fakirs, scattered about the ghats in greater numbers than Vicky had seen anywhere else—apparently, that was one of their religious duties, according to Fabian. From what Vicky could gather, he was intent on sharing their onerous task as much as possible. Snorting with laughter when he told her about Rakhi, misinterpreting his serious sincerity for a sardonic sideswipe, she apologised and explained that she had four brothers, and could only imagine how hellish her life would have been if they'd got a whiff of their being any 'duty' involved in their relationships. Fabian couldn't seem to grasp her explanation.

A small, oak-bark Saddhu covered
haphazardly in white ash, rolled an elaborately
pricked rangavalli tube before various stalls, creating
odd chalk patterns on the dusty earth. Small tokens
for his actions or blessings were pressed quietly into
his hands by an occasional person; otherwise,
people continued with their preparations for the day
ahead. A chai-wallah's child helper mumbled and
wove through the throng with a large pot, and
multiple throw-away clay cups; his voice low and
soft, he chanted the 'chai chai chai' incantation—the
smallest glimpse or twitch of an eye was enough to
stop him.

§

On the rooftop Drew smoked on another joint and
watched the potatoes boil for some minutes before
draining them, listening all the while to an argument
rising from the floor below. Hearing random English
words in the middle of Hindi conversations still
surprised him. Once he'd drained the potatoes,
Drew added them to the frying pan with some oil,
and put that on the heat. The rest would go in on
top of those after ten minutes, and once it was all
well-cooked, he'd add the beaten eggs with a little
curd mixed into them. Not trusting the water, or the
milk, which had an odd taste—as though somebody
had pissed in it—it made him retch, so he avoided it.
　　With some reinforcements from its troop sat
alongside, the monkey returned to the building next
door and was once again on the same side of the
street as Drew. Watching Drew watching them,
watching him, Drew checked his catapult nervously
and picked a couple of copper bullets up; just out of

range, he didn't pose an immediate threat, but they fidgeted nervously at the sight of the catapult. Setting the weaponry down again, next to the single ring of cooking gas flame, he set about prepping his eggs.

§

Leaving the open area of the market stalls, Vicky resumed her meander back to the guesthouse through the narrow alleyways. The ironing man was already up, slurping his chai as he half-listened to his boy telling him something in an excited fashion; wearing a khaki coloured pair of shorts, a gleaming short-sleeved white shirt, and a striped neckerchief held with a woggle, with his hair damp and pressed flat into a military-style side crease, his over-sized school satchel hung across his back, and the straps held as he spoke, to relieve some of the weight of the books, the boy looked like a parade scout. He stopped talking when he saw Vicky looking at him; adding some hot coals to the top of his iron, nodding all the while, his father's eyes twitched and also narrowed slightly as Vicky passed by his corner, taking in her bare shoulders, but otherwise he didn't acknowledge her. Beyond his squatted spot of the alley, a small labyrinth of narrow lanes with tall buildings kept the area cooler during the day, and already Vicky could feel the temperature drop a few degrees as she mooched her way along the shade with her second bag of bracelets of the week.

Nearing the corner for the last lane before the guesthouse, a large bull sauntered into view some twenty yards ahead of her, and stopped; a beautiful beast, with impressive wide horns—if you were looking at it from the safety of a bus, or a barrier between you and it—it also had those unusual humps at the top of the shoulders, and a long dropping throat. It reminded her a little of camels, especially in the languid way they loped about. Tilting its head, and looking at her square in the eyes, it drew Vicky to a halt.

Aware that in Varanasi the cows and bulls meandered at will, completely unrestricted, Vicky paused for a moment. Hearing a loud snort behind her, she turned to look and almost collapsed in a heap when she saw another identical bull blocking her intended retreat. The creatures by and large ignored humans, unless they were feeling particularly cranky on a hot or wet day, or had been bothered by dogs or monkeys and were similarly riled, or if they had to squeeze past people in the narrow lanes, and felt threatened. Street fighting bulls are common in Varanasi and often cause traffic chaos across the city, or even mayhem by the ghats themselves; however, in the narrow lanes of the old city, a more immediate risk of being gored, stamped, squashed, or even getting caught up in a mad bull charge is the real danger.

Both bulls snorted loudly, and the one in front of her raised its head and sounded what to Vicky's ears and body felt like a threatening bellow. Her feet began to shuffle backwards. Utterly terrified and trapped in the narrowness between the houses, she froze uncertainly; the alley went eerily quiet and turning Vicky could see that both bulls were now ready to charge the other, oblivious to her minor obstructive presence. She contemplated dropping flat to the floor—being stamped, somehow seemed preferable to a goring. Reaching for a doorway, only slightly set into the house wall, she banged it fearfully without looking at it. There was no outer handle. Ahead of her, the massive bull charged; at the same moment the door slid open and a man's arm reached out and grabbed Vicky to pull her in. Feeling the force of the animal's charge as it thundered by her, and where she'd been standing moments earlier, she then heard the loud coming together of their hardened skulls, and the clickety-clack battle of their horns.

"Okay! All clear now," her rescuer unceremoniously shunted Vicky back into the alleyway, and shut the door behind her; barely catching a glimpse in the darkness, she had no time, or opportunity, to thank him. In a city of ceremonies, manners tended towards the abrupt.

Arriving at the hostel, Vicky took in the mess of the entrance before going inside. It was something a squatter in England would go past, preferring the open, exposed, airiness of the bus-shelter to it. Circling the balcony beneath the roof terrace, where several families lived, often four or five to each room, Vicky stepped over a small girl squatting and shitting by the drain while talking to her mother in the nearby room as she awaited her colon to empty. She winced at the youngster's waft, but it faded as she neared the stairs and got the first wave of breakfast smells from above. Sighing with relief, it was still well before seven, Vicky felt as though she was ready to go back to bed and was looking forward to some food. Atremble from the bulls, she climbed the stone steps leading to the roof; her hand reluctantly touched the greasy flaking wall-plaster to check her balance. The handrail had long gone, and three empty holes at either end of the steps were the only sign that there had ever been one. Potatoes, eggs, onions, peppers, garlic— each step brought a stronger and more distinctive smell.

Stepping out on to the balcony smiling, she looked around in dismay.

Squatted and cowered to one side, Drew held his arm over his face; with a bag of oranges between its legs, an alpha monkey loomed near him. In one of its hands, the monkey held another orange and a fistful of some human-food in the other. Three smaller monkeys scrabbled around grabbing frenziedly at steaming food spilt on the ground near the cooking area.

Their breakfast.

Vicky screamed in frustration and then roared as loud as she'd ever screamed or roared anything in her life. The monkeys dispersed explosively in shock; the second person changed the power balance, but they grabbed everything in an instant and disappeared over the side. Looking to Drew to see if he was hurt, Vicky tilted her head in a concerned fashion.

"You okay?" She bent her knees and came down to his level.

"That big male they told us about yesterday is back," Drew replied sheepishly. "They attacked— that thing is-?"

Fear in his eyes told it all; they'd been warned about him, but as he hadn't shown up, or been about, they assumed he was no longer something for them to worry about—another myth of the rooftop, they half-hoped.

"The gallybander-catapult thing?" Vicky looked around for their only protection.

"He ripped it off me," gesturing to indicate the monkey had flung it over the side of the building and showing a long scratch on his arm, a pitiful Drew shook his head.

"What happened your face?' Vicky asked, noticing the redness on one side for the first time.

"He—he slapped me," Drew mimicked the monkey's swipe. Touching the redness, and meeting Vicky's eyes, he challenged her to disbelieve him.

"He slapped you?" Vicky rattled her lips and shook her head; she nodded to assure and let him know she believed him; flopping next to him she looked about at the mess the monkeys created.

"What did you make?" Vicky asked.

"Frittata," Drew looked about at the mess.

"Varanasi Frittata," her mind montaged her morning so far, as she rubbed her face with dirt-sticky hands and immediately regretted it. Stifling another tired yawn, she looked to Drew until his eyes met hers.

"Yogi Lodge," she scanned again and resolved to leave any clearing up to someone else; this wasn't her mess or her problem anymore. "Yogi Lodge!"

"You want us to go to Yogi Lodge?" Drew's face curled with disappointment; in his eyes, the monkeys were a small set back, and he was sure they could get around it. Chewing his lip, he shook his head as though let down, before looking to Vicky once more following a small cough from her.

"No," speaking quietly, decisively, she narrowed her eyes and looked closely at him to ensure he understood her words fully.

"I'm going to Yogi Lodge, Drew."

Below, and along the street, beyond the ironing man, further along than the narrow alleyway, beyond the ghats and next to the bank of the Ganges, a new group of black-clad pilgrims streamed excitedly through the temple doors and set the bells a-clanging frantically, awakening the city and her gods to their newly arrived presence and their fresh offerings. The shift in noise drew the gazes of the monkeys; the distinctive Durga bells clanged and echoed through the narrow alleyways, bouncing off the walls, the cows, the bulls and the buffaloes as they stopped and tilted their heads to read the sounds. As one, the troop shifted; their focus arrowed across the roof-tops to the distant bells and an excited chatter swirled in their effortless clambering. Drew and Vicky, forgotten behind them, avoided each other's eyes and didn't notice their departure.

***

Varanasi Frittata

Ingredients
4/5 medium sized potatoes
5 eggs
1 red pepper
1 onion
1 leek
4 cloves of garlic
50g mature cheddar
1 splash of milk
salt/pepper

Making Varanasi Frittata
Slice or cube the potatoes, give them a good wash to clear the starch, and boil them in lightly salted water for ten minutes. Drain and let moisture steam off for a few minutes.

Frittata essentially means frying/fried, so after that, fry them separately (oil/butter combination) until they're browning and crisping nicely. Set them aside, or whilst they're frying, start a new frying pan.

In the second pan, sweat the onions, then add the leeks for six or so minutes before adding the pepper and garlic, and gently fry them until the peppers have softened nicely (ten minutes or so).

In a large bowl beat up the eggs, milk and add the cheese. Add the potatoes to the other pan for a couple of minutes and lightly shake it. Add the egg mixture, cover, and gently fry until the eggs are ready (12-14 minutes)

Serve as you would a quiche, with a side salad, and some rustic bread.

***

Dog for Sale: Abandoned by Husband

THE PHOTO OF THE SUPERMARKET ADVERT from his daughter arrived as Lachlan walked along the garden path towards the front door.

Clicking it, just as he came to the porch step and reached for the bell, he growled to himself.

"Oh, you! You bloody bitch!" Lachlan stared at the phone, and his finger froze seven inches or so from the bell.

His daughter had warned him that his wife had put an ad out, and little Trudy was upset about it when talking to him on the phone the previous evening; she'd been upset every evening since he left, but Lachlan was trying to stay strong. Janine needed to know he was serious this time. Slowly leaning forward, he allowed his finger to carry the few extra inches and reach the bell which he then pressed twice.

It rang multiple times within and seemed to go on forever, echoing all over the house, before he saw the oncoming shape of his friend in the smoky bubble glass.

The door opened.

"Oh g'day Lock!"

"G'day Tommy," miserably looking back at his phone Lachlan's face told a story.

"What's up mate?" Lachlan showed him the text.

Tommy read it, and re-read it, but he didn't understand it, or its connection to Lachlan.

"It's from Trudy," Lachlan sighed in a self-pitying desperation. "Janine stuck that bloody thing up on two of the Coles local ad-boards yesterday! Trudes told me about it last night. Just down the bloody road mate! Y'know, for the whole neighbourhood to have a good old gander and gossip!"

'What?" Tommy put one hand to his head as though to hold his thoughts inside. "She's selling old Bingo? Oh mate, I guess you'd better come in, eh."

Lachlan followed his friend along the hallway towards the kitchen at the back of the house, muttering the whole time about what a bitch his wife Janine was until they came to the kitchen, where he looked about nervously. The worktop was full of food in the process of being prepped.

"Is Chrissie about?" Surprised at the food, his ears had told him nothing of her presence. "I thought she-?"

"No. You're 'right mate—that's my stuff; she's out—up at the school kitchen today—got her old Monday-Tuesday shifts back," Tommy explained. " Just getting a bit-a-grub sorted out for meself for the week. We're back on the sixty shift, mate."

"Oh, good shit fella? I thought that was all finished and you guys were back down to forty-somethings?" Lachlan checked why the news he had was already old.

"Seems we landed that Chinese order," Tommy filled the gap for him. "That'll keep us all busy over there for at least eight months Locky. I need it to fella—tellin' you now. Gotta knock a little chunk of me mortgage bills while I can, y'know."

"Too right," Lachlan agreed. "It'll be good for you guys if they keep the sixty shift running Tom—you doin' all the weekends too mate? Yeah? What's that you're making there with that stuff anyway?"

"Month-on month-off for the weekends, so we gotta juggle the kiddies every couple, which isn't too bad. Chrissie just wants us to pile any extras into the bank. Get the numbers down, y'know? 'No holidays for us Tommy', she said. Y'know what Chrissie's like mate," Tommy spread a narrow sheet of filo pastry onto a chopping board and kept his focus there as he spoke.

"She's a good girl, your Chrissie," Lachlan's tone changed and he shook his head.

"What's happening Lock?" Tommy tilted his head upwards, holding a spoonful of filling in his palm, and Lachlan looked at him questioningly without speaking. "You and Janine mate? I thought you guys were solid, y'know? What's goin' on? Chrissie was sayin'."

"So did I, mate," Lachlan replied. "So did I."

Pausing for a moment, he watched Tommy create a small ball in his hand with the food before him; squeezing it together, Tommy added it to the pastry and began an elaborate process of folding it in triangles.

"You heard about the teacher bloke? Yeah? What the hell are you making there, Tommy? I never realised you've become such a dab hand in the kitchen, mate," Lachlan's curiosity grew as he watched his friend. Tommy nodded and smiled as he concentrated; criss-cross folding the pastry he finished the triangle before putting it on an oiled tray.

"I think we all heard, mate! Not the specifics like, don't get me wrong!" Tommy twigged Lachlan's horror and skilfully adapted his confirmation. "You know what the girls are like … shit fella, they probably even knew all about it when it was going on. They always seem to be a step ahead of us, yeah? Especially on this kind-a-shit."

Lachlan nodded; he was over the humiliation now, but reminders still touched a nerve and brought colour to his cheeks. Sometimes it made him want to weep.

"Chrissie said you moved out too? That right?" Tommy probed, partly curious and partly to fill Chrissie in later.

"Had to Tom." Lachlan took a deep snuffle. "Might-a-killed her, mate, if I stayed there, y'know? I was seething inside, Tom. Burning up with the anger like. Felt like a beast, I did. She wasn't, or I can't be sure, but it felt she was kind of gloating too, y'know? Somehow, everything was my fault on top of that. Me head is down, me arse is up, and if I ain't workin' mate, it seems I'm gettin' shafted one way or the other from that lady."

"Still, Locky mate, you could end up losing your rights," Tommy added a fourth triangle of filled pastry to the row. "You might want to bite that bullet fella and just get your head back under the roof for a wee while. Don't rock the boat too much until-? Is this goin' the whole way to the courts this time Lock? She could end up blocking you seein' Trudes. Shit! You don't want that Lock—y'know what I'm saying?"

Lachlan nodded. Tommy had touched a nerve on something that was keeping him awake at night.

"You had words with that teacher bloke over in Ozford yet?"

Staring blankly, his mind went over Tommy's words as he watched his friend fill another pastry before neatly folding it once more; Lachlan rose and put the kettle on to boil, deciding he needed a cup of tea or something to distract him. Just thinking of his wife at the moment was enough to set him shaking inside; crying and raging himself to sleep for nearly a week, he then got drunk for another week and was due to go back on nights in his own job the coming evening. It wasn't a thing a man could do really—going around blubbing and whinging to his mates—but Tommy and himself went way back. Lachlan's brother had been his best man at his wedding, but deep down he'd known it should have been his old mate Tommy.

"Went up there to see him, mate," he reluctantly began to talk about the teacher. "Was goin' to knock his head off too. Proper riled I was mate—proper riled—I'm telling you, Tom. Waited outside, just sittin' in me car. Must-a-missed the bugger somehow. Wasn't full sure what he looked like but I didn't see anyone I thought might be him, y'know."

"Oh, he's a big lad, Lock. Must be six and a half foot of him—with a big beard. One of those big—salt and peppers? Is that what they call them? You know half-black half-grey—looks like a big bear, mate," aware of who the teacher was, Tommy couldn't help but check if Lachlan's bluff would have carried through when he caught sight of the monster.

"Oh shit, I saw 'him'! Really—is that the bloke?" Disbelief in his voice, Lachlan gulped a swallow. "He's a bloody monster! Was it him for sure? Janine was having it off with that big-? What is he—Russian? Oh, Christ, mate, I don't even know what to make of that. Shit. Bitch'd make me shave before getting into bed, even if I'd been on a sixteen-hour stint."

"I dunno either, mate," Tommy lined up his first two completed rows—he'd prepped ten, and there was space enough for ten more once he tightened them up. Lachlan needed a consoling man-pat on the back or shoulder, but his hands were greasy and he was on a roll with the pastries.

"Has she stopped seeing him?"

Lachlan didn't know the answer and rocked his head from side to side as he stared at the tea; removing both tea bags, he added milk and a touch of sugar to each cup and placed Tommy's to one side for him, getting a nod of thanks, as Tommy continued with his task.

"Maybe find that out, mate," Tommy lifted an eyebrow at his friend and waited until their eyes met. "I mean, Lock, you've been doing nights on and off now for what … three, four years? They only change you guys one week in three, and that's just wrong! That's bad practice, mate. You get a week off, and you're on your back fella—you're trying to catch up with sleep, and just as you're getting there, you're back on the shit again. All you boys up there are fucked! What's it they say … killing you softly, Lock? Eh?"

"Don't have a choice, Tom. You know what she's like. Wanted a bigger place, mate. I have to put the hours in to hit the bills. She's not like Chrissie, mate; Janine likes her coffee mornings with the girls, and that, bitch always said she'd never be a working mum. If she dropped the kids, then it was down to me. That was the arrangement, anyway, and she's never tired of reminding me," weariness sat heavy in his voice.

"You gotta get back in there, mate. If you don't, she'll still have you payin' for it, but without any access or anything. That's how they read it today, Lock," Tommy reflected on the situation and gave the best advice he could.

"I know, Tom. I know that, fella." Lachlan agreed with his friend but struggled to pull his thoughts together. "I'm just a bit crook, mate. It's like a knife in me. I can't really get me head in the game, y'know."

"I can imagine, Lock," Tommy nodded and blinked back his thoughts as he sipped his tea. Janine was a bitch. Tommy knew that himself first hand. Eight years now; he was only twenty-one at the time, and he remembered clear as day, despite the passage of time and the fact it was late in the evening. Four days after his twenty-first. Up St Kilda's walking off a buzz. Just after eight; he remembered looking at his phone at the time—it was one of those old Nokias. Janine cycled by and saw him when he waved. She stopped, and they'd chatted for a few minutes. They were all friends back then. Once she realised he had a bit of weed on him, she locked up the bike and came for a walk too. Only beginning to get dark, and it had been a warm day for November—he remembered that she was wearing the engagement ring Lachlan bought her the previous month too and seemed to look at the bugger every ten minutes, that Tommy could tell. They stopped in the middle of the hill for a while, after meandering into the long grass where they'd be invisible; there was no one around anyway, but it was always best to be careful. Melbourne cops always seemed to pop up just where you didn't want them. They sat together hidden in the long grass and Tommy made up a little cone for each of them; afterwards, they lay back and watched the sky for a while, talking about this and that, as you do. Janine started talking about things happening too quickly, and how she didn't want to miss out on life. Tommy agreed with her, in truth, but he would've agreed with anything. He was happy, twenty-one, summer was just beginning, and he was stoned. When she made a play for his balls, Tommy was slow to react. At twenty-one, how would any fella react? Janine was a hottie. Always had been. Locky had nabbed her at seventeen, and nobody else got a look in with her after that. Even now, sayin' no to her for sure would still be tricky in Tommy's mind; looking back, he didn't really get to think about it. Before he knew it, they were both upside down in the grass giving each other as good as they got. It happened a couple more times that summer—pretty much the same spot each time too. That was it though. Tommy walked up around the hiking paths near St Kilda's the following summer a few times but never came across her there again; he met her out with Lachlan loads of times, especially after he and Chrissie got it on, but it was something they just never seemed to have taken out of the park, so they never spoke of it again.

Folding over the last of the pastries, he set the oven, before turning once more to his friend.

"You gotta decide, Locky mate. It's your family, and it's up to you if you want to keep it together. You can forgive, and move on, and maybe try to come to a better work arrangement. If it happened because you're never about anymore, or always working, or too tired, then something's gotta give, mate. Either that, or she's gotta step up too, y'know? Tear up the old deal! If it ain't working, it's a no-deal, Lock! Maybe if she has to put in a bit-a-graft as well, she'll soon change her tune."

Lachlan said nothing; he watched Tommy fuss with his tray of pastries before putting them all in the oven and tidying up. In a matter of minutes, there was no sign of all the work he'd been doing and Lachlan shook his head in amazement. Finishing his tea, he looked on, lost in his own thoughts as Tommy began removing more items from the fridge and cupboards, as though to start preparing something else. Putting his cup in the sink, he cleared his throat.

"I'm off, mate," putting his hand on Tommy's shoulder he gave it an appreciative pat and squeeze.

"Where to, Lock?" Tommy knew the answer would tell him where his friend's mind was at.

"Home, fella," Lachlan nodded decisively. "I'm going home, Tom. I gotta family, mate, just like you said, and I gotta sort through this shit."

"Good on you, Lock," Tommy squeezed his shoulder again in encouragement.

"Cheers, fella. You're a good mate, Tom. You're a good mate. I think I just needed the right nudge, y'know?" Lachlan made his way out of the kitchen to the hallway.

"Righto, Lock," Tommy followed him out to see him off and picked up his phone as he did so.

From his car Lachlan waved at Tommy with a jokey salute before pulling out from the kerb; his new Shogun purred as he put his foot down. Tommy turned and made his way back to the kitchen and opened a text from an unfamiliar number as he did so. 'Remember the long grass in St Kilda's?'

Perched on his tall kitchen stool next to the food he'd spread across the surface, Tommy scrolled through his phone diary for the coming weeks, checking and double-checking his shifts and the kids' activities into which he was scheduled.

'Cycling up that way this Wednesday evening', he fixed himself on the stool as the thought alone began to get him going.

§

Tommy was right. Lachlan took his foot off the brake and allowed his car to roll the last few yards silently before stopping in front of the garage door. A man should look out for his family first, and put his own concerns second. Family first! Even his old man could agree with that. Remaining in the car for a few minutes, he spoke for a while with Wayne Williams, his co-foreman up at the plant. Together they re-jigged their shifts so Lachlan could effectively get some time out and sort his life out, but at the same time wouldn't lose out on any upcoming extras. Life just had too many bills. Thanking Wayne, he made his way to the front door. Janine was out. He knew that already, and also knew that she wouldn't be back until she picked up Trudy after three o clock. Today was 'Pilates day', and a leisurely lunch with the ladies after.

John Finn's van rolled into his driveway just as he put the key in the front door. Lachlan stopped to greet John himself. An old school friend, they'd always joked that he'd stolen Locky's destined career. Walking him around the house to the three doors he wanted everything changed on, the front, the back, and the interior door to the garage, Lachlan explained his need for urgency. Finn set about the work once Lachlan left him to it. Indoors, he made his way upstairs. Taking the three suitcases they used for holidays, he removed his wife's clothing from the wardrobes and drawers and filled all three in moments. After that, he improvised and set about filling sport's bags and a couple of boxes he'd stashed in the loft; he took everything outside and piled it in the garage. His nerve shook a bit, and he thought to write a note but decided against it. Lachlan knew he had to stand his ground. No doubt, she'd want to ring the police. The deeds of the house were in Lachlan's name, as was the mortgage. Janine didn't work, and adding her to the mortgage application reduced the funds they could raise, so they kept her off all the paperwork for the house. Sometimes small blessings are disguised, as his nan used to say. Lachlan knew the whole thing was going to blow tits-up in his face at some stage, but at least this way the complications of finding a place to live, or stay, or anything else that the world might shit out, would happen to Janine. Possession was nine-tenths; he remembered hearing that once. He didn't know if it was true and he didn't care anymore either. Janine had no reason to throw him out, and he hadn't taken anything with him to say he was gone—he had plenty of reason to fling her out, though. The top window was what he felt like, so in some ways, she was getting off light.

Ringing his mother, he told her what he was up to, and she volunteered herself to look out for

Trudy until they got a minder in place. Lachlan knew she would; it gave her an excuse to get away from his old man too, and she'd never liked Janine much, his mum. 'Don't trust her shifty little eyes' she used to say when they got together first, and every now and again when she'd supped a few too many Chardonnays, she'd repeat it to anyone who'd listen.

"I'm on me way. I'll sort the little bitch out, Lock! Don't you worry 'bout her, son," she said, before hanging up.

Shaking hands, John Finn gave Lachlan the three new keys before leaving; he hooted and stamped his feet when he realised what Lachlan was up to. Lachlan would spot him some cash over in the Fifth Province on Fitzroy Street, where Finn hung out on Friday nights. Still single, he liked a few beers when the week was done. Lachlan couldn't remember the last time he'd been in the pub.

"Life's about chapters," Lachlan spoke the words aloud to himself and the clear November sky, as he watched Finn pull away. "Time to begin a new chapter, Locky mate. Time for a change! Fuck knows a man needs a rest every now and again."

No rain fell in Melbourne for the next six weeks; the grass around the hills in St Kilda's grew tall and turned golden earlier than usual. It was lovely up there as long as you didn't snot up with hay fever. Tommy Kennedy cycled up around a few evenings but never met a soul he knew; it was mainly kids and shifty fellas in their twenties looking around for other fellas to go into the grass with. He didn't hear from Locky for a long while, but with both of them doing odd shifts, the kids, and everything else life throws at young men trying to get their shit together, that wasn't strange. Saw Janine up in Little Bourke Street one Saturday when he and Chrissie were out and about shopping for clothes and the like with the kids. Didn't notice him, did she? Tricky to notice anything when your nose is stuck up in the air like it was. With a big fella and holding on to his arm like she was about to fall over; he didn't have a beard anymore. Liked a close shave, Janine. Always had, that he remembered. Always had.

***

Feta and Spinach Triangles

Ingredients for 8
100g fresh baby spinach leaves
250g block of feta cubed
8 sun-dried tomatoes chopped
Half a cup of raisins (6 or seven in each triangle)
Half a cup of olives diced
Half a cup of pine nuts (optional, as these seem to be now more expensive per gram than gold)
salt and pepper
I pack of Filo Pastry

Preparation
Lightly steam the spinach just to shrink it a bit for about a minute or so.
Then put everything into a large mixing bowl and mix it all together with a fork until it becomes a large block or ball. Weigh it, divide it into eight equal pieces, and set them aside on a plate.
Take four sheets of filo pastry and cut them in half lengthways. Brush them lightly with rapeseed oil.
Lie one of the strips out flat and add one of the prepared mixes to one end. Then take one of the corners from that end and bring it across the mix to create your first triangle fold. Bring the farthest corner of the triangle forward to continue the triangular shapes, and continue doing this until you've run out of pastry to fold. Repeat seven more times. Keep the finished shapes beneath a damp

tea-towel as Filo can be tediously dry sometimes. Brush lightly with oil before putting them in the oven at 180 for about twenty-five minutes (check them after twenty).

Serve with tabouleh or a side salad for a light and healthy lunch.

***

Catching Up

The body of a young woman sat propped against the trunk of a mature beech tree just behind the graveyard of the castle grounds. Found by an elderly lady, Mrs Denning, who lived in the village, it was while she was walking her small terrier, a small border her husband had named Billy-Bob, and she was quite shaken over the incident. It was Billy-Bob in truth who found the body, but even the young police officer omitted him from his report, and on later reading, he realised he'd made it seem that Mrs Denning was somehow scurrying about beneath the bushes when she came across the body. Hoping nobody noticed, he said nothing.

The body wasn't there that long; the blood was still sticky and wet to touch. The woman's face looked sad and hollowed more than anything else; the young police officer having got over his initial excitement, then felt a bit sick in his stomach, which also made him pale, and a little dizzy. His supervising officer, WPC Sheringham, took him aside and set him the task of asking questions of people who were walking about the area. This was more to give him some relief, than in the hope of gaining anything useful. After forty minutes he came back with copious notes of all the conversations. An unnecessary screech of tyres told them CID had turned up. WPC Sheringham watched from next to the body as a bulky moustached man with a wind-swept comb-over struggled out of his car; she continued to watch as he wrestled himself into an over-sized rain mac, after which he then stomped his way through the castle grounds straight across the old graves to the crime scene. Blowing his nose loudly, he walked around the crime scene twice half-picking at the end of his nose, before finally looking at them both.

"Does anybody know her bloody name yet?" Detective Inspector Crawley scratched at the tip of his reddened nose again and snuffled back a headful of snot as he bent over to take a closer look.

"Laura Esta-something," Acting Constable Duff struggled to read aloud one of the flapping paper pieces from a bag he held. "Hang on. Estaban! Sounds like she might be Colombian or-?"

"What? Here in bloody Warkworth?" DI Crawley sneered a retort at the young constable. "Next you'll be saying she's a drug dealer, Constable, and Alnwick the centre of her international bloody network!"

The Woman Police Constable and the Castle Warden who'd been watching over Mrs Denning laughed nervously at the Inspector's joke.

Duff glared at the Castle Warden before answering.

"'Acting' Constable, Duff. Sir. No Inspector," Duff kept his response factual, but couldn't help the terse edge. "I was merely thinking out loud. Spanish maybe?".

"Probably Duff? Probably. An exchange student, do you think?" Crawley bent to take a closer look at her face.

"Possibly, sir. She seems a little old for that though—they're usually just kids aren't they?" Duff was a little reluctant to fully contradict his superior's inferior observations.

Crawley looked at Duff and shrugged before bobbing his head to indicate a likely agreement.

"Mmmm," Crawley noised as he scrutinised the body. "Are the swabs and all the photos finished?"

"The medics are waiting for the nod to take her, sir. WPC Sheringham instructed them to wait until you'd surveyed the crime scene and given clearance, sir," Duff enjoyed reporting facts and nodded in satisfaction as he responded to the Inspector's query.

Crawley gestured with a thumb to the WPC in acknowledgement of her decision; still getting used to working with WPCs, Sheringham was only the third Crawley had met professionally, but within twenty years Crawley reckoned there'd be at least one or two in every station-house. They wouldn't be making the tea either—a revolution was coming.

"Let them have the poor little blighter," Crawley's hard mask slipped a little, allowing the human behind it to peep through. "Let's find out who she really is. WPC Sheringham?"

"Sir," Sheringham met his eyes and awaited instruction.

"Can you take young Duff here and check out Warkworth House. Also, look in on The Sun and The Hermitage while you're at it. I suspect she'll have worked in one of those. Anything at all you can find."

"Laura Estaban … how did you end up here?" Crawley knelt once more and muttered quietly to the body.

"Sir," Sheringham watched the usually stone-faced Inspector talk to the body with sadness and compassion filling his face.

"I'll be in The Bull or The Masons. Call me there if you need me. Jones hasn't sorted the car-radio yet," Crawley gestured a phone fist to his ear as he looked up at her.

"Vicious fucker whoever did this. So much for thinking it was an April fool's call this morning. Rape and murder in bloody Warkworth! Who'd bloody credit it?" Crawley shook his head at Sheringham and Duff before he tip-toed his way back across the graves and out of the Castle grounds.

At his car, he wondered if he might just walk down the hill to the two pubs, but decided against it. In Northumberland, March and April could be contrary months: the rain if it came properly, with this biting wind, could soak and chill a man to the bone. Crawley got into his brand new mud-splashed Volvo 740se and turned on the engine. Releasing the hand-brake, he frugally rolled the fifty yards instead—Nena's 'Ninety-nine red balloons' filled the air for a few seconds, before he turned it off—lost in his thoughts as the car rolled.

§

"Some stupid tosser has concreted over the river path!" Jay James spoke loudly to himself as he made his way down the disabled access slope.

A local cut through, he'd walked this path as a teenager mostly—a rat-run for the youth when he was growing up—it got you from the centre of the town to the small suburban estates quicker than any of the paved streets. Only ever a hard dirt path back then; dark strips of grass either side made it easy to see your way, even on a moonless night.

On a moonless night, the river path was always busier than other nights.

There were unwritten rules for the river path too.

The first rules of the river path were, no looking, or messing with couples getting it on in the darker crevices.

Break the first two rules, and you'd likely end up in the river.

At least when he was young, that was standard protocol. The grass was gone—overhanging trees that created private, sheltered snugs along the walk were all cut back hard and couldn't even be seen from the path anymore. Fake antique-style streetlights linked their illumination every thirty meters, and a high concrete breeze block wall ran as far as Jay could see. What was once a scruffy but busy artery from the countryside into and through the heart of the town was now an urbanised footpath, tidy, and utterly devoid of people.

Thirty years had passed since Jay last walked along beside the river towards his parents' house. Thirty years since he'd been in his parents' house; it was also twenty-something years since he'd been back anywhere in Lincolnshire.

Much had changed he thought, so much had changed.

§

Maddie Macabe was nervous. In her kitchen, she fidget-arsed about all afternoon in an effort to remain calm, but her heart still beat too quickly in her chest, and her thoughts just couldn't seem to settle; she was trying hard to get everything 'just so'.

Her husband, she still thought of him as that, even though he was now dead two months. Duncan had been his name; he'd kept a kitchen garden, and Maddie over the years became accustomed to it; and although reluctant to get involved with it at first, she now loved it. Her initial reluctance was down to her husband's stinginess. What they saved, in his estimation, from their grocery bill, Duncan Macabe deducted from Maddie's housekeeping money. Had he been asked to estimate anything, Duncan Macabe always worked his sums to a conservative, miserly amount—Maddie's savings with the patch, however, were calculated to a maximum and deducted as such from her already paltry allowance.

Maddie dug up a whole bunch of perpetual onions, which she topped, tailed, stripped, and then fine-chopped, filling an entire breakfast bowl with them. Welsh onions, she called them, but Duncan had insisted the official name was 'perpetual' onions—he had a thing about the Welsh too. Maddie made her croquettes; lost in thought, she watched a grey squirrel trying to defeat the new baffle she'd put beneath her bird feeders.

At a loss, Maddie was making what she remembered to be her son's favourite food—her son had just turned seventeen when she last saw him, and the dish her mind pictured him loving was likely when he was somewhere between eleven and thirteen, and still her innocent little hero.

How different must he be now, Maddie wondered.

When they spoke on the telephone, some five days earlier, and he'd agreed to come over and catch up and visit her after all this time, Maddie suggested that they might have a bite to eat. Always more comfortable doing things than just sitting about, food was something she did well, and her son had agreed to the suggestion. Having become mainly vegetarian too over the years, she hoped that wouldn't be awkward; sometimes she thought her diet choice had been just to counter Duncan, who ate meat at every sitting, and with the inactivity, his complexion reddened year by year. If he hadn't died, Maddie thought he might just have exploded, or combusted, like an over-ripe seed. She liked vegetarian sausages anyway, and it wasn't like they'd ever eaten those fancy gourmet sausages—the cheaper end of the chilled cabinet was where she shopped, and bits of gristle shocking the teeth at least once per sausage had been a run-of-the-mill experience. Most men ate their food too fast anyway to know what was even in their mouths half the time, Maddie thought, so she put her concerns to the back of her mind.

§

Stopping at a bench, where the river had a small bend, Jay sat down to look about the once familiar spot. Behind him, the high wall hid a car repair garage that used to spill out its endless bits of junk and car left-overs onto the river path. Memories of fighting in amongst it all with two of his friends graced his reflections—it wasn't pleasant, but the memory was clear. They caught two young boys their own age, but from an estate at the other end of the town, jogging through after dropping their girlfriends home. It was all of half a mile to the other end, but to their young minds, they might as well have invaded from another country.

Jay remembered how he'd joked about how few girlfriends they'd have after they finished with them; his memory showed him the young boys lying in pools of blood, and he suspected that he'd been right.

That evening set off a chain of violent revenge, and counter retributions over the whole summer; Jay still bore scars from that time in his life.

Sea-bound, two small black-headed gulls negotiated their way skilfully above the river against the wind. Watching them, Jay enjoyed the simple pleasure of seeing them up close.

§

Snipping the twelve remaining asparagus spears from the garden, Maddie plucked ten good-sized broad bean pods, which she shelled and put in a small bowl. Fancying garlic buttery broad beans, she remembered her son counting them, before tucking in.

"DON'T PLAY WITH YOUR FOOD, you bloomin' half-wit!" Duncan used to bellow at him.

After that, he would eat his food quietly, with his head down, and he'd avoid eye contact with either of them for the rest of the meal. His plate was always clean though. Duncan didn't allow an option there, and if needed be, would have made him sit at the table all night rather than allow anything go to waste. Encouraged to come home earlier from school, so she could feed him before his father came in from work as he moved into his early teen years, Jay cared less and less about the consequences of anything he did. Sport, he enjoyed, and would have played football, and some of the other activities after school, but Duncan refused to cough up any extra money for the kits and subscriptions that were needed. Not a sports fan either, there hadn't been a lot Duncan liked about life. In some ways, Maddie reckoned that with his dislikes and everything else, Duncan was probably as well off dead. Some people were just like that Maddie had come to learn over the years: alive, but in truth, there was no real life in them.

Quickly scanning about, Maddie realised she was on top of everything in the kitchen, and even ahead of herself.

§

'A heinous act committed by two heinous individuals' was how the Judge described their actions; he said a lot of other things, but that was the sentence that stuck with Jay. Neither of them had ever heard the word before, and it was a while before Jay ever got to look it up and find out what it meant. At the time, both he and Walty felt they were harshly treated. They were only boys. 'The Blood Brothers', they called themselves, and the fighting against the Mitchell Estate Mob was already going on for months; beatings had also been doled out to them on several occasions. 'They' hadn't complained or reported them to the police. Finding one of their perpetual persecutors along the river walk on their way home one Friday night, after they'd been drinking cider, was just too good an opportunity to pass up. Fumbling with his girlfriend off the path, heeding protocol, Jay and Walty sauntered past the couple pressed against the wall in the darkness. Groping at her a bit more than she liked, the unfortunate angry words "No, Wacker" hissed loudly as Jay and Walty went by. Stopping, a quick peek was enough, and they attacked. Smashing Wacker head first into the wall when his hand was still in the girl's knickers, it was enough to rip her short skirt apart. Grabbing anything to hand, they kicked and beat Wacker until he stopped moving. In shock at the sheer brutality of them both, the girl stood frozen. Walty, seeing her ripped knickers and bare flesh, suggested that she was the spoils of war. Claiming first go, on account of it being his birthday, Jay grabbed hold of her; he raped and beat her brutally with promises of far worse should she try to come against them with the police or any other way. Walty tossed himself off when watching Jay on the girl, and in the end didn't touch her.

Being young and stupid, they somehow thought Wacker would share some kind of thug's code with them. He didn't. Identifying them both early the following morning in the hospital, both boys were taken from their beds where they'd been sleeping off their teenage hangovers. Swabbed, sampled, finger-printed, photographed, interviewed, and then beaten with wet towels once there was no more need for them, and the solicitors had gone home, neither boy got a proper wink of sleep for the five days in the holding cells. By the time they got there, Borstal was a welcome relief.

§

Chopping onions and garlic, Maddie wondered to herself when she started liking garlic so much, and then remembered putting lots of it into Duncan's dishes, especially after him saying he didn't care for it. Finding it easy to grow, as long as she planted it in October, that became her stock piece of advice to anyone who might have cared to listen to her. At least she got that much from Duncan. Gardening was her refuge now. All her nurturing went there.

Gone out the Saturday when the police came, Duncan refused to go to the station later when Maddie told him; he reasoned that if Jay committed the crime, he was no longer his son, and if he hadn't, he'd be home soon enough. Jay's name was forbidden in the house once he was prosecuted. Despite wanting to visit him in Borstal, and later in Prison, after she received the letter advising her of his move, Maddie couldn't; Duncan never let, or taught her to drive. Finding a bus and train might have been an option, but Maddie had no money spare that could have got her there. The odds and ends she managed to whittle away from Duncan's endless auditing of her purse didn't amount to much, and her life would have become even worse if he found out about her defiance of him.

§

Borstal was a learning curve. After a year, both Jay and Walty were moved to prison to serve the rest of their seven years. Parole was an option after five years, but only Walty was granted it; not having shown any recorded remorse, and being involved in multiple violent incidents in the recreation area, Jay was excluded from the option.

Having passed up the free education birth in England offered him, it took prison to prompt Jay to finally get one. By no means a scholar, he could write, read, and do as much maths as a regular person of his age might need in their life when he finally got out. Applied to specific machinery needs, things that had escaped him in school, now finally made sense.

Released after serving six years and ten months; upon being released, he used the little money he'd made when in prison to get himself sorted. Jay first spent four weeks in a 'Refuge half-way house', just outside Skegness, when he still didn't have to think about rent and the general day-to-day cost of living. During this time he changed his name to Jason 'Jay' James by deed poll, and removed himself from most official administrative records; his juvenile crime, despite its severity, wouldn't follow his adult profile. His birth name, Macabe, had been in a few papers, including one of the more popular national red-tops.

Deciding to leave the area he'd grown up in, he made his way northwards, hugging the north-east coastline as he went. The mechanical skills and his seeming affinity with machines prompted him to make a career choice. Not confiding in the officer, after the four weeks were up, he left without a word and boarded a national express bus heading north. Stopping in four different places along the way, one of them, Louth, more inland from the sea than he wanted, he only stayed for a week before moving on. The work he got there was poorly paid and involved filling lorries for a warehousing company. It paid cash though, and used to a frugal life he did at least end up ahead financially. In Grimsby, his luck struck, and things took a turn; after a couple of drinks with a foreman in a Docker's pub, he was given a start as a welder-cum-fitter. Good work to get, it was also well paid once he showed his ability and a desire for the shifts. For three and a half years a small one-room bedsit on the Grimsby side of Cleethorpes became home before he moved onwards again. Unhappy to lose him, as they drank together most Friday nights, the foreman ensured Jay went north with a reference in hand.

In Alnwick, he stopped for two nights and took a bus to Alnmouth from where he walked the windy beach to Amble on the second day. He'd spent most of his early childhood summer holidays on caravan sites in the area, and even in summer, the wind off the North Sea would still have an edge to it. On the way back along the beach Jay planned to pop in and see the castle at Warkworth, for old times' sake, and perhaps have a pint in The Black Bull, as he'd never been old enough when in the town as a kid. From there, he'd grab a taxi back to Alnwick, as it would likely be getting dark. As things turned out, Jay decided not to pop into the pub in the end, or get a taxi and so didn't get back to his guesthouse until the early hours of the morning. Sleeping most of the following morning away, he even missed the breakfast included in the charge. When he rose, he paid, left, and got on a bus to Kirkcaldy at two o clock, arriving there at half-past four. Eating at The Victoria Hotel, he treated himself to chocolate brownies for dessert. At seven o clock that same evening, Jay alighted another bus heading further north.

With an hour left of his twenty-eighth birthday, Jay sat in a dark regional bus with rattling windows rubbing at the soreness of two deep scratches on his hand. Passing a brightly lit road sign, he read it aloud to the darkness, 'Welcome to Aberdeen, Bon Accord'; he idly wondered why they had a French sign in Scotland.

After two months of trying to find work on the offshore oilrigs, multiple interviews, and numerous rejections, he was finally accepted when someone was taken ill and ended up as a roustabout on a Lerwick rig. Five years on, he knew what he was doing, and worked as a roughneck for a few more years before becoming a driller. Shunning any opportunity of taking charge of any of the crew, even when he'd become one of the oldest and was senior enough to be the father of half of them, he kept his head low. Jay knew he struggled with authorities of any sort. His workmates were often men who fought with people in power too. Any people in power. They just wanted to get on with the work. Not too much thinking. Work, eat, drink, sleep, and more work, with a pay packet at the end of the week. A simple pattern, for Jay it suited his needs. As much as he knew he struggled with authority, he also knew he struggled more with being in charge; if challenged, Jay only knew one way to deal with it. That was a brutal way. Even the densest of fools come to see, that whether he likes it or not, the world at large doesn't like brutality. The world has also spent a lot of time making rules and laws against it.

§

After fifteen minutes the oil in the top of Maddie's oven was piping hot and perfectly ready for her batter. The mushroom gravy was sweating, so Maddie added the stock mix. About to pour a glass of milk she stopped, realising it was unlikely a forty-seven-year-old man would want one. Instead, to steady herself, she sat down at her kitchen table and lit a cigarette. Back down to one or two now, for years she'd been deprived them. Duncan just didn't allow smoking - it was the first thing she had to give up once they were married. 'Simply too expensive and stunk the house out', Duncan had declared. Finding a shop near her old primary school where they still sold them separately, she occasionally treated herself with the few coppers cadged from bits and pieces of shopping forays into the town.

The notice in the paper Maddie remembered as though it was yesterday; the council in its wisdom decided to post notices on the 3rd of April 1984 once both boys were past eighteen. Stating that due to crimes of Jason Duncan Macabe, born of Wainfleet, 1st April 1966, and Walter Arnold Bright, born of Thorpe St. Peter, 2nd January 1966, the River Path Walk of Wainfleet was to be renovated and properly lit, to prevent such further disgraceful crimes shaming the town ever again.

Going on into full details about their actions and backgrounds, the paper printed school photographs of both boys, now that they were eighteen. Oddly, they also printed a photograph of Duncan at work in the hardware shop in Skegness.

Maddie thought Duncan never fully recovered from the shock of that photo. He'd never been a popular man by any standards, but give folk an opportunity to legitimately vent their hatred, that green light will potentially open a floodgate. It did. Within a month Duncan had to quit his job, even though it was over in Skegness and six miles from where he lived in Wainfleet. Never venturing out much after that, a fear of the outside world overtook him, and he was under Maddie's feet for pretty much the rest of his life; seventy-two when he died, which might seem a fine age, but Maddie knew it was young. His heart got him, she thought; his cholesterol readings were off the charts, and he was also having problems in the toilet for years too, about which Maddie knew he'd never talk to anyone. Finally diagnosed with clinical depression, they at least got some money from the social that way.

For twenty-five plus years Duncan didn't work a day and stopped leaving the house completely some years before he died. Maddie had full responsibility for her housekeeping budget after that; she did much as she wanted without any real interference from Duncan for the later years they were together. He even lost what miserable heart he had to care about that. Moving into her son's old room Maddie boxed everything she found and put it all out with the rubbish, but kept the photos. Eventually, Duncan ate less, did less, moved about less, and talked less. Then, he just didn't get up, and after a few months he was gone. With a whimper, Maddie thought, he just petered out. Only Betty and Tony, her husband, and thankfully two people Duncan had worked with in Skegness for years, turned up at his cremation service. She'd been relieved to see them, as she'd asked Betty to come in case of being alone; they didn't stay to talk after the service, and once they told Maddie they were sorry for her loss, they left. Maddie didn't get their names.

The doorbell rang.

Bracing herself, Maddie stood up. Weak at the knees and her stomach somersaulting like her tumble dryer she dipped the cigarette in the basin and dropped it into the bin; one last look about the kitchen, she waved her arms at the smoke and opened the back door to help it disperse. Taking a deep breath, she kissed her wrinkled clenched hands and fixed a soft smile on her face. From the hallway, a dark shadow loomed in her yellow bubble glass. Reaching for the latch she opened the door inwards, tentatively leaning forwards with her mouth trembling in anticipation of seeing her innocent little hero come home.

Something about the shape tickled at the back of her mind.

"Mrs Madeleine Macabe?" Detective Inspector Sheringham pushed a stray lock of hair back over her ear with her middle finger and wrinkled her eyes as she awaited a response from the small elderly lady before her.

***

Toad-in-the-Hole Recipe

Good comfort food, easy to make and warming on a cold Winter's day.

Ingredients
100g plain white flour
2 eggs
300ml of water
teaspoon of salt
teaspoon of mustard powder (optional)
4-8 veggie sausages (depending on how much protein you want)

Gravy
2 onions sliced
6 mushrooms wiped and quartered
4 garlic cloves chopped and crushed with sea salt
300ml of onion stock (stock cube/onion gravy pot)
1/2 teaspoon of marmite added to the stock (optional)

Making Toad-in-the-Hole
In a small non-stick pan begin frying the onions gently to slowly caramelise them. Add the mushrooms and garlic after about fifteen minutes. Once the mushrooms have begun to sweat add the stock and allow it to simmer gently until everything is ready.

Place a large deep baking tray or Pyrex dish with at least 2mm of groundnut oil in it on the top shelf in the oven for fifteen minutes whilst you're prepping the rest.

Gently fry the sausages in a frying pan until browned and dry with kitchen paper once cooked.

Put the flour in a large mixing bowl and sprinkle in the salt and mustard powder. Add the eggs and some of the water. Whisk it to a batter and add water to get the consistency you like. Watery will be fluffy and high-rising.

Pour the batter into the very hot oven dish and add the sausage. Into the oven, top shelf, oven at 200. Check after twenty minutes and keep an eye. It shouldn't take longer than twenty-five minutes.

Top with the gravy and serve with roast potatoes or croquettes and greens of your choice.

***

Six Million Dollar Boys

1974...

Moira Tindle fixes the last hairpin in place and
checks herself in the hallway mirror; pursing her lips
to a kiss she quickly scans a peek up her nose
canals. Twenty rollers, neat and tight, she wraps
her headscarf over them and deftly ties it at her
neck. Her husband Alan sleeps in the armchair;
three buttons waistband open, brown underpants,
orange trim, mullet hair, skinny moustache, he's
born and bred Cavan. Sunday afternoon. Six pints
after twelve o clock mass—two of them after the last
bell at two; a feed of boiled salty-bacon ribs,
buttered-cabbage, and a mountain of spuds washed
down with tart and custard barely touched the sides;
Maxwell House, whiskey, and a spoon of cream on
top followed.

The sleeping farts drove her to the hallway.

Mr Sheen next to the rubber plant. Abba on the
radio. Waterloo! Napoleon's surrender fades away
for the pips. Cosgrave condemns a happy Sammy
Smyth. Thirty-three unnamed dead in a matter of
days. The announcer stumbles over Michael
Gaughan: forgotten in a week, an unmemorable
name helps no cause. The Price sisters call an
end—force-feeding women, leaving men die is
official. Harold Wilson, again and again, Harold
Wilson; it's the beginning of his time. Strikes,

Provos, Red-hands, and booming northern
nonsense bombast the airwaves. Six counties of
nine always the bloody lead; six counties say no, six
counties say yes; the Ulster conundrum prattles on:
a dance of words, a dance of death—Woodrow's
principles gather dust in an unused library.

A tsking Moira turns it down; the top forty is still
an hour away—a dose of Casey Kasem needed to
lift her spirits and fill the afternoon.

Tonight, and every Sunday, is whiskey-mac
night. Alan due early at the club with Joe for a darts
competition. Moira and Noreen plan for eight. Sky-
blue mascara, thick clumping lashes beneath the
curls; back on with her best! It's been hanging on
the door since Mass ended. Sausage and chips
after for the walk home, at home, a Pernod-and-
black nightcap, just the one before a tumble. Sleep
in the wet patch, plugs in to block the snoring. Alan
up at six, back to the carpet factory, and the week
grinds forward once more.

The boys would be back Monday. The birds
were held up by the weather Mary next door
reported. The lads had eaten what she'd given
them already, and were worried they might starve.
Stuart rang Mary. Mary's phone, the only one in the
street.

§

A mustard Hillman Hunter sits on a country lane
beside Ballyliffin Golf Course. A welded shut, rusty,
red driver's door remembers an incident, and a brick
sits tucked by the front wheel—old handbrake
cables fickle things. Two boys camp in a hollow
amongst the reeds in the sandy earth; used pink

toilet paper sticks to the spiky-tipped clump behind their spot. June. Malin Head. Force 13 for three days. A mile up, it's near twice that. Squalls swing in every hour. Now force 7, it feels like the doldrums.

"Wait! I told you, wait!" Holding both sides of his head in frustration, Stu remonstrates with Henno, who closes the gate of the box cage once more. "Start taking down the tent, and get the stuff back in the car, Hen. That way, once they're in the air, we can race them home."

Henno trills his tongue at the birds within, hoping it settles them. Fed and watered an hour earlier, checking his quartz digital watch, the red numbers blur in his gritty vision.

"How long, Stu? Fifteen minutes?" Rubbing his eyes, he asks and answers his own question impatiently before resuming his pressing of the watch buttons.

Stu nods towards the headland and shrugs. "We'll hold them for four or five minutes after they've been released over."

"Right," eyes closed, he mouths his calculating thoughts and agrees. "Will that be too much? Won't they all have gone by then, Stu?"

"Not at all," Stu assures him, rubbing his palms. "They'll circle for ten minutes and go higher as they do, Hen. What we have to hope for is that one of those big Belgian cocks got a few knocks last night and is in no mood to fly after being held over for an extra couple of days. Once he sees all our little girls in here, he's bound to come and have a look, so he is."

"Is it always this freezing cold up here?" Henno shivers in his flimsy anorak, "I mean it's June. I'm still cold from that tent, and we got up ages ago. Why didn't we sleep in the car, Stu? That tent and those sleeping bags mammy bought us are rubbish."

Stu looks at his younger brother and frowns, wiping some crisps and the remnants of a scone from the side of his face. Henry wasn't the hardiest kid in the world: an intermittent asthma sufferer, it was often triggered by the damp and cold and made him cranky. Mid-summer too he seemed to suffer. Stu shakes his head; being eldest brings its own weight. From his bag, he takes out the last scone which he hands to Henno before scooping the crumbs into his palm for himself.

"The birds were in the car, boy. You can't sleep in the car with birds anyway, not the way your lungs are. The doctor's already told you to avoid them, and mammy wants us rid of them. You come back coughing and spluttering all over the place, and we'll be wringing bloody necks all week!"

"We can't get rid of our birds, Stu. Look at them. Bluey and Snowy are the best pigeons in Cavan. It'd be criminal! Criminal, so it would," Henno licks at the butter in his scone, dismay filling his face as he squints at his brother through one eye in the bright sunlight.

"Leggy's the best bird in that basket," Stu tickles the top of a large female silver dun. Henno has a soft spot for the blue-bars and whites. Two blues make whites; Stu finds himself pairing the birds just to see the smile on his kid brother's face when the squab begins finding its colours. Checks and reds he ignores, but the blues and whites Henno visits each morning before school to make sure they're eating and drinking—cleans the shit up every Saturday for pocket money too.

"Do you think we'll get one this time, Stu?" Eyes full of hope and dreams, he watches his brother.

"I do! I really do, Hen. I've a good feeling this time. Real good, don't y'know."

Squinting one-eyed across the mile or so where their prize will be released, Henno rubs at his closed eye. Straining with him, wind, salt, and sun tickle the unwashed sleep still sticky along his eyes causing Stu to blink and sneeze.

"They don't like it cooped for a long time," Stuart strokes his chin sagely as he speaks. "Some of the wee birds get stressed out and bullied by others, Hen. There'll be plenty of bruisers, and bigger than our fella too in there, so there will. I'm telling you, Hen, if we're lucky we'll get a good cock and we'll be getting half the hens up the pole before we have to send him back to Belgium."

"Can't we keep him—not tell anyone like?" Henno checks. "I mean nobody'll know, and we can do what we want then."

"But that's not right Hen. Not right at all, so it's not," Stu shakes his head at his brother's lack of understanding.

"Tubby's da kept one … that's why he gets more for his eggs and squabs than anyone else, don't y'know," Henno checks the birds once more.

"You heard dad," Stu reminds him, lowering his voice. "The Tubritts are wrong—wrong-headed, Hen: what they do is wrong; it's against the pigeon breeder's code, so it is."

Henno nods, accepting Stu's explanation; the fullness of the code's rules is beyond his ken at eleven. Stu, nearly eighteen, straddles the divide between young and old. Allowed to drive with his provisional, as long as he puts petrol in the car, he weaved the way to Malin Head alone this time, even though it was against the law. Dad showed them the route two years earlier. They avoided the six counties on his advice. The Peelers there were 'right bastards'. They'd have locked him and Stu up, and thrown away the key too, according to dad. Prisoners of war they'd be—starving all the time! Living in their own cement, whatever that meant—it didn't sound good. They sneaked along the backroads to Bundoran and made their way up to Letterkenny keeping the 'L-O' for Brit-Peelers all the time; after that, finding Ballyliffin was easy. Two Americans stopped in a lay-by to read a map and asked them for directions. They even had golf clubs in the back seat, right where you could see them. They took off after re-checking their map.

"We'll follow them," Stu announced, and Henno could see the wisdom in his decision. They wouldn't be able to park that car in Cavan. No chance boy. Brick wheels in a minute.

"Anyway," Stu interrupted his brother's thoughts. "There might be a reward Hen."

"A REWARD?" Releasing a whoosh of air, Henno rubs his hands together.

"Sometimes," Watching the sky above the distant bird trailers, Stu nods. "Not always, but sometimes—depends on the bird I think. Some of those Belgian birds would cost the same as our wee house Hen."

"That'd be grand, boy," photographers flash away before Henno as they bump each other for the best position—front page in the Anglo-Celt on a Wednesday; the Mayor shakes both of their hands and presents them with their medals.

"What would you do with the money, Stu?"

"Buy a ticket to America!" Stu tilts his head, and half closes his eyes dreamily, "Chicago or Boston. I'm not a big fan of New York, Hen. Too much crime and too many black fellas doing the jive-talk there. I think it'd be Chicago. I'd fly first class too, and pick up a hostess as a girlfriend for when she's in town."

Henno looks at his brother silently: the answer is not what he expects.

"You'd leave mammy and me here alone with dad?"

"They're fine, Hen," Stu raises an eyebrow and checks his brother's confused face. "All parents are like them. Everybody fights all the time. They're not even that bad really. Not compared to Clarkey's!"

"They're all stone mad, though!" Henno shakes his head in disbelief. "Everybody knows that, Stu. Clarkey's lot should be all locked up in the Mental!"

"You'd join me when you're eighteen though, fella. We'd have all sorts of businesses in America; we'd be like your men on the telly, y'know, Hen—the one mammy watches, 'The Brothers' thing. Except we'd be in America, and Irish brothers."

Henno nods in pleased agreement with how his future is panning out. Rubbing his eyes again, he yawns widely as they water. Popping the last remnants of the scone into his mouth, he sucks at the stodgy dough stuck in his fingernails. Both boys look across the expanse of water and land just in time to see the release. Hundreds of pigeons take to the sky and swirl about looking to flock but are unfamiliar with the birds about them. Henno's hand trembles on the release hatch, and he fixes on Stu for the nod. Stu's focus narrows; he watches the birds batch up and after a minute or so gives the sign. Eleven birds burst forth—four novices, seven experienced—all hens. Three of the hens are on eggs back in the loft. The boys faced them north in the hope of sending them across. The birds batch and circle for a few minutes and then begin to rise; the Belgian birds already above them disperse like a giant firework at Halloween. All directions lead to Belgium. It's in the hands of fate.

"Come on!" Stu urges. "We'll get back in time for tea, I'm bloody starving. We've got hours ahead of us."

Henno stops and watches a couple of trawlers pushing outwards—Cavan's inland, the sweet-peat quiet of Sweelan Lough lapping the grassy bank, a stranger to the untamed ocean.

"Are they going to fight?"

"Fight?" Stu queries. "Fight what, Hen?"

"In the war," Henno points north. "The Cod War is on. I heard it on the radio, Stu. It's all going on up there by Iceland, don't y'know."

Entranced, the boys watch the hypnotic movements of the boats. Horizon bound, through seas still abundant with cod, their wakes diverge. The herring have already failed. Killybegs is still thriving, but nobody is listening. Nobody is watching. Nobody has time to care. Plundering fills the hours; it fills the hearts and minds too. Paper in the pocket today! Legacies for grand-children and tomorrow frittered away: selling on the cheap fills freezers and bins for the supermarket scramble.

Kittiwakes peel from the cliffs to plead scraps from the boats. Hundreds of the crying birds circle a trawler—screams of lost tormented souls, theirs is a decimation still to come.

The boys remove the brick and put it in the boot before climbing into the car to head home; their scones and crisps have gone, and both ache with hollow hunger. Enough petrol for the journey but nothing else. Stu knows a couple of wells they stop at for water to drink, and Henno whispers his prayers to the statues of Mary above them. The radio crackles and farts and warms the car with sound. Talk from Cosgrave. Wilson defends Direct Rule. They sing Shang-a-lang before mourning the dead in Monaghan—it's close to home. Merlyn Rees? Henno wonders if he's magic. Why a man is a secretary? Stu laughs. Twenty miles to go. Sugar Baby Love. Good time made. Under three hours with stops for Henno to puke. In Cavan. Near home. The junction next to the industrial estate with the crooked tree. Factory Fields, dad calls it. What fields? A bang on the car! Dad, and his friend Joe Toban. A black line rings their lips from a stout lunch. Out! Dad needs the car. They walk the rest. Tired legs going in the front door. Mam has a kiss and a hug for both of her boys. Hot scones with currants and milky sweet tea. Henno's eyes tear with relief.

Stu shouts from the garden.

Nose to the window.

An unfamiliar bird gently cradled.

"Belgian!" Stu mouths, showing Henno the ring.

Tears for both.

Sinatra's New York, New York blares behind Henno and Moira sings along.

***

Recipe for Scones

On a cold winter's day, back from school, and it's already dark. The dog still needs to be walked, but the inclination is not there for anyone to move. The scones are in the oven, and the house smells warmly of them. You can taste the melting butter. Nobody's getting anything until he's at least been around the block. Every step of the run increases the drooling thoughts, and whoever takes the dog is allowed first choice.

Small problems were often easily solved.

Ingredients

350g self-raising flour
1tsp baking powder
3 tbsp caster sugar
80-90g butter (cut into small pieces)
175 ml milk
salt (a good sprinkle)
(Add raisins or chopped figs if you fancy them)

Prepping and making the scones

Put the flour, salt and baking powder into your mixing bowl. Add the butter and work with your fingers until it has the texture of breadcrumbs. Add the sugar and stir it in.

Create a well in the middle and adding your milk caress it all together with a flat knife. Once you have your dough ball roll it onto a floured board. Fold it into itself a couple of time and then pat it flat.

Use a floured 4-6cm cutter (depends how big you like them) and create your four shapes. Roll up the remains and flatten once more, either making a couple more, or a rough chef's treat, if there's not enough dough.

Brush them all with a beaten egg, place them in your hot oven (220/GM7) for ten to eleven minutes. Eat them hot, or warm—there's really no other way!

Clotted cream, jam, or just simple, gorgeous melting butter.

***

Arnold and the Herring Welly

ARNOLD HERRING WAS NOT WHAT ANYBODY would ever call 'quiet'. In fact, nothing about Arnold Herring could ever be regarded as quiet in any reasonable sense.

His clothing, brash and uncoordinated in a way that only a fashion student attempting irony, or a complete madman, could achieve, was also loud.

Arnold's inner life was noisy too.

Most nights he slept soundly and snored loudly between the hours of eleven and four. After that, his brain ascended from deep sleep and regurgitated as much information, randomly remembered facts, and absolute nonsense as it could to Arnold's semi-aware sub-conscious; this resulted in Arnold awaking each day with a fresh smorgasbord of blithering bilge with which to assault the unready world.

When he spoke, and often did, Arnold spoke loudly.

His mother, with whom he grew up pretty much alone, had been hard of hearing. Whether this was because of Arnold's blaring chunter, or whether it was a pre-Arnold condition, nobody knew for sure: she'd never had it treated or diagnosed correctly, and died a week after his thirtieth birthday before anybody ever thought to question her about it.

Except for Arnold and the unusually titled Humanist Celebrant, Doctor A Field, nobody else attended her cremation service. Harriet Herring passed quietly into the non-after-life without much ado; there hadn't been many quiet moments in Harriet's harried years, so perhaps her peaceful passing was something she might have enjoyed.

Arnold returned home with his mother's ashes some four hours after the ceremony finished. The Humanist Celebrant, Anthony Field, a rather ordinary looking man with a leathery withered skin now too large for his body, and a head too big for his hair to cover (a former General Practitioner), feeling, as any decent person would, a certain amount of compassion and sadness for the young man seeing his mother off alone, well, he engaged Arnold in what he thought would be a small, gentle chit-chat about his mother's life. It was why Dr Field left the medical world early: as a committed humanist, understanding both the need and benefits of clergy to one and all, once the end came, Dr Field ascertained that there was a real need for compassionate and caring individuals in the community to assist people in their most profound moments of despair, without a reference to a mythical upstairs, amongst the seraphim, cherubim, and the four living creatures, whatever on earth, or the heavens, they were supposed to be.

Following his question, Arnold described his mother to Dr Field. Being Arnold, he began with his first real memory of her leaving him at primary school—a traumatic day for Arnold, he described it in detail to Dr Field.

It was a traumatic day also for a Miss Laffin, who, doing her two-year overseas stint from

Australia, was hoping to find a nice cushy number to fund her fun in London. Her first problem had been a wretched, incessantly shouting child, displeased to be where he was, making it clear that he was indeed miserable, and oddly explaining in detail when and where every piece of clothing he wore had been acquired once she touched it. The first day wasn't perhaps the best to bother a new and unknown entity which the Headmaster was, so Miss Laffin and her class of twenty-five four-year-olds all listened to Arnold's story of his preparation for school, and after that, his life to date. There was crying after a while, and Miss Laffin, having taken and worn out the paracetamol tablets she usually only used for white wine headaches, finally managed to get a young Mr Christian to look after her group.

"Only a minute," she'd promised, and braved the walk to the Headmaster's Office. Stopping for a vape to gather her thoughts, in the porch outside the staff room, when she did go in, she stood her ground to insist the Headmaster come and witness for himself Arnold's odd behaviour. The class ran riot in her absence and being subjected to Arnold's relentless outpouring. Extremely unhappy that Miss Laffin had returned with the Headmaster to witness it all, Mr Christian was nonetheless relieved, but unable to help himself bearing a small grudge against Miss Laffin for showing an aspect of his ineptitude on her first day in the job, which, though understandable, was oddly unchristian-like of him.

Arnold didn't remember any of that.

Informing Dr Field that he was deemed, after considerable assessments, unsuitable for the school, and thus requiring home educating from thereon, or to find, what Dr Longbottom, the man from the Education Board, who had a very large nose, yet still found glasses that were too big for it and kept sliding to the bottom, suggested: 'a very special school for very special children'.

Home educated after that: home did indeed become his very special school.

In the eight years between his fourth and twelfth birthday, when Arnold was to be re-assessed for school integration once more, Arnold encountered twelve different specialist primary school teachers—the names, sexes, nationalities, and attributes of whom Arnold explained, in some detail, to Dr Field.

Happy with being home-schooled, each day after school was deemed done Arnold and his mother met in the kitchen to bake and cook together. During this time, Arnold relayed to her his day in detail while they cooked and ate, after which Arnold was sent upstairs to his room, and did his homework. That was when his mother watched television and spoke to his father, so she couldn't hear Arnold anyway. Instead, Arnold just talked to himself, and worked on his exercise books; afterwards, he warmed a glass of milk and got into bed. Always in bed early, he learned to count to very large numbers from a young age, and it took him a long time to make a mistake watching his mind sheep.

Following some later assessments Arnold continued to be home educated through his teen years; his academic success in finishing secondary school established his route of access through the myriad of qualifications available, and without feeling any need to attend institutions, three different degrees from the wonderful Open University, and

Masters credentials in two other subjects now adorned his wall. All of these he'd managed to achieve by the time he was twenty-five.

Dr Field couldn't help but be a little impressed.

Trying for various jobs, but never succeeding at interview stage, Arnold decided he would have to work remotely and never meet those for whom he might work (or provide his not inconsiderable range of services). This lack of acceptance by society, Arnold informed Dr Field, was because of his hyperthymesia—as diagnosed by a Doctor Legg when Arnold was only fifteen. Enquiring in an off-hand fashion what type of doctorate Dr Field had acquired, to enable him to describe himself thus, Dr Field obliged in explaining his former General Practitioner status very briefly. Disappointed, as his GP misdiagnosed him as hypomanic, which he wasn't, and as anybody with proper scientific training could obviously tell, Arnold shook his head sympathetically.

Mirroring the head shake, and ignoring the unwitting insult, Dr Field still managed to smile politely. Thinking Arnold was definitely hypomanic, he had been tolerating him with this in mind.

"Work!" He clapped his hands together intending to follow the word up with 'duty calls', and after that, run for the hills.

Arnold described his work at length.

Restricting himself to writing code for two internet security firms, since his mother had stopped him spending so much time on his computer, Arnold only did three or four days of paid work in any week.

Computers were why he wore thick glasses, according to his mother, but having worn the same type of glasses since his first proper eye test at eight, when a Mrs Patel (an Indian lady from Ealing, with two girls, who hoped to have a boy as clever as Arnold) diagnosed his needs, and picked the glasses she felt would suit him most, Arnold disagreed. Seeing Mrs Patel every second January or whenever he needed new glasses, Mrs Patel picked them for him, which was much easier than him looking, as she knew all the glasses that were available, and Arnold would have had to spend far too long remembering them to make a choice easily.

But work, about which Dr Field had asked: work, was no longer straightforward. Arnold still wrote code, but now it was just analysis of code someone else had already done, and Arnold checked.

Only on Mondays and Tuesdays though.

Wednesday was baking day, which was not strictly work of course, but it involved thinking and doing, which was the same as work in Arnold's mind but just wasn't valued by people in the same way, because of money, unless of course, you worked in a kitchen.

Thursday was his scientific journal day, and on that day Arnold reviewed a lot of articles that were sent to him to check and analyse. Often spilling over into Fridays, unless he worked late, which his mother never liked as it disrupted their meal, and her television viewing, and subsequently her chats with his father; it also meant Arnold got to bed late, after which he was always very grumpy the following day.

On principle, Saturday or Sunday was out of bounds for work.

On Saturdays Arnold and his mother always had breakfast in the park café; if it was summer they ate outside because there was too much glass, and it was too hot inside. In winter, inside, they were nearly always alone, and Mario, who ran the café, brought Arnold an ice-cream with a chocolate flake when he finished everything on his plate, even when Arnold was too old to be rewarded in that way.

Sundays used to be for church, but Arnold proved to his mother when he was seventeen that God didn't exist; his mother eventually agreed, so they no longer went, but sometimes they sat on the bench behind the church overlooking the graveyard where they had buried Arnold's grandparents. Always quiet there, they used to close their eyes and guess which birds were making noise. That was only ever in the summer though, and after The Archer's Omnibus—which they listened to all year, but didn't always go out after. In winter, they read books and magazines; sometimes they went for a walk after dinner, which they ate around two o clock. Sunday was the only day they ate around two o clock, even though they knew God didn't exist. Every other day they ate between seven and eight. Taught by his mother not to get too hung up on exact times, it was why he'd arrived a little early today, Arnold explained but reflected that it could have been the taxi driver too, who seemed to drive a bit too fast.

Proceeding to describe the meals they generally ate, he eventually came to Thursday, which was today, and he detailed a dish called Herring Welly to Dr Field, as he'd intended making it that evening. After listening to the meals, Dr Field's left knee gave way, and he almost fell over from a standing still position. Apologising for not being able to keep him company much longer, as he was getting hungry, and thought he would have been on his way back before now, Arnold helped him upright enquiring about the chances of taking his mother home.

Dr Field demanded the ashes himself from the administrative clerk with the hope of finally extricating himself from the racket of Arnold—hoping then to find a pub, any pub, in which to have a large drink, any drink, to assist in clearing his mind of the previous three-plus hours. He also now knew how to make a somewhat unusual dish called Herring Welly, the procedures for which spun endlessly around and around in his head with a myriad of facts, ideas, thoughts, recollections, hear-says, and a multitude of other stuff that he felt he was condemned to carry with him to his own grave. He briefly wondered if it was punishment for not believing in a god.

Arnold took the bus home from the crematorium.

It was cheaper than the taxi and Arnold hadn't liked the way the taxi driver, Izzy Batty, from Maxi's Taxis, kept interrupting him on the way there. Talking and laughing at everything he said, as though his own words were a complete surprise to him, he interrupted Arnold so much that Arnold didn't take his card, which he'd intended doing before setting out, as that way he'd know exactly how much to pay on the way back. Uncertainty was something Arnold always disliked. With large ginger whiskers, and a bulbous pock-marked nose, looking at Izzy made Arnold's face itch and twitch. He drove too fast too and used his brakes far too much for Arnold's liking; every time Arnold felt he was just getting to the good bit about what he was explaining he was hurtled forwards and half-strangled by the very long seat belt, after which Izzy Batty told Arnold another story about somebody else Arnold didn't know, and how a similar thing happened to him, and how funny Izzy thought that was. Reminding himself to remind himself when he got indoors once more to put a thick red line through the taxi firms details in his mother's telephone pad, Arnold blinked three times to capture the reminder.

Thinking about Dr Field, and their conversation, Arnold realised again how hungry he was, and how little he'd eaten that week. When alive, his mother usually made them both some breakfast before they began their day. Arnold hadn't had a proper breakfast for five days now, and having eaten most of the freezer meals he and his mother had cooked, and put his name on, he knew he should make something for himself later. With the fridge checked before he left, he knew he had all the ingredients for his favourite Herring Welly, which he must have been thinking of to have spoken to Dr Field about.

Anthony Field ordered himself another pint of bitter, but declined the barman's gesture towards another brandy. The racket in his head quietened with the less abstruse nature of pub and television noise, and he seated himself at the bar away from the now annoying screen with its repetitive loop of half news and gossip. Covering his eyes with his fingers, partly in relief, he shook his head and released a groan.

"You alright?" The barman asked, leaning back in a half-concerned curious fashion.

"Oh, I'm fine. Fine." Dr Field shook his head wearily. "Just a very odd day. A very, very odd day."

Eyebrows raised, the barman twitched his head just the once, indicating receptiveness to hearing odd stories about people's odder days

Starting with the brevity of the service, Dr Field explained to the barman what his function as a Humanist Celebrant was, and then why he was described as a Celebrant—of life it turned out, death after all, for humanists, being the end of the whole shebang—he digressed unintentionally. Finally getting away from matters about himself, he got to young Arnold and the lonely emptiness of the service hall for his mother's cremation. Describing the lone young man in his red and white Grand-Prix style blazer set off by his bright yellow shirt, and his mournful ankle height black trousers, with his oddly festive red socks coupled with the sensible brown shoes: Dr Field added the picture of Arnold gripping his Sherlock Holmes style hat and caressing the pheasant's feather in the side as he stood before him with his head swivelling all over the place as though in search of someone, or anyone, who might also have cared about him, or his mother. A touch of sadness caressed his words.

The barman touched the corner of his eye.

"Oh God, that's tragic."

"My feelings exactly," Dr Field agreed. "But the young lad suffers from some kind of hyperthymesia? I'm not completely sure myself if that's the only thing too!"

"What? What's hyper whatsit?" The barman picked a glass and began to polish it with a white towel.

"Seemed to have an eidetic memory too apparently, on top of that! To the best of my knowledge the two aren't linked?" Dr Field mused, missing the barman's question but seeing his confused face. "You know? Eidetic, sort of like a photo memory. Not a photographic thing that people think—he remembers everything, and everything he's ever done. Combined with his hyperthymesia, he can't help it and has to share as much information about himself, and anything else he knows with you too, and as much as is physically possible in whatever little time he has. That's what hyperthymesia is in a way, I think; he remembers everything about himself! Every last bloody minute! There's only about thirty like him on the planet. Compelled to share the lot in an incredibly loud voice too, he was. As I said, it was a strange day!"

"What? Just goes around shouting things about himself to everybody he meets?" The barman tried to get his head around the odd condition being described.

"Got a call from a cop about him too," Field shared his confusion with a questioning shrug. "Pretending he was just asking about the service, and that, but he wanted to know if the poor blighter was dangerous or mad. One of them had interviewed him, and couldn't figure him out; he had to get away from him in the end. Afflicted, I told him. Afflicted! That's what I said. What are they teaching them today? Poor little blighter, alone in the world with all that weird madness in his head that he can never forget."

Feeling better, after getting what was inside of him out into the open, Dr Field decided he should perhaps leave the pub, while he was ahead.

Suspecting that by sharing what was in his head he'd somehow passed it on, he thought it best to clear off, before it got passed back to him, or anything else reminded him of Arnold. "Can you get me a taxi?" He asked, "I seemed to have left my phone at work in the rush to get away."

Nodding, as he mused over their conversation, the barman took a few steps towards the bar end where the pub phone sat. Picking it up, he pressed an autodial button.

"Izzy, my man," the Barman laughed aloud upon hearing the answering voice. "At your earliest convenience please."

Perched on the edge of his porridge coloured recliner armchair, Arnold watched his reflection in the smeared glass of the TV screen. Still off, unusual for Arnold, he hadn't removed his blazer since getting home either, and wasn't entirely sure what to do next; he was caught off-guard by the silence and cold of the house upon entering. His mother usually had both radio and television blaring away, and if a song came on she liked, Harriet used to croak along to it at the top of her voice. Somewhere between the bus and the kitchen, Arnold lost his appetite; suddenly, his world seemed a little out of kilter, and for a moment, he was uncertain and felt utterly alone.

Still cradling the urn of his mother's ashes in his arms, he finally stood up and placed the urn on the mantle shelf directly above the fireplace; he shunted his father's urn to one side a little, nearer the dogs Holly and Squire. Squire was his first kill after his mother had shown him how with Holly. Arnold liked, even needed order, and up until now his father always occupied the middle so his mother's newly introduced presence was confusing things as the numbers were now even and it didn't look right. Lost in thought for a moment before continuing, finally, on his mother's side he spaced the cats Crackers and Spider so everything there was even—both of those he'd done together, tying their tails and tossing them over the two sides of a fence, so he retained a special memory of them. They were still Arnold's favourite, and he remembered as though it was yesterday his tantrums with the incompetence of the police for not having arrested all the teenagers whose names he'd given them. On a whim he put a family photo of all three of them in the middle, and re-spaced everything once more. Finding a certain symmetry to that, Arnold felt his chest relax as though the jigsaw of his world had once more settled into place. With his jacket removed he returned to his chair and sat rocking forwards and backwards with a little less uncertainty in his movement.

"What am I going to do now mum? Huh?" Opening his hands at the urn, he shook his head in query.

Waiting a couple of moments in case his mother did reply, and he just wasn't listening, something she'd often accused him of, and Arnold had always found immensely irritating, he smiled and nodded to himself in satisfaction. Silence. Nobody else's voice in his head. Nobody else's voice anywhere.

Three years of trace amounts of Aconite, or Wolfsbane, was all it had taken; he'd first discovered it reading a steamy series of science fantasy books some years earlier, and couldn't believe how common it was in the countryside. Always the wolf in his life, as far as Arnold was concerned, he never forgave her for walking in on him. That slow withdrawal from his room, and the reflected look in her eyes he could never shake: disappointment, mixed with disgust. Disappointment, he understood. Disgust with her own son he could never forgive or forget. Minute amounts of the leaf sporadically and carefully added to occasional dishes. It made him wish he'd studied medicine, because Arnold was sure he could see the subtle changes in his mother and had asked the doctor to keep a closer eye on her, because of his own particular needs. All over with now. Natural causes. Just like his father, and that had been her idea!

Arnold decided to tell her what he thought he should do.

After fifteen minutes of giving himself solid sounding advice, with a couple of humorous asides about the living and the dead, which he knew she wouldn't have enjoyed—she never liked losing at anything—Arnold felt much better. The heating timer triggered not long after he came in, so the house was feeling cosier, and Arnold could feel his tummy gurgling once more. Switching on the television, he found their favourite programme. Smiling at the urn, he advised his mother of his intentions to cook their favourite dish, asking her what he might have with it as they were out of asparagus and beans, and the only green thing he remembered seeing that morning was frozen spinach, which wouldn't do at all. Offering nothing back, which made a nice change, Arnold continued his dialogue uninterrupted.

In the kitchen, he switched on the radio for the comedy half-hour he liked, but of which his mother hadn't approved. His hunger growing, Arnold prepared his favourite dish, but just had potatoes alongside. Pleased to see that he would easily get three more nights from it, as long as he went out and bought some vegetables, he announced the meal when he brought it to the table. It had always made them laugh when she served it up, and he announced to the room, that "TONIGHT", they were having the famous 'Herring Welly!'.

You just have to be a Herring to appreciate it, Arnold thought and smiled again at the quiet urn as he chomped, chewed, and slurped loudly through his dinner.

***

Herring Welly Recipe

Ingredients

2 onions fine chopped
3 cloves of garlic chopped with sea salt
1 leek fine chopped
1 medium parsnip, peeled and grated
200g mixed mushrooms, wiped and finely sliced
6 veggie sausages, lightly cooked, and then mashed
(with the mustard seeds)
100g cheddar/hard cheese, grated
butter and groundnut oil
1tsp of mustard seeds

Stock

100ml of mushroom or onion stock (cube with
boiling water.)
2 stems of rosemary leaves only fine chopped
small bunch of thyme, leaves only fine chopped
3 sage leaves fine chopped
salt & cracked pepper
1/2 teaspoon of marmite (optional)

Add all ingredients to stock pot and allow to sit on
very low heat whilst cooking is ongoing.
    400-500gram block of shortcrust pastry. This
can be shop bought, or if you wish to make your
own pastry, put some time aside a few hours

beforehand, or the day before, and follow instructions here.

Making Herring Welly

Sauté the onion in groundnut oil for five minutes before adding the leek. Sauté both for five more minutes before adding the garlic and mixed mushrooms. Stir together and cover for a five minutes to bring up the heat and draw the moisture from the mushrooms. Remove the lid, stir and add the parsnip. Stir well and add the stock. Cover and leave to simmer gently for ten to fifteen minutes, after which you can just stand it to one side off the heat. If the mixture is runny (watery) add two heaped spoons of plain or malt flour for the last couple of minutes of cooking and stir together with your wooden spoon to give it a firm moist texture. If left in a colander sitting in a pot it will cool and drain the excess moisture, which you can use for a gravy, after which it will be easier to use, and there'll be less chance of the pastry splitting too much. I often make it without using any stock in the mix, but turn it into a gravy instead.

Add the lightly fried and mashed sausage to the mix and churn it all up. It should be firm (not runny or watery)

Home-made Pastry

320g Spelt White Flour
110g Butter
1 teaspoon of salt
Some splashes from a glass of very cold water
A good butter knife to help

Put flour and salt in a mixing bowl. Add the butter. Rub the flour through the butter with your fingers until your left with a bowl of floury breadcrumbs. Wash off your hands. Add a little water to the mix and begin caressing it with the butter knife. Keep adding splashes with your fingers as you caress it into a coherent pastry lump. Remove it from the bowl and roll it into a ball. Wrap it in film and put it in the fridge for 1-36 hours.

Or use a block of pastry from the shop.

Final Prep

Remove the pastry from the fridge and roll it out into a flat rectangle on a floured surface. Place in on a large flat lightly oil-wiped oven tray. 10x18 inches pastry length is good. Butter one narrow end for about two inches (to help it seal).

Spread the (not wet) sauce mix evenly across the pastry, allowing an inch gap around the edges, and the two-inch gap where you've buttered. Cover with cheddar or your choice of hard cheese (hard goat's cheese works very well). Begin turning the narrow end with the one-inch gap and roll the whole thing over on itself (roulade style) finishing with the two-inch buttered fold sealing the top. Brush with a little milk or beaten egg. Straight into a hot oven on the middle shelf at about 180 (gas mark 5) for around 35-45 minutes. Keep an eye after half an hour, it's quicker in a fan assisted oven, obviously.

Serving

Slice as you would a roulade or cake. Serve with a side of asparagus and broad beans sautéed in garlic butter, or any greens work nicely with it.

***

Fish Supper

THREE YEARS HAD DISAPPEARED SINCE Paudy Fitz' returned from Boston to the seaside hamlet of Ballymacaw in County Waterford. His kids, adults now, whined in that nasally American fashion about their decision to return home to Ireland and acted as though they'd been abandoned in orphanages. Paudy thought he'd done better by them, and had at least taught them to stand on their own feet as they faced the world.

Paudy and Marian made sure the house they bought on coming back was small and unable to entertain large groups: a three roomed cottage, with an eight-foot square vegetable garden, a flower bed, and a grass patch that needed next to nothing doing to it; life couldn't have been made easier. If they had visitors, and they knew they would, then Dunmore East, and any hotels people might need, was only three miles or so away.

The weekend finished, and with the kids still confined in school, a quiet emptiness whispered through the winding lanes around Ballymacaw. Paudy was intent on spending his Monday mackerel fishing on the flat rocks near Dunmore East; there was little to interfere with his intentions, and retirement for Paudy was about doing the things that pleased him most. Taking his middle rod, he fixed it onto his moped in the style of a lance and set off. Along the way he stopped to pick up a couple of

floury blaas which Mary Fortune in the shop buttered
for him; he had her add four slices of red-lead to
each, as the cheap luncheon meat is known locally.
Checking his moped basket, he picked out the
blanket and mentally ticked the reel, hooks, glue,
cotton, a large flask of tea, an assortment of
spinning weights, and finally, on top of them all, a
delicate tissue bundle of pigeon feathers. Paudy
tucked them all back into the bag with his blaas and
continued on his way. His wife also put a kitchen
roll in the basket before he left, and he added an
extra bit of padding to the feathers from it.

"You always get the sneezes out on the rocks,"
she reminded him, and Paudy, in truth, couldn't fault
her.

Early in the day still, when he began his
descent down Coxtown Hill, the breeze chilled his
ears as he free-wheeled past the Lemon Tree Café,
and onwards towards the sea. Dunmore East
confronts the sunrise from the southeast; on a fresh,
bright sea-sparkling morning, such as this was,
Paudy felt it was surely good to be alive.

Once on the flat rocks, he spread his blanket,
laid out his bits, poured himself a cup of tea, and sat
down with a contented sigh to prepare for the day's
fishing. Knowing he probably should have done his
prepping at home, his itching mind had urged him to
just get out, and once out he didn't care. Arranging
the hooks into two rows of six he ran a length of
cotton from the reel about a foot long and snapped it
before opening the glue bottle. Tentatively selecting
a silvery-blue feather from the tissue, about three
inches long, Paudy aligned it along the hook,
carefully wrapping it tightly with the cotton. Holding
it firm, he released a little glue onto the cotton coil

and gently caressed it in with his forefinger and thumb. After a few seconds examining it, and feeling it drying out to his touch, Paudy propped it against a long stone on his blanket and began the process once more with the next hook.

§

Rummaging in her kitchen cupboards, Marian Fitzgerald placed various unearthed items along the length of her worktop and draining board. People didn't refer to her as Marian Fitz'. Just Marian, or Marian Fitzgerald. There weren't very many Marians, but there were a few Paudies around Ballymacaw. With her Paudy out for the day, Marian was having a clear out. By her reckoning, he wouldn't be back 'til early evening, and she wasn't in any mood to go anywhere in the car.

Finding the usual suspects in the back of her cupboards: a mysterious tin of lychees she was sure she'd never bought, a selection of half used bottles of various soya sauce-like condiments, and a jar of a Polish pickled vegetable not readily identifiable, all of which had been shunted into hiding by other things, Marian also reached into the back and drew out a neglected small hessian sack that still held some winter vegetables; a couple of parsnips, swedes, a small turnip, and three large carrots peeped sadly from the semi-darkness, softening and sprouting quietly in the stillness. With the sun finally arriving, and ever frugal, Marian thought to put them to use. Tumbling them into the sink, she turned the bag inside out to beat any dirt or bits out of it and continued with her tidy-up. Marian removed everything from the cupboard intending to tidy or throw it. The bay leaves, brown and dry as a bone, found the bin. Three small glass containers of paprika removed, she decided to keep the smoked Spanish stuff and binned the rest. A small near-empty tub of cumin seeds sat alone on the top shelf, and holding it, trying to remember when last she'd made a curry or any kind of hot spicy dish, she put it to one side and her mind itched at it. Wiping the spice cupboard down with a bleached hot cloth, Marian selectively replaced the spices she used regularly and decided everything else was for the bin. The cottage kitchen was small, the cupboards few, and within the hour Marian completed what she'd set out to do for the morning. To kill any further domestic tasks for the day in a single swipe, she dumped the winter veg in the bowl and in a matter of minutes topped, chopped, and peeled the lot into a semblance of respectability adding three extra potatoes and a couple of chopped onions. Marian had no plan, but with everything sitting there clean and ready, somehow, she felt better.

Making herself a pot of tea, she opened her bread bin to make a piece of toast, only to find she was down to a single crust. Toasted and buttered, she looked back at the vegetables as she munched; her mind worked over what she might fancy later. Paudy might or might not come back with mackerel; it was way too early for the boats, or any chance of a decent catch. They should be in the water he'd said, but it hadn't been that warm so far, in the early fingers of summer, so Marian thought he mightn't have as much luck as he hoped. Paudy was ever the optimist, especially when it came to fishing.

§

With twelve hooks propped at angle drying on the blanket, to stop himself fiddling with them before they were properly set, Paudy poured another cup of tea and patted the flour from one of his blaas. With the tide having turned an hour earlier, and from the look of the water, Paudy was confident that if there were mackerel out there, he'd definitely get some. After eating and waiting a bit more, he watched a cranky row between the gulls and kittiwakes resolve before he cut a length of catgut about seven feet long, and he set about making a casting line. Weaving and knotting the line through a set of six of the hooks, Paudy then spaced them just under a foot apart, before attaching the spinning weight to the bottom and a small circular closed jump-ring to the top, to prevent the line getting tangled in the eyes of the rod. Next, he fixed his reel and ran the gut through the eyes before tying it to the jump ring, locking it, and placing the whole lot to one side on the rocks. Tenderly tissue-wrapping the remaining hooks, he replaced them carefully back in his basket. Paudy had never seen the need to make crazy coloured feathers: the iridescent water-repellent feather of a blue-bar, or a silver-dun pigeon, were all he ever used; it wasn't like mackerel had a thing for colour that he knew, and most of the sprats or bait fish he'd ever seen were a silvery blue colour anyway. Picking up his rod, he tentatively trod his way as close to the water's edge as good footing allowed.

Briefly closing his eyes and whispering a prayer for luck, Paudy sucked a deep breath of the sea air into his lungs and began his day of rhythmical casting and reeling.

§

From the square of blue and white sky out of her kitchen window Marian could see the high cirrocumulus clouds scuttling across. Paudy was right, she thought. Once the tide turned, with the water swelling and chopping, the signs were that the fish would surely come. The clouds told the story of the sea, her father always said, and she nodded in agreement with his folksy wisdom as she surveyed her preparations. A stack grated, she scooped two parsnips worth into a large baking bowl as her mind wandered to imagine where Paudy had got to. Sticking the bowl to one side she dabbed the corner of her eyes and wondered why the body now needed so little sleep, with so much idle time to spare. The thought of her daughter, scheduled to arrive later in the summer, raised in her a sense of dread and guilt; a mother should look forward to seeing her kids, Marian thought—especially when opportunities for seeing them between now and her own doom would be few. For Marian, that had been the toughest part of coming back home with Paudy. A bright shaft of sun streamed onto her, bringing her grimacing reflection into sight and causing her to shake her head at the kitchen window and her own maudlin thoughts. Putting aside the grated parsnips, Marian sieved her wholemeal and malt flour combination. Adding what was left of the cumin seeds, and a good sprinkling of salt, with a second shake to make sure, brown sugar, baking powder, baking soda, and finally a good large knob of butter followed. She held back the buttermilk. It was a shame, she thought, but no matter how she looked at it, she knew her own daughter to be a bossy little cow. Even the fella she was with had lost his balls. Gutless! After four years of her bossing and domineering he was a mere shadow of the fella she'd met. A life down that route her daughter would find, no doubt, as there's a life to be found down any road, but she'd never find happiness; to Marian's thinking, that was all a mother ever really wanted for her kids. Mixing everything together, while it was still dry she tumbled it and squeezed and rubbed until she could no longer find the butter and the mixture looked like moist breadcrumbs; with the parsnips and buttermilk added, the masala soda bread was ready for the oven. A pair of choughs landed in her patch of grass outside the window; their red feet caught her eye, and Marian looked about for something to throw into the small garden to ensure they returned. Paudy would envy her this little treat.

§

Rising further as the morning passed, the tidal swell whip-cracked and whacked and walloped off the flat rocks. Three smallish mackerel behind him, in a tiny sheltered rock pool out of the gulls' sight, Paudy knew he had three more than anyone thought he might catch. The wind had upped and gusted more, throwing up a bit of salty spray, and Paudy cast directly into it, watching the weight gracefully arc its sixty-odd metres, before the distant chunking splash sounded in his ears fractionally behind its disappearance from his eyes. Counting to five, he reeled and drew the rod behind him to vary the path and speed of his feathers, just like a small sprat shoal; a slight jerking motion in his forearm told him he had another, and Paudy eased the rod again, laughing aloud at the sky. Alone on the rocks, looking along water's edge, the spray thrashing into the air, Paudy could see the twenty or thirty men that would be there most evenings through the summer—all of them shouting, roaring, and egging each other on if a decent shoal struck.

It was for such moments as this that Paudy Fitz' lived and dreamed.

§

Marian sautéed the onions while the kettle boiled; she put a vegetable stock in a jug, two chopped garlic cloves, and half a teaspoon of Marmite—an ingredient that was never mentioned to Paudy. Once the onions began browning at the edges, everything else was tumbled into the pot, stirred a few times, and Marian added the stock, bringing the heat up for a minute before covering it, turning it down and leaving it. Later was time enough to decide whether to blend it or have it as a chunky soup. If Paudy did manage to get a couple of mackerel, they'd also go nicely with the bread, she thought, as the fragrant cumin aroma filled the air. With her tablet removed from under the telly, she opened her emails. Planning initially to say something to her daughter, and get rid of her irksome thoughts, after fidgeting about for a few minutes she closed it and put it back; her daughter would only ask what was up and if everything was alright, and proceed to talk to her for hours when she was home from work, which for Marian would be long after her and Paudy's bedtime.

§

It was six days before Paudy's body showed up.
Another two days passed before Marian got to hear
of it. Found in the jurisdiction of another county, he
was lifted from the water on the rocks before Hook
Head some three and a half miles across the bay,
she heard. A wave must have hit him, Sergeant
Halpin sagely suggested; his voice cracked as he
tried to find the right tone. The tidal swells and
surges were unpredictable after the wet late spring,
and Paudy wouldn't have expected it to have hit the
rocks so high and hard on such a sunny and clear
day. A hole in his middle had been eaten by the
fish. Mackerel, most likely. On Marian's work-top
the masala soda bread remained un-eaten, and
mould began to colonise. The soup remained
chunky but was now starting to sludge beneath the
lid.

That he died doing what he loved most was no
consolation whatsoever to Marian.

***

Masala Soda Bread Recipe

Ingredients

300g wholemeal brown flour
100g malt flour (or plain flour)
2 grated parsnips
1 teaspoon of cumin seeds
2 tablespoons of brown sugar
1 teaspoon of fine sea salt
3/4 teaspoon of bicarbonate soda
3/4 teaspoon of baking powder
60g butter
300 mls of buttermilk (or 200 mls plus some milk)
2 medium free range eggs

Soda bread is made throughout Ireland but seems to have originally come out of the Waterford and Wexford area and is even occasionally referred to as 'Waterford Soda bread'. If a hearty soup is being made, often the soda bread will incorporate some of the left over ingredients to use up things like a last parsnip or a carrot, or even yesterday's potatoes. The addition of cumin seeds creates a wonderfully aromatic bread, and for variation you can easily substitute the cumin with fennel seeds, and the parsnip with carrot for something different again. Don't leave this hang about once your mix is done … get it straight into the oven. Remember too that the soda needs the dairy catalyst like buttermilk or yoghurt to trigger the rise. I've had friends try to avoid adding the dairy ingredients and they invariably end up with bread-frisbees.

Making Masala Soda Bread

Get your oven on and build up the heat to 200 plus, or gas mark 6-7. Spray before you put the bread in—if you have a spray.

Put the flour, salt, bicarb and baking powder in a mixing bowl. Add in the butter and rub it through with your fingers until the butter disappears and the mix is like breadcrumbs. Add the grated parsnips, sugar and cumin seeds and mix them in by hand. Pick up a solid spoon. Add the eggs and buttermilk to create a moist gloopy mix your spoon can stand up in. It's easier to mix this by spoon and you don't have to spend ten minutes trying to clean yourself off. Once it's mixed, scrape it into a mold or create a ball and place on an oiled tray or greaseproof paper on a tray. Make a cross in the middle with a large sharp knife and sprinkle with plain flour. Spray some water into the oven if you have a water spray and put it on the middle shelf at 210 for 35-45 minutes, depending on the efficiency of your oven. Tap the base when it's browned and if it sounds hollow, it's good to go. Leave to stand for at least half an hour before cutting into if you can. Try not to eat the whole loaf at one sitting.

It's also fantastic with any kind of dahl.

***

The Babysitter

JAMES PURCELL WATCHED HIS WIFE'S FINGER
nails dig deep into the soft flesh between his thumb
and forefinger, but with his mind elsewhere it didn't
register, and he felt no pain. He was busy counting
the number of times he felt happy in the last six
months.

James was struggling to get off the mark.

His wife Miriam grunted, groaned, and
grimaced her way through a difficult birth. Their
third child was rather large, or his head was—the
twelve-year gap in birthing hadn't helped Miriam's
cause. Bearing down once more, encouraged by an
enthusiastic 'Yes' from the attending midwife, she
unwittingly drew blood from her husband's hand,
and as her head tilted in exhaustion, she saw his
lost, distant-cast, stare. Aware of the limp
disengaged hand she was now clinging to, looking
at it, she saw the blood she'd drawn. The shock
triggered another spasm. Miriam pushed and
pushed, until she heard cheering, clapping and
crying all at once, and she could finally close her
eyes. Wanting so desperately to sleep, even now,
she dreaded the months ahead of breastfeeding and
broken dreams.

Briefly holding the child that the midwife
placed in his arms, her voice danced around him as
she spoke; she registered his confusion and called
the nurse over to assist him. After a minute of
staring blankly at the bundle he held, James walked

around the bed and tucked the baby in next to an exhausted Miriam. Utterly spent, she didn't open her eyes or acknowledge either of them.

"Let me take him to the nursery, and allow the paediatrician look him over. We need to log his details and wash him. The poor dear is exhausted," the midwife looked sympathetically at his wife. Without any input from James, she proceeded to act on her suggestion.

Feeling as though he as far, far away, he watched her pick his third son up and prepare to leave the room before she called an orderly; together, chatting about something they'd been discussing earlier, they rolled his wife's bed back to the ward, leaving him standing and looking about to see if there was anything that might have been forgotten—other than him.

Other than him, nothing remained in the clinical efficiency to suggest they'd even been there.

Shaking himself a little, James found his way back to the ward, where he met and startled the same nurse by accidentally walking into her.

"Oh, Mr Purcell? I'm sorry," the nurse apologised reflexively.

"My fault, my fault," a bumbling tired James mumbled. "I wasn't concentrating, sorry."

"It's not surprising after what you've been through," the nurse folded a sheet she held as her eyes consoled him. "She's sleeping now. I suspect she'll be out for the night, and most of tomorrow: that was a tough one, Mr Purcell. She's been through the mill. We'll monitor the baby overnight in the nursery, in case of any complications. It's routine after a difficult birth. You understand? You should get some sleep yourself.

"Is there someplace-?" James began.

"Not here Mr Purcell," the nurse interrupted the question she'd heard a thousand times, "You should go home, and get a proper sleep. You can pick her—you can pick them both up tomorrow. If all goes well, you understand, but I don't think so, or don't think you'll be able to, if I'm honest. She has lost a bit of blood, so the doctor may want to keep her for forty-eight hours just as a precaution. You understand. That's routine in this situation."

"What? Yes. No-, aah?" James's tiredness left him a little lost. "Okay. I think so nurse; I'll just pop and have a look at her before I go. If you don't mind?"

"No, not at all Mr Purcell," the nurse nodded and waited for their eyes to meet before she stopped. "But try not to wake her. For her own sake. You understand?"

The nurse's need for James's understanding caused his tired mind to feel more confused. Creeping into the ward where his wife slept a familiar dry-throated cough sounded from one of the beds at the rear. Slipping through the curtain gap, he stood at the bedside looking down on his wife. Fast asleep on her back her head lay sideways on the pillow with the tip of her tongue peeping between her lips; her breathing was laboured and wheezy. Looking haggard and old, an unsightly mole had grown gradually on the left side of her chin, and James found himself looking at it and noticing too how her hair was greying at the roots; James realised he had no idea who this woman before him truly was. His wife, yes. But what did that mean? They'd raised two children together for thirteen years, after a brief romance and a quickly arranged marriage: the children arrived after seven months, and twenty-one months; James couldn't remember a real conversation they'd had since that hadn't somehow revolved around them. What were her desires? Her loves? Her hates? Or even anything she was passionate about, other than their children? If it hadn't been for the sex, they probably would have split years earlier. A holiday in Spain the summer gone by Miriam had forgotten her birth control pills, and neither of them had ever gotten on with condoms. Meaning to sort out the morning-after-pill, once they returned, somehow Miriam forgot, and James hadn't given it a second thought. Going through a second honeymoon period, they'd even been getting on great as a family. Always having something to do at the weekends too, even on a Saturday night they sang karaoke and danced with the kids on one of their games after the family television programmes, and before they went to bed. Later when the kids were gone, they'd have sex on the big sofa and finish a bottle of wine together, before Match of the Day. Both worked hard during the week at jobs they even enjoyed. Once the morning sickness kicked in, everything changed. All sex stopped: the endless rounds of bickering about nothing began; invariably, this resulted in James sleeping on the couch and drinking himself to oblivion after she'd gone to bed. As the stubborn weeks and months went by, both of them became ever more miserable and resentful of the other. Quitting her job, without telling him, caused a massive fight as they lost her maternity leave pay which she was only a couple of weeks away from receiving. Re-joining the gym to get away from her, he now found himself working out for a couple of hours most mornings, and on an occasional evening, just to avoid the fights.

"I can't do this anymore," James whispered to his sleeping wife. "I just can't do this anymore, Miriam."

Turning, he left the ward as quietly as he'd entered.

The blanket of oblivion wrapped itself around her. It was dark. Darkness and a weight sat on her chest holding her down. Miriam struggled but couldn't move. Deep sleep came, and her struggles finally ceased, allowing her exhausted body to begin the slow process of regeneration and healing.

§

In his Volvo S60, in his driveway, looking through the windscreen at the house he lived in, James rubbed his face and eyes and fought back a yawn. No recollection of the drive back from the hospital, but having lived in the town all his life, he presumed an automatic homing instinct had kicked in, and he'd allowed it to dictate the mechanics of driving and navigating. It was twenty-past-one in the morning.

His front door opened as he approached, and a tousled teenage girl looked out at him in the porch light. Blinking back sleep, James looked at her as though seeing her for the first time: eighteen or nineteen now, he thought; she'd been babysitting for them for a few years when the rare need arose. Wearing a short skirt, and a too-tight scoop-necked top that showed off her oversized young cleavage, her long black hair was tied back, accentuating a fresh, but not-so-pretty face, and clumsily lipsticked red lips.

"Are you—is everything all right?" Her eyes scanned the passenger seat, "I heard the car pull up ages ago, but I didn't know what-?"

"Everything's okay Sandra," James yawned and stopped at the step. "It was a long birthing process, and there were some complications—I won't go into details if you don't mind. I think it wore us all out."

"Oh God James," Sandra covered her mouth with her hand. "Are you back to stay now or-? Can I go—or are you going back? It's just I'm not sure what-."

"No. Of course you're not," James yawned again and smiled as he tried to buck himself up a little. It wasn't the young girl's fault his life was a mess. "I'm back and yes! Yes, you can go, and thank you, but If it's not too much, I just need a quick word with you about tomorrow?

Hesitating, uncertain what to say, his mind struggled with tiredness and a bleak uncertainty. "I'm here all day tomorrow for the boys," he began, his eyes looking her over once more now they'd adjusted to the light; he could see she'd removed her bra and imagined it must be uncomfortable for girls like her. The late night chill had brought her nipples up, and they pushed against the light transparent material of her top. His mouth felt too dry to speak on.

"I need a cup of tea I think. Shall we go in?"

Inside, the house was dark and dim except the living room, where a lamp remained alight. Sandra's laptop sat on the coffee table next to a wine glass with the remnants of some red wine drying in the bottom.

"They're asleep?" James asked, gesturing with his head to his sons upstairs and beckoning Sandra to follow him to the kitchen.

"Hours ago," Sandra replied. "They had a match after school, so they seemed to be pretty knackered and went off early."

Feeling the weight of the water in the kettle, he plugged it in, nodding along to Sandra as she filled him in on the evening, and waited for her to pause.

"I've got to go back to the hospital tomorrow night too, I'm afraid. I know it's Saturday-?" James cut in once the opportunity arose.

"That's not a problem James. Honestly. I'm getting more done here than I would at home anyway," Sandra put her hand on his arm and smiled. "What time will you need me?"

Looking at her hand and feeling her grip, he felt his mouth dry once more. Turning away he picked a cup from the cupboard and popped a tea bag in just as the kettle boiled; pouring the water in quickly he swivelled for the fridge just as Sandra bent over to remove a carton of milk for him. His outreached hand hovered before her arse.

"You want milk?" She asked, scratching her breast as she stood and turned.

James sipped at his steaming cup before holding it out.

"What time will you want me to come tomorrow?"

"What?" James, a little fuddled, had lost the thread of their conversation.

"What time tomorrow will I come over?" Sandra clarified. "I'm out with Dad until after three. I'm going to test drive a polo. Oh! Peter and Daniel

Levin are coming over for the day. The boys said it'd been arranged, and you'd know about it?"

"What? No! Who said I'd know?" James put the cup down and shook his head.

"Well, not you specifically I suppose? But you'd both probably know I thought. It's on the fridge list. I don't think the boys expected Miriam to go in today, and I suppose they didn't think to cancel. Boys are like that I'm afraid?"

"Bugger! I'll cancel them once I'm up. I could've done without that," his head felt a clearer, and his mouth a little less dry after the tea. "If you could come over around five, that would be super Sandra. I might be late there again though. There's a bed upstairs. It's got fresh bedding on it. Please, make yourself at home. I would've stayed tonight, but Miriam was out of it completely, so I took the opportunity-."

"I'll come whenever you want," Sandra smiled affably at him. "Don't worry about being late, or if you don't make it back. I can crash anywhere. Mum and Dad know I may, or may not, be home, and that's okay. I should go now though, and let you get some sleep."

"Shall I walk you over?"

"Don't be daft," Sandra shook her head at him and smiled again as she gestured to herself. "It's only down the road. I'm a 'big girl' now. I'll be over as early as I can tomorrow near five. Good night James. You should get your head down. You look like you really need it."

James went to bed once Sandra left, and slept fitfully; his dreams were full of breasts and bums and lips, and he woke around six, masturbated, and went back to a deeper sleep.

Sandra Giovanni was regarded by several of her friends as a cock-tease. Wearing short skirts most of the time, she also pushed her cleavage up high, and when drunk, or even tipsy, she became physical, losing any awareness or care of people's personal space. It wasn't a premeditated type of tease: Sandra was young, mentally but had physically matured early; her breasts were forming from before she was eleven, and her first period had arrived the day before her twelfth birthday. By fourteen, her breasts were already a larger size than her mother's, and Sandra had spent much of her self-conscious early teen time with folded arms and hunched shoulders. At sixteen, she lost some of her puppy fat, grew taller, and already looked nearer nineteen. Soon used to the attention from boys, her confidence developed as she saw through their bluster and nonsense. Her upbringing was strict, at least compared to many of her friends, and she was denied her desires to work part-time in bars or shops during the school holidays. Limiting her strictly to babysitting, her father encouraged her to study during these evenings and even set tasks for her as a monitoring device. Livio Giovanni was ambitious for his daughter; he felt it more productive, and safer for his girl, to make use of the secure, protected life in the suburbs of Harpenden, rather than be exposed to the ugly reality of drunken weekend town life in Harpenden centre or St. Albans. When she came through college unscathed and went on to university, he was immensely proud, despite the trips to Durham being tediously long. Seeing her resume her childminding duties of earlier days when she came home on spring break was a relief for him; in doing so, she was, he and his wife felt, still part of their community.

Sandra didn't like boys her own age; some still had runny noses, among other personal hygiene short-comings, and much of the humour revolved around pranks and juvenile school-type nonsense. Even at university she'd found too many cliques and covens for her comfort, and she'd kept herself pretty much to herself unless there was a special night out. On those nights the boys seemed to like her, even if nobody had quite managed to bed her. The girls on the other hand disliked her vehemently, and as she'd fumbled and kissed with most of the boys at one stage or another they bore her resentful grudges. School years in St Albans High School for Girls inured her to girl grudges.

Sandra Giovanni lay on her back in bed and thought about James Purcell. Not much more than thirty, which being younger than any of her university lecturers, meant he was still young, even to her. Also looking pretty fit and muscular; she noticed him fidget and spasm and ogle at her, and she'd had her own fun playing with him. If Sandra Giovanni was going to finally put her virgin years behind her, she didn't want it to be a fumbling snotty-nosed boy. Sandra fell asleep smiling to herself and didn't wake until her father shook her in the morning with a cup of tea in his hand for her.

§

Shaken gently to wakefulness by a Medic she hadn't seen before, Miriam Purcell realised that she wasn't in the ward any longer, and could feel the pinch of needles in her arm and hand when she moved.

"Mrs Purcell?" The unfamiliar voice drew her gaze. "You had a bit of a turn in the night. You've lost quite a lot of blood I'm afraid. We've stabilised you for the moment. Do you feel okay?"

Dizzy, dry-mouthed, very sweaty, and very cold, Miriam dry swallowed.

"I'm fine," her instinctive no-fuss attitude kicked in. "Thirsty. Stabilised? What does that mean? Thirsty."

"I'll get you some water," the medic promised her.

Miriam passed out again.

§

Waking to the sounds of boys cheering and whooping in the room beneath his bedroom, James groaned with dread and tiredness. Allowing himself to adjust to wakefulness, he lay looking at the ceiling. After a couple of minutes, he rose and stretched wearily. Picking the tissues from the floor, he dropped them down the en-suite loo and returned to change the bedding. After showering, he felt better and made his way downstairs,where he loaded the washing machine while waiting for the kettle to boil; he looked in on the boys.

The Levin boys were already over, and all four boys were intensely focused on the television and the banality that the boys called Minecraft or some variation of it.

"You can't stay over lads," James advised the room.

Nobody answered for a while, the boys evidently deeming themselves to be at some crucial point. Moments later, as one, all four looked up at him and his own two asked why.

"There were complications with Mum," James watched their faces change as he gave them the news. "I have to go back tonight, and it's not fair on Sandra. You'll have to arrange pick up."

"What time?" Peter Levin, the older of the boys, asked.

"What time what?" James asked.

"What time … Sir?" Peter replied nervously, his schooling showing.

"What? No. What time what? What time for what?" James clarified.

"Oh! To be picked up," Peter laughed with the others.

"Around five I suppose," James suggested.

"Dad?" Anthony, his eldest tentatively got his father's attention.

James looked at him and raised his eyebrows quizzically.

"Can you do us some lunch?"

"It's only-" James looked at his watch. "Twelve thirty! Aaaah, Christ! Give me a bit, and I'll sort something out. I need a cup of tea first. God!"

Returning to the kitchen, he swore to himself; he still felt wiped and had planned to do a lot over the day. One of his plans had been to get in his car, drive north or south, or west, or anywhere until he ran out of petrol! The idea then had been to begin a new life wherever he ended up; that didn't seem possible now, in the cold light of day, but it had helped him sleep. His tea made, he opened the fridge door. There wasn't a lot in there. Miriam usually did a big shop on Saturday mornings, which was now, James realised. Taking a pen from a glass jar on the table, and a notebook from a drawer, he began a list of things he might need later that day. Looking in the cupboard, he found there were a few potatoes, and he tumbled those into a large colander. There were some red onions, which went on the worktop, next to the egg rack and its 'egg' sign; after which he returned to the fridge. It wasn't looking great, he thought, but it was getting there. He wrote potatoes, mushrooms, onions, spring onions, beetroot, carrots, parsnips, cucumber, peppers, chillies, broccoli, cabbage, salad leaf, figs, tomatoes, avocados and bananas on his list.

"Dad!" Simon whined loudly from the other room. "Anthony's hitting me!"

Ignoring him, James continued with what he was doing, and removing spices and other bits he was finding from the cupboards, he set the oven to two hundred and twenty, filled and boiled the kettle again, and began his prepping.

His phone cuckooed for a received message, and picking it up as he continued about the kitchen, he checked it. It was from Sandra and warned she might be a little late that afternoon as the test drive was further away than she thought. James went back to the food. Half an hour here or there made little difference, he thought, but he admired her thoughtfulness. Cornflakes, Weetabix, muesli, bread, milk, sugar, honey, Marmite, peanut butter, tea, coffee, breadcrumbs, stock-cubes, and biscuits got added to his list.

Once the mince for the burgers was prepped and seasoned, he set about slicing some wedges for the oven.

'Cuckoo! his phone again sounded. Sandra texting once more. This time she reminded him to leave some money for Pizzas. He acknowledged with a simple "Cheers X".

After a brief check on the boys, James began his chopping and organising in earnest.

'Cuckoo!' the phone went again. Sandra again. The message just had an "X". Shaking his head once he'd looked at it, he didn't give it another thought. If he were nineteen, he thought, he'd probably have to send her an "X" back, and the whole bloody nonsense would go on all day. Giving the mince mix a good stir, he squeezed it through with his fingers feeling how soft it now was, as his mind drifted to thoughts and dreams of another life he might have had.

Anthony appeared at the door and asked after the availability of snacks; he shooed him away impatiently. Washing his hands after finishing his prep, he read his list aloud as he dried them; it helped him see if there were gaps in it.

The doorbell rang. Shouting to Anthony and Simon to answer it, after a couple of minutes when it rang again, he went himself and opened the door still holding the kitchen towel. It was Sheila from next door on a visit to see the baby. Following James in, as he explained the situation at the hospital, Sheila was full of sympathy, but seemed to think the whole thing fairly routine. Apologising for his lack of manners, he explained that he was in the middle of making lunch for the four boys. Also on a mission, mainly to get away from her husband Malcolm for an hour or so, Sheila was probably after a cup of tea to boot, which James didn't fancy having to do for her: his plate was full enough.

"You should've just given them something from the freezer," Sheila suggested, ignoring her awareness that James cooked for a living, and Miriam was vigilant about keeping crap out of the boys' diet. On a normal day, James would've got both boys prepping with him, but today their friends were over, and he didn't really fancy the conversation and endless nonsense questions, and ludicrous scenarios they posited, that came with their help. Meandering to the living room to look in on them, after a few moments she came back for a final word with James before leaving.

"They shouldn't spend so much time playing on that thing," she advised, in a disapproving tone. "It's better for boys to be out in the open air. Playing proper games like football and rugby, or tennis. It can't be good for them all that computer stuff."

Nodding, James grunted his agreement with her sentiment, and for a while stuck his head in a lower cupboard in the hope that Sheila would be on her way out when he looked up again. Thankfully she was and he shouted his good-byes, promising he'd keep her updated if there was any news, before returning to the food and his list once more. Kitchen roll, loo roll, sanitary towels, deodorant, bleach, toothpaste, cream cleaner, softener and washing powder to the list; he was in the zone, but the zone was different aisles of the supermarket. He also wrote down condoms, with a question mark.

Slotting four seeded pittas into the toaster without pressing it down, he prepped a quick side salad and some salsa. Miriam didn't like the boys to eat a meal without something green on their plates. A House rule, it sat prominently on their fridge.

Looking in on the boys, Anthony looked up.

"How long for food?" He was on the verge of looking stroppy.

"Twenty-minutes tops," James glanced at the screen.

Still playing Minecraft, none of the other three removed their fixed stares from the monitor. A man framed in a small square window on the screen spoke about something related to the game. Listening for a few minutes, conscientious after Sheila's comments, the utter pointlessness of what he was dribbling on about to James made it impossible for the words to penetrate any part of his brain, and he returned to the kitchen bewildered at his kids' fascination with this particular game.

Not for the first time, he thought.

Looking to get a crispy edge on the wedges, he turned the oven up to two hundred and thirty. Finely slicing five gherkins lengthways, he put each next to their allotted onion slices and checked for a larger tomato to fine-slice also, but didn't find one. Boys often don't like sliced tomato, for some reason, whereas most men don't seem to have a problem with them, so he wasn't bothered. Wondering when it changed, he wrote the question on the magnetised fridge pad they kept for such oddities and put it under 'Interesting Family Questions". Finding an old browning lime, he removed it, halved it, and squeezed it over the four salsa piles.

His phone flashed, as though to ring, and he picked it up only to see it turn itself off. A dead battery. Electrical gadgets of any sort seemed to somehow end up in the boys' room. After a couple of minutes rooting around in there he gave up, before stepping on the charger coming down the stairs. Muttering and swearing to himself, he came back to the kitchen and scanned the area, trying to remember what he was doing.

A large pan on the heat, he fried the burgers, while trying unsuccessfully to get his phone to pick up his mail as it began to charge. Rice, lentils, balsamic, mustard, brown sauce, butter, cheese, milk and gherkins went on the list. Taking four ceramic camping mugs from the cupboard, James filled each with a stash of upright wedges; placing each cup on the plate with a dollop of ketchup and mayonnaise next to the base. The burgers in pitta bread with gherkins went next to them moments later. From the cupboard, he removed a pack of tortilla chips and added a few to the sides of the salsa on each board. The boards were ready, and he laid them in a row along the kitchen island. A knife and fork in kitchen paper next to each board with a glass of milk, and he was done.

"FOOD!" James shouted and turned to get on with finishing his own, so he'd have something inside him, for what promised to be a long day ahead. Eating the remaining wedges from the basket tray, he wrapped his own burger in kitchen roll as he walked about seeing what he needed to do, checking his list, and racking his brain to think if there was anything else Miriam might need. Wine, beer, vodka, and brandy went on the list. Wine would most likely be Miriam's first demand; they'd covered everything baby related multiple times beforehand.

The boys meandered in with Simon slagging off Anthony, having apparently done something better than him.

"Dude!" Peter Levin nodded his appreciation; Peter was growing fast, and like Anthony food was high on his list. The younger two, still animated over some facet of Minecraft, began eating and drinking without ado and were soon involved in a milky moustache masticating conversation that made no sense whatsoever to James.

The phone rang, and everyone looked at each other before all four boys looked at James. "It's the house phone," James looked at their confused faces in surprise.

"Nobody rings 'that'," Simon looked at James in confusion.

He was right. The walkabout handsets weren't anywhere James could see or locate, so he eventually found himself answering the original old telephone they still kept connected in the hallway. It was the hospital, and after listening for some moments, only saying the words "Yes" "Sorry" and "Okay", James thanked the caller and hung up.

"I HAVE TO-!" James began to shout into the boys, but as he turned, both of his sons were framed in the doorway watching him.

"-go to the hospital."

"Is everything all right?" Anthony's voice quivered, and Simon next to him was as pale as a sheet; James reached out to them both.

"Everything is fine," he hugged them close. "Mum's just lost a lot of blood in the birth—it's not unusual. It's not, but it means she's sleeping, so if they need to do anything somebody has to be there to give the okay. You understand?"

The boys nodded.

"Sandra will be here at five, or thereabouts. I think you guys are big enough to see your way through 'til then?"

They nodded their agreement again.

"Don't mess about lads—this is not the time. I've got to be there. I'll try get back for tonight. I'll leave money for pizzas for later and Sandra can order them in, but the boys can't stay over. Okay? I need you guys on-side here. Mum won't be home for a couple of days I think. This is not kid-time, okay? Are we good?"

The boys nodded once more.

"Come," James gestured to the table. "Let's finish our food, and I'll go. I've still got to pack some extra bits for mum. She wasn't expecting to be in there more than a day, and I've got to get to one of the supermarkets at some stage—just in case. If I end up taking mum home later in the week and she's got nothing to eat, she'll eat ME alive!"

The boys nodded and laughed, a little weakly, but he'd broken their fear.

§

Staring at the red traffic light through the rain splashes on his windscreen, his mind fighting with multiple dialogues, James blinked himself back from them. The main thrust of his concern he realised was his own dread. Not fear. Just utter terror of being left with three boys on his own. It wasn't that he was a bad father—he was a somewhat reluctant father most of the time, which he believed most men were, but he did the tasks expected of him. Children, in general, were something he just wasn't that fond of. Loving his boys, as most fathers might; they still bored him senseless if he spent any serious time with them. Without Miriam, James feared life would soon become a drudgery of endless chores, with sheer physical and mental exhaustion, coupled with tedium, and children's endless inanities filling the void of countless days, before his ultimate death from the loss of a will to live on. James realised his fretting and the palpitations he was having weren't for Miriam, and her predicament, or anything she or the baby were going through; his entire concern was for the effect of how whatever happened to them would ultimately play out in his life. It was insanely selfish he knew, but he consoled himself that at least he was being unsentimental, and emotionally honest with himself—that had to mean something. He couldn't leave Miriam with the three kids to do it all alone, no matter what he'd been thinking. To his mind, separation or divorce after more than two kids was just wrong; whatever else he'd been thinking, he now knew there was no simple escape route for him. The traffic began moving again, and a James more reconciled with his world followed the hospital signage to the various parking options.

§

Awake once more, a medic and an orderly called her name and shook her persistently from her deep slumber. Miriam blinked the darkness away and stared at the two vaguely familiar heads above her.

"Mrs Purcell?" The Medic repeated, in a soothing voice. He smiled at her. "You're awake."

Miriam's foggy mind felt he was stating the obvious, but her eyes roamed his face and throat in close proximity; she wondered if being so hairy was uncomfortable.

"We have some food for you. We'd like you to eat something," the orderly interjected and drew

Miriam's eyeballing towards him. Nodding to her, he gestured to the tray behind them, which he brought forward.

"You've stabilised," the medic informed her. "We'd like you to have some food, and begin re-building your strength. It'll also make you feel better."

Miriam nodded. Still weak, she was hungry and especially so now that she could smell food. Combined with the antiseptic clinical smells, it wasn't any food smell she could identify but her olfactory senses had information to support them and she moved to sit up more. Helped by the orderly who slid the trolley-tray across in front of her he gestured once she was settled again.

"Do you want me to feed you?" He asked.

"What? No. I'm fine. I'm just a bit weak I think," Miriam looked at the medic in horror. "When can I go home?"

"Not for a couple of days at least, I believe," the medic answered.

"Oh thank God for that," Miriam sighed with relief. Her boys and the world they offered were something she wasn't ready to return to just yet. Slotting back into being "Mum" without some rest, some real rest, was more than she could face.

"Oh!" Miriam remembered. "My baby?"

"He's fine, Mrs Purcell," the medic smiled at her. "We'll take him along to you a little later once you've had some food and settled again. Tuck in while it's hot. It's an Italian bean soup from the 'staff' canteen." Lifting the plastic food cover, she smelt the soup as she fumbled with the serviette and spoon. A cut of bread dunked and sucked before biting, a heavy weight lifted from her. The soup was just above tepid. Chewing slowly, she sighed deeply. Part relief, part misery. Relief that she and the baby were okay, but the sadness felt deeper: things weren't right with her life and her marriage. Even now she couldn't seem to shake the dis-engaged gaze of James during her birthing struggles; the endless fights and bickering of the previous months caught up with her. Supping and chewing mechanically her still foggy mind tried to find a solution, knowing there really wasn't a simple answer. Life, and especially life with children and all the baggage that they generated today, was too complicated. Pushing the empty bowl and plate away, Miriam was surprised that it was all gone; barely remembering eating it, she lay back, thoughts circling her head. In moments she fell back to sleep.

§

Framed in the doorway holding his swaddled new-born, James looked at his wife sleeping in the hospital bed. Already having been in to drop her extra bag in the locker of her new room, James also went to the nursery and checked on the baby. Finding all reports to be good, he saw the medic dealing with Miriam, who informed him that she was now a lot better, but was still being kept for forty-eight hours. 'A couple of weeks' he said before she'd be back on her feet properly, so she'd need all their support as much as possible. Assured by James of their competence, the medic shook his hand, and in relief with everyone being alive and safe, James found his way to the café where he had a double-shot Americano and a slice of carrot cake. Picking up an extra one for Miriam, when he finished, he visited the hospital shop and picked up mineral water, grapes, tangerines, and a couple of her favourite chocolate bars. Back at the ward, he spoke for a while with the sister who suggested that he take the baby into his wife and wake her, gently. Arranging for her to remain in a private single room for however long they kept her, he paid the advance fees for the satellite television package while she was there. With relief, he saw that Miriam looked much better than previously.

Opening her eyes as he neared, their gazes met; she burst out crying, and for a while they both sat holding each other, sniffling and sobbing all the while. Each apologised in whispers for how awful they'd been. They blamed hormone changes, stress where they could, the boys, life in general, and after much hugging, stroking, hand-holding, and promises for the future, they finally settled back into the bed and chair, and together, they looked down at the new-born cradled between them.

"Are we going to try again for a girl?" James asked.

"My arse we are!" Miriam weakly punched him. "It's the snip for you!"

Laughing, for what felt like the first time in months, James, after a few pretend sceptical moments, agreed and laughed with her.

Together, quietly, their fingers touching, they sat into the early evening and watched Miriam's favourite Saturday night family shows, nibbling on the snacks and treats. James went over the days without her, how the boys had been, how helpful and accommodating Sandra had been, how much he missed her, the neighbours wishes and Sheila's visit. At nine o clock Miriam reluctantly suggested he should head back to the boys. Agreeing, after half an hour he managed to finally depart from the hospital taking a detour on the way home to one of the major supermarkets that remained opened twenty-four hours.

Once there he did an extensive family shop, taking his time so as not to forget anything which might be needed that he hadn't listed, and felt that he spent an inordinate amount of time in the sanitary aisles.

Arriving home shortly after half-twelve the house and street were in darkness. Unloading the car, he quietly stocked the fridge, the freezer, and the cupboards. Pouring himself a large brandy when it was all done, and realising he was still hungry, James opened some crisps. When he finished his drink, he topped it up again. After fifteen minutes, sated, he found himself staring at the weekend's sports news headlines as they ran silently across the television screen beneath the endless news loops. Pouring himself a final drink, he decided after a sip to go to bed with it. Switching off the television and lights, and in the darkness, quietly and tentatively holding his drink before him, he set out to climb the stairs to his bedroom, before standing on a gadget charger, causing him to spill his drink all over himself. He hopped about in blind agony for some minutes before finally calming himself. Furious with the boys, he removed his brandy-soaked trousers and put them by the washing machine, before resuming his journey upstairs. James looked in on the boys; both were fast asleep in near identical sleeping poses, and his anger with them dissipated.

The guest room was quiet and dark and James tip-toed past it and along the landing to the back of the house where he and Miriam slept; he yawned wearily when he finally came to his own bedroom door and the promise of his bed.

Opening the bedroom door quietly he turned on the overhead light, automatically dimming it as he pressed; he stepped into the room and felt the welcoming soft carpet pile beneath his bare feet. Lying on his bed, a semi-naked Sandra Giovanni gazed mischievously at him. Watching his eyes the whole time to gauge his reaction, as he approached the bed she tracked her gaze down his body to his boxers for a sign of a response. Sliding down further in the bed with a small inviting groan, her thong rode up high between her arse cheeks. Sandra Giovanni smiled warmly up at him, blinking slowly, in a seductive way she'd seen women do on television and in movies, and in a way she'd practised many, many times before her bedroom mirror until she felt she'd got it just right. The tip of her tongue peeped through her lips. Slipping the thin straps of her lacy babydoll from her shoulders and drawing it down a little, she allowed her full young firm breasts to pop through, and spread her legs a little wider; her arse lifted slightly from the mattress, tantalising, teasing, tormenting, she swayed slowly from side to side.

***

Veggie Burgers Recipe

Ingredients for 4 quarter-pounders

Dry

350g of a soya, quorn or vege-mince
1 onion, very finely diced and chopped
3-4 garlic cloves crushed and mash-chopped with
sea-salt
2 hot red chilies (optional)
1/2 bunch of coriander (leaves only) chopped
3 sprigs of rosemary (leaves only) chopped
3 tablespoons of breadcrumbs
3 tablespoons of gram flour
1 teaspoon of cumin seeds
1 teaspoon of smoked paprika powder
1 teaspoon of salt & cracked pepper

Wet

100ml mushroom/onion stock (with a dollop of
marmite optional)
1 large egg (2 small or med)

Mix all the 'Dry' ingredients together in a good sized
mixing bowl. Add the stock and mix through
thoroughly. Add the egg(s) and fork mix it through
once more. Cover and set aside in the fridge for a
couple of hours. It can be used straightaway, but it

retains a tighter compaction if left for a bit (overnight is best).

Remove from fridge and weigh the mix on your kitchen scales. It should come in under or around the 560g mark. A quarter pounder is about 114g so anything between that and 120g gives you a good version. Divide the mix into 4 even pieces (using your scales). You can either shape them by hand, rolling them into firm balls and pressing them into patties, or if you have a burger-shaper, use that. A wide deep heavy based frying pan with a splash of groundnut oil on a medium heat, add the burgers, allow them to seal before turning and turn them regularly for seven-eight minutes.

Meanwhile, slice open four rustic white bread rolls, or seeded pittas or ciabatta—your preference. Either pop in a wide toaster for 30 seconds or put in a hot oven for a few minutes.

Slice two medium to ripe tomatoes thinly, four gherkins (optional), chop a little green leaf (basil works really well). Pick out 4 slices of Emmental or Cheddar. Add in a little chutney if you have some, and have the mayo, mustard and ketchup on standby. Once the burgers are ready, put some chutney or mustard on the bottom piece of bread and place the burger on top. Add the cheese slice, leaf, tomatoes and gherkins, and dress to your own desire before putting the top on. You can wedge it in place with a cocktail stick.

Serve with a side of home-made sweet potato wedges, and a small bowl of salsa and guacamole. Good for a sunny Saturday in the garden!

***

Sticky Nurses

A LOUD SIREN CUT THROUGH THE TRANQUIL night air, gradually fading as the ambulance negotiated its way through the traffic towards the Harrow Road, and away from the hospital.

Praed Street, Paddington, was otherwise eerily quiet for a Friday evening. In the alley behind the monolithic monstrosity of St Mary's Accident and Emergency building, a window sat slightly ajar, and from within words drifted into the night air.

"No-no-no-no. No! I do not think so, Angela," a shaking head caused the words to rise and fall as the contrasting high pitch and deep bass sounds of an African woman's voice danced their way to the window.

"They're coming on Sunday, so I need to know how to do it," Angela pleaded. "Just go through it for me. I'll remember it. I promise. Really, Adanna. I will remember!"

Adanna shook her head and drew her chin inwards; she gave Angela her sceptical glare; feeling she had no choice but to help the poor girl, she gathered her thoughts and began to speak in her teacher's voice; it was a vocation she knew she'd missed.

"Oh child, what am I to do? What am I to do with you? Okay-okay—I will try do this, just for for your sake," she shook her head at her younger colleague who nodded desperately with wide, pleading eyes.

"Okay. To begin with, you will need two or three green onions. Green, yah? Four cloves of garlic. Two, no, three scotch bonnets. Maybe two for you. You would not be used to them so only use two, but be very careful when you chop them, Angela. Try not to get them on your fingers when you cut, so just chop them with a big chopper knife and throw away the green stalky bit that you cannot eat. Try not to touch them if you can," Adanna frowned as she spoke and held Angela's gaze to ensure the seriousness of her advice was being taken on board.

"Why?" Angela knew she had no choice but to ask.

"It burns like a fire on your fingers. Really like a fire! I am not joking, Angela," Adanna splayed her fingers before her and grimaced in pain to simulate the experience.

"Um, okay. What else?' Angela, stopping her folding, yawned loudly and covered her mouth. "These night shifts kill me you know."

"I know," Adanna agreed. "It is not natural this night working, you know. If God had wanted us to work through the night, we would have owl eyes and not be feeling all hot and dizzy after every shift."

"I thought that was just me!" Angela held both of her cheeks and looked at Adanna in surprise.

"Oh no! No-no," Adanna's voice changed to her wise-woman tone. "All us ladies suffer like this. It is our burden, Angela. It is the burden all of us ladies everywhere must bear for the sins of our mother, Eve."

"So, onions, garlic-?" Angela nodded her agreement but brought Adanna back to her original teaching voice. If they visited the Bible, they might never get back to the everyday before the shift ended.

"You also need about three hundred grams of split peas, which you should soak overnight. Add some bicarbonate soda to the water when they are soaking too," Adanna reflected for a moment as she visualised herself cooking.

"Bicarbonate soda? Wha-Why?" Angela enquired.

"I am not a scientist, Angela," Adanna questioned the questioning. "It is what we do when we soak these things like split peas, or chickpeas, or black beans. Is it not? Do you not do this here?"

"Aaah? I-? Not that I'm aware of," Angela raised her eyes, apologetically uncertain.

"That man was very messy," Adanna scrunched her nose in disgust as she took in the bench before her. "We're going to have to mop everywhere in here now. There is mud all over because of him, and all his dirt. He was a very dirty man!"

"Let's finish the tidying first, and then we can call the cleaner," Angela suggested.

"That is a good idea, Angela," Adanna agreed and looked at Angela as though surprised with her useful input.

"What else do I need? I need to make this right, Adanna. I like this guy," Angela joined her hands and smiled dreamily.

"I know you do, Angela, but I don't know how to make this wrong, so I am going to tell you how I make it. Is that not what you want from me, I am asking you now?"

Angela nodded her agreement and for Adanna to continue.

"Yes of course it is. Let me see, now. Of course, you need to get four or five good maduros, and you must first chop the ends off all of them and remove the skin too, of course. After this, you must slice them into inch size pieces. You know, about this big," Adanna demonstrated the approximation of an inch to a confused looking Angela.

"I know what an inch is," Angela looked at her in dismay. "What on this earth is a maduro? That's why I looked at you that way."

"A maduro. Really? You do not know? How can you not know what a maduro is?" Adanna raised her eyebrows in confusion and disbelief at Angela's mystified head shake.

"They are in every shop between here and Shepherd's Bush market," Adanna continued. "On the pavement in boxes, or in all the markets. They are everywhere, Angela, you know—the big ones that look like rotten bananas."

"Oh. Plantain? I thought-" Angela began.

"They are all types of plantain, but when they are ripe-ripe, you know, almost gone off—really-really ripe! Then, Angela, then they are called maduros," Adanna fussed at her fingers beneath the tap; the dirty man was clinging to her.

"Why?" Angela asked.

"I am not a scientist, Angela," Adanna repeated her earlier explanation, but her focus was fixed on her fingers. "That is what they are called when they are very very ripe."

"So—what do I do with them?" Angela let it go and thought it might be more productive to get on with the cooking.

"If you fry them first in butter—I will not say palm oil to you anymore because of what you told me before, and I don't want to have that big conversation again, so I will say to you to fry them in butter, or a different oil, for ten to fifteen minutes, and then you must add them to the curry in the last ten minutes only. It is very simple. And don't be telling me that it is fattening again. How on earth are you supposed to stay warm in this country without a little bit of something on you?" Adanna beamed up at her, satisfied her hands were once more her own and free of contamination.

"But we haven't made the curry yet?" Angela shook her head in dismay.

"Oh that is easy," Adanna looked in surprise at Angela's lost look. "My God, girl, how do you manage to eat? Do you ever cook anything at all, Angela?"

Angela defended herself briefly with a look and a head shake before bringing Adanna back on track; wiping down the sink area she then sprayed the disinfectant everywhere across the surfaces.

"Okay, what's next?" She nodded her request and consent for Adanna to continue.

"Next? Let me just first summarise quickly a little bit for you Angela, if you don't mind—it will help my mind. You must boil the split peas in clean water before everything else. No salt. That is very important to remember; I cannot tell you how important that is, but do not ever use salt with those pulses or beans when you are having to make them soft. No-no-no. Before you ask, Angela, I am just telling you what I know. Okay. Next job. Where was I?" Adanna closed her eyes for a moment and back-tracked in her thoughts.

Angela looked at Adanna and shrugged; nothing ever happened quickly with Adanna.

"All done here," Angela buffed the last few smears on the stainless steel sink. 'There was a funny smell off that bloke, wasn't there."

"I don't think that man washed very often," Adanna visibly quivered. "Will you get the cleaner or should I?"

§

Outside, a loud siren noise interrupted the quiet night; the swirling blue of the flashing light created a sense of bedlam for those unused to it. The city was slowly coming to life as people drifted out of their homes and offices to begin their weekends. Here and there those who'd gone straight from work to get on with their Friday night were already into the swing of things; for some of them, their night was already coming to an end. For Remi, it had already been an eventful night and for a brief moment, the whole evening swirled and flashed before his eyes just before the triage supervisor appeared and called loudly for a nurse.

"HOLD ME BACK!" Remi staggered forward. "HOLD ME BACK YOU BASTARDS OR I'LL KILL HIM! I'LL RIP HIS POINTY FUCKING HEAD OFF!"

The focus of Remi's rage was a tall, thin, gangly man with a long hook nose, dark eyes, jet-black hair, and skin so white it almost looked powdered; he was like a wannabe vampire. Shoving Remi over, after Remi had been bothering him and his girlfriend as they sat kissing and fooling about beneath the garden heater in the pub's beer-garden, he then continued chatting to her and she to him as though nothing had happened.

There wasn't anybody to hold Remi back.

"YOU LANKY STICK OF PISS!" Remi continued his rant.

Meaning to say or shout 'streak' his brain and mouth slipped out of synch with the drink; lanky stick-man turned to Remi once more and squared to face him as he staggered directly towards him; he was at least eight inches taller than Remi, although weight-wise there probably wasn't much in it. His arms were at least five inches longer than Remi's, and his hands made two large fists that looked as though they were at least half again the size of Remi's. Remi swung at him furiously. Leaning back, easing out of the way of Remi's clumsy haymakers, he lashed one punch and caught Remi on the side of his head just below his ear.

People later agreed, he had very fast hands.

Also kicking Remi in the middle of his gut with what looked like a size twelve plus foot, on which he wore a walking boot of sorts—it was hard whatever it was. Remi doubled over, and he kicked Remi once more, this time on the upper part of his left thigh, on the outside, causing Remi to collapse in an undignified heap; the last kick hurt more than the first two wallops combined. Raising his head, not intending to get up, but just to fling another profanity, another massive fist—this time with a gold signet ring on the end of a very fast moving arm—caught Remi on the upper cheek below his eye and sent his head spinning. Blood spurted in a spray from his face.

"Enough," the girl behind the lanky man murmured the word nonchalantly, and the long-limbed shadow hovering over Remi stopped and looked sideways before snorting a laugh.

The shadow then nodded and departed from Remi's view. Staggering to his feet and holding his thigh with a grimace, Remi watched the couple quit the beer garden hand in hand. The man clicked his car-key, and the lights of it flashed. Leaning on the tree at the side, trying not to throw up, and hidden by the box hedge, Remi smiled when he saw the lights flash once more and the couple change their minds; they angled their footsteps instead towards the footbridge that took them over the carriageways to another parade of bars.

Remi threw up. His stomach cramped in pain, and lowering himself to his knees he threw up again, only then feeling marginally better. Nobody helped him. The four or five people in the beer garden who witnessed the beating knew Remi deserved it and didn't care too much about him. Trying to spit the bloody mess in his mouth onto the grass his mouth and jaw malfunctioned and it stuck to the side of his face briefly before glooping onto the table.

"Oi!" One of the bar girls on a smoke break just coming out the doors shouted at him in disgust.

Staggering away, he limped out the gate towards the car-park before the girl could take it any further; he hobbled along the path beneath the overhanging shrubbery until he was out of sight. Finally reaching the large public car-park, he sat on the kerb behind a large white van and in front of two re-cycling units. He tried to gather himself together. There was a lot of blood on one side of his shirt, and he traced it upwards to beneath his eye where the last punch had landed. Smarting when he touched it, Remi stood up and looked in the dark reflection of the van's window where he could see a deep black gash from which blood was still pouring.

"Bastard!" Remi looked up to see if he could see the man who'd scarred him and growled to himself as he prowled across the carpark. His assailant was gone. No sign of him anywhere, looking about, Remi realised that there was no sign of anybody.

The car he'd seen the lights flash on wasn't anything special. An Audi A3 with a leather roof. It was five years old too, so there'd been no reason for the arsehole to have behaved so flash and full of himself, just because he had a pretty girl on his arm. With the sharp point of the bottle opener gadget on a Swiss army knife he carried with him, Remi etched the words 'Wanker' on one door, and 'Whore' on the other. Chuckling to himself, and feeling avenged, he sauntered across the car-park to the bus-stop. His luck was in and the bus to Paddington where the hospital was located pulled in just as he arrived at the stop. Concerned at the state of his face the driver wanted to get the police, but Remi convinced him otherwise, and eventually he reluctantly drove off. Giving Remi a small soiled hand towel to stem the flow of blood, the driver only stopped the bus twice for people to get off; he didn't stop on three other occasions where people waited and stuck their arms out. Pulling up at the back of the hospital, he shouted to Remi.

"You're here! Go get that seen to before you end up losing an eye."

Remi sobered up a bit on the ride with the fresh night air blowing in his face from the opened window and the after-effects of having thrown up; he thanked the driver and got off the bus, following the signs to the accident and emergency ward where he saw them.

§

Sent straight in behind the curtains after someone shouting for a nurse Remi's head spun and he tried unsuccessfully to step the world swirling about him before closing his eyes and giving himself into the nurses' care.

Once cleaned up, the nurse applied a surgical glue to the fold of flesh before pressing it all back in place; she assured Remi that it was standard practice now and showed much better results than stitching. The heal-scars, reputedly, were much less prominent and usually invisible within a year, she suggested. Remi was chuffed. Holding it and him in place for a few moments, as Remi didn't want to lie down—the room spun when he did, after first being sent behind the curtain, and Remi didn't want to throw up again—an older nurse also asked Remi a variety of questions about his injury. Claiming it had happened in a drunken fight with his friend who'd gone home to sleep it off, Remi's focus tried to keep a grip on a still world. When asked his name, he then gave her the name of a former school friend whose details he remembered almost as if they were his own. They used to look a bit alike, and Remi had no idea why he did it. It was probably because they'd been through junior school together and Roger Waters had never moved, so the details had never changed; it was the second time that he'd used his name like this, and the nurse scolded him when she saw that the incident wasn't Roger Waters' first of this nature. With some of his composure regained, Remi did a good job of looking contrite and agreed with the nurse that he was too old for things like this to be happening. To convince her of the sincerity of his repentance he promised he'd avoid places from now on where it could happen. The first nurse declared herself done and straightened to go to the sink to wash her hands. As she stood, Remi's face came with her hand. Looking at him following her in surprise, she gave a tentative experimental tug.

"OW!" Remi yelped, and his eyes leaked tears.

She tugged again, half instinctively, half confused.

"OW! STOP THAT!" Remi yelped again.

All three stopped; both nurses burst out laughing, before realising that Remi was anything but amused.

"Oh my God! You're stuck fast to me!" The nurse declared and struggled to speak as her laughing instinct overcame her.

"I can fucking feel that!" Remi retorted.

"There is no need for bad language, Mr Waters," both nurses immediately responded angrily back.

"If you'd laid down like I asked, this probably wouldn't have happened, Mr Waters," the stuck-nurse neatly passed the blame back to Remi and held his glare.

"I'd have thrown up on you," Remi lowered his tone and felt a little contrite once more.

"Again, not my fault really—is it Mr Waters?" The stuck nurse scanned the area around her. "Adanna, please, can you ask triage what the best thing to do is, in this case? I don't want just to pull it quickly. I might pull his face right off?"

"NO!" Remi squeaked his protest loudly. "Don't do that!"

"I said, I 'didn't' want to do that, Mr Waters," opening her eyes wide, Angela clarified her mischievous comment with doe-like innocence.

Raising his hands to her wrist and looking at her all the while before he took hold of it, Remi's fingers fully circled her wrist, and he tugged it slightly towards him to remove the tautness and stinging her movements were causing him.

"I'm sorry," his regret was clear, as was his anger, and the beating he'd taken was catching up. "But it hurts when you move. Not wanting is not, 'not doing'. That's all. I was just asking that you not 'do' that. I don't feel right, and this is not helping me."

"Okay, okay Mr Waters," Angela adopted her soothing motherly voice. "Stay calm, and we'll figure this out. I've never heard of anything like this happening here, but we'll be out of this in a jiffy."

Returned, the other nurse fixed the curtains and smiled widely at them both as she waggled a bottle of Tippex thinner between her thumb and forefinger.

"This should do the trick, Angela," a single eyebrow raised quizzically suggested humour for her, as she raised the bottle and shook it. "Jeannie found it in the stores."

"Should?" Remi's voice trembled.

"Oh, don't be such a big baby, Mr Waters," Adanna dismissed his fear offhand. "It will sting, maybe a little bit, but it is a good idea. What is it called when something breaks down glue? You know? A de-?"

"I don't know. I'm not a bloody scientist," Remi hissed the words through clenched teeth, first looking at Adanna, and then to Angela. "But could I ask that 'you' apply it, and 'you' keep still? Please!"

"Okay Mr Waters, okay. Keep your boy pants on," Adanna's comment set Angela chuckling and caused her hands to move and Remi to wince. "I will put it here Angela. I will pour lots of it. Close your eyes, Mr Waters. CLOSE!'

Adanna complied with Remi's request, and once Angela felt the wet dribble she yanked her finger away; she didn't know if the thinner worked, but she knew she had enough of Mr Waters and his smelly beer-sick-cigarette breath.

"There!" A spinning Remi holding his hand over his cheek and eye glared at her when he'd come full circle.

Angela checked her finger, in case the skin fold had stuck to it and come away with her pull. It hadn't.

"Adanna," Angela used her officious voice to change the mood of the room. "Can you finish Mr Waters for me, please. I must go remove this glue and return this thinner chemical to the front, and I should thank them for their assistance."

Nodding with a suppressed smiled after calming a tearing Remi down, and getting him to sign his release form, Adanna kept him on the opposite side of the trolley to where Angela was, before she finally advised him that he was free to go. Angela came back through the curtain once Remi departed the room.

"This is going to be a long night, Angela," Adanna looked at the clock. "It is only ten o clock, and we have already had two crazy people! That Mr Waters was lucky you did not pull his eye out, girl!"

Falling about with laughter, they set about tidying and cleaning down the area in readiness for the next admittance.

"So once everything is in the pot and cooking, other than the rice, is there anything else I would need to do?" Angela asked, returning to where they'd been.

"Have we put in the maduros? We have. Okay, now you need to add a little bit of water to the two big spoons of maize starch and beat it all very fast into a paste. Just five or six spoons of water should do it. Once everything is cooked, and you are happy with the look of it, then, ten minutes before serving you should add the maize and stir it in, and it will thicken your curry nicely. You could chop some coriander leaves and scatter them on top when you serve it, Angela. You do know how to cook rice yes?" Adanna sprayed the bench-bed where Mr Waters had put his dirty hands. Pulling another long strip of blue tissue to cover it, she noticed Angela's nod in the corner of her eye.

"Have you seen that new Locum covering for Mister Prendergast?" Adanna hummed her pleasure.

Shaking her head, Angela laughed at the dreamy face Adanna was making.

The draught from outside picked up as the double doors swung open once more. A new admittance was on the way in with the ambulance crew. Picking up the pace, in moments they were finished and pulled the curtain back around. With the refuse disposed of, they ambled their way back towards the front of the ward where two consultants were sipping tea and watching them approach.

"Too skinny," Adanna whispered without moving her head, and Angela smiled and nodded.

***

Maduros Curry Recipe

Maduros Curry is an Indian-Ugandan-Nigerian hybrid, with a Spanish/South-American name. Having lived in Shepherds Bush for over twenty years, I've been given multiple methods on the 'best way' to make this dish (amongst many others). What I've suggested is what worked best for me in the end. Do be careful with the scotch bonnets though, Adanna wasn't kidding! I had to ring St Mary's in Paddington to speak to a Nigerian lady my wife worked with at the time for her advice on how to stop my hands burning. I had guests at home but had to sit by a sink for nearly an hour with a cold tap running over them before the burning eased. I did also get stuck to a nurse using the surgical glue after a night out, and the Tippex thinner was my own suggestion after traipsing a few corridors with her. The nurse had planned to push my head away fast whilst pulling her thumb away. I held her wrist a little tighter than she liked. Trust ran thin after her idea.

Ingredients

300g yellow split peas, soaked overnight in cold water with a spoon of bicarbonate soda.
3-4 medium onions, finely chopped
6 cloves of garlic, finely chopped with salt
1 small piece of ginger
2 scotch bonnets
1 large red pepper cubed

3-4 large maduros cut into inch thick pieces
1 300ml can of coconut milk
1 glass of water
groundnut oil and butter

Spices

3 cloves
5 deseeded green cardamon pods
1 teaspoon of fenugreek
1 teaspoon of cumin seeds
1/2 teaspoon of fennel seeds
1/2 teaspoon of black peppercorns
1 teaspoon of palm sugar
1/2 teaspoon of sea salt
3 tablespoons of curry powder

Making Maduros Curry

Cook the yellow split peas in a large boiling pan until
they are no longer hard but not gone soft (al dente)
and set aside. Remove the scum that arises on the
water as you boil them.

Heat a small dry frying pan and add the spices
with the exception of the palm sugar, salt and curry
powder for about two minutes. Add all the spices to
a pestle and grind the mix to a powder.

Put two pans on medium heat, one a large
frying pan and one a deep heavy pot. Add a good
splash of groundnut oil and a dollop of butter to both
pans. To the frying pan add the sliced maduros, to
the other start with the onions. The maduros will
cook gently over 10-15 minutes and should brown
and caramelise nicely for you to set aside. Once the
onions have sweated a bit, add the ginger and

scotch bonnets. Sweat these for a couple of minutes and then add the chopped pepper. Sweat for a couple more minutes and add the powdered spices and give it all a good stir. Add the coconut milk and stir for a couple of minutes. Reduce the heat, cover and leave to cook for seven to eight minutes. Add the split peas and some water to keep a runny mixture. Leave to simmer gently for twenty minutes to half an hour. Add the crushed garlic, stir in and add the maduros. Allow to simmer for another fifteen to twenty minutes, adding water to keep the mixture moist and runny. You can leave this simmer for another hour and it will be even better. Scatter some torn or chopped coriander leaf on top when you serve.

Serve with rice, mixed salad and flat breads, and very cold beer.

***

The Conversation

LUCKY PEAK STATE PARK IS THE PERFECT place for swimming, picnicking, fishing, boating, or even biking, according to officials from the Idaho Tourist Board. They forgot to mention hiking. This was not for any comparative lack in standards, when put up against the other outdoor pursuits, you understand, but just one of those things that an official inadvertently omits to add when looking at a brochure dominated by a lake, or a stretch of water, with people engaged in those activities aforementioned, and with a deadline looming in his or her head. Oddly enough, hiking is what most people come to Lucky Peak for; whilst it can't be assumed for sure, there's a high probability that the Idaho Tourist Board man, or woman, because that too can't be taken for granted, well, let's just say whoever described their various perceived perfections of the park, they themselves are probably not much for hiking, given that they forgot to mention it.

A desk jockey perhaps? Even a race of desk jockeys, if the collective still applies to that particular class of jockey. Maybe even carrying a little too much of themselves around, unlike the skinny little silk wearers we're all more familiar with, but, very like many a man and woman I see sitting sucking sodas in their cars looking out at the world, and all in need of a proper hike in these here beautiful hills of Lucky Peak.

Slightly south of the Park, and probably still less than five miles from Boise, on highway twenty-one, north-side, a small diner sits tucked in the shelter of an enormous overhanging boulder. This rocky prominence has likely jutted in this fashion for over two hundred million years and has sheltered many a creature seeking refuge over the millennia, no doubt. Now it's mainly truckers, miners, tree-planters, fellers, mill workers, potato farmers, and end-of-life day-visitors out of Boise who seek refuge, or respite, in the diner that sits beneath the boulder. Not rare as big bears in Idaho by any means those type of folk, but, in an out of the way pass-through spot like this particular diner, for any one person, being there at all is rare enough; for me, it's always nice to hear them talk and have an opportunity to listen in on conversations from other parts of Idaho, and the world too for that matter, if someone from afar comes by. That way, I get to find what this planet far from Boise is interested in, and might even be talking about these days.

It's rarely what I expect.

The diner beneath the boulder is famous today for two things. Or two dishes really I should say, and fame is obviously a relative thing, so put that aside for now. Its first item of esteem is a particular potato dish that could cause a grown man to weep with satisfaction, and sits beside a rack of ribs, or a steak, or any kind of fish or pie dish, and brings nothing but joy to, in this case, the aptly named consumer. But I won't go there just now, as Idaho, I'm sure everybody in the civilised world must know by now: Idaho, is famous for its potato dishes. Heck, one in ten here claim to be of Irish origin: a few of those even claim to be original Murphys.

It's really the other dish that locals come out to this roadside diner for.

Martha's a local girl you understand, born and bred in Boise, and like most of the people from around these parts, potato is what Martha knows best. Her husband, a smaller stocky fella, sports a pencil moustache, boasts jet black hair, and moisturises a skin that's a tad sallower than most in these parts; he came north one day some thirty years back for the picking season. Suffice to say, he just never went back south. He met Martha Quinn. There's one thing we here know about flame-haired Martha, and even some who've never met her might even know this—the Quinns here have a reputation of sorts you see—the thing about Martha is, well … if Martha wants something, she gets it, and if she gets it, and she likes it, she darn well keeps it. It's simple enough, and Eduardo never really disputed Martha's keeping of him, or even keeping him all this way up north the way she did.

There was a shack beneath the boulder when they first got together, and rumour has it that it was behind that erection that Martha first tasted Eduardo's New Mexican sausage and found it hit the spot, and was very much to her liking. They acquired the site some months later, were wed in the Foothills Church over on West State, and eventually put up the three-roomed house and the diner that sits out front of it, complete with the bright yellow lettering spelling out their names across the six-foot-high red paint 'diner' sign. They've not looked back since, and Eduardo has never found himself further south than thirty-five degrees north.

Today, Eduardo is known simply as Ed by people 'round these parts, and having always been a man of few words, his voice too has lost its southern Latino affectations, and only one real reminder remains for us to be aware of Ed's New Mexican heritage.

"FOUR TACOS, FOUR SAUSAGES AND TWO PITCHERS!" The waitress bellowed across the diner, her shout loud enough for every head to swivel towards her—even those busy eating. Bo bit down on a large piece of chilli, wincing as the heat filled his mouth and stopped him talking for a moment; his eyes followed the waitress's hips as she went past. His pause finally allowed Lou to add his five cents worth to the pot.

"There's an old saying Bo-? Well I'm not entirely sure if it's exactly a saying, or a proverb now. Anyhows, it's one of those things, but someone said it a-long-ways back, and it should help clarify that point I was just trying to-," replying with an explanation and expansion of his earlier effort, Lou watched his friend anxiously mopping his brow before gulping water, and in his pause for concern, he allowed Bo to come back in.

"Who said what again?" Bo wiped his arm beneath his nose to remove the sweat that ran down and tickled the end of his glistening fleshy protuberance; blinking back the tears the heat had triggered he released a sighing whoosh of belly-air straight at Lou.

"Well that ain't exactly clear now, Bo," Lou tilted his head out of Bo's wind, "but it ain't of no great importance either!"

"How is that so, Lou?" Knocking back another swig of water Bo's bulging eyes kept his friend's focus on his question. "Surely it matters who said a thing, if anything matters about a thing? I mean, we ain't gonna listen to any old fool now. I ask you?"

"I don't agree with that now," biting a spicy sausage neatly in half without stopping for breath, Lou shook his head dismissively. "I think it more important 'what' was said, than by 'whom' it was said. That's what it is I'm thinking, Bo."

"But any old fool can say any old shit," taking a break from his plate for a moment, Bo questioned Lou's assertion. "Surely if we know who said something, we can tell if it's worth our time to listen to it or not."

"Bo, a fool can sometimes see things right, and call it as he sees it," Lou picked himself a thin paper napkin from the dispenser on the table to wipe his brow. The chilli was hot and spicy, and watching Bo's profuse perspiration was prompting an infectious response in Lou; he paused for a moment to take a rest from the food, picking at a space between his front teeth where food habitually stuck before continuing. "And a wise man too!" Lou sucked his fork clean and used it for timing to emphasise his point. "A wise man can be blind to a truth as a three-day-old pup, if his mind is elsewhere on a given day."

Bo blew his nose, using near half-a-dozen of the slippery, waxy napkins; he sucked a deep laborious breath back through his cleared nostrils.

"This is fine chilli here, Lou," he nodded at the plate before him.

"Use some-a-that-there sour cream, Bo," Lou advised his glistening friend. "They call this here

'The Special'! That cream'll stop this special thing blowin' our heads off before we're done. Try one of these here sausages while you're at it—they're a special of Ed's too I hear."

"What was it you were saying again?" Bo picked a sausage and dipped it in Ed's special brown mustard.

Lou looked at his friend and queried the question with his eyes.

"You were talking about something somebody said before I distracted you. I'll have some of that-there sour cream you suggested. I'm gonna have to take this here sweater off too," Bo wheezed; heat pumped from his body, and he waved his hand before his mouth taken aback with the extra zing in the mustard.

The sweater clung tight across Bo's broad shoulders and the little space offered by the fixed bench seating arrangement wasn't enough for a man of Bo's size to begin removing any piece of clothing, short of a hat perhaps; he stood up and out of the restrictive space. Removing his sweater over his head, he pulled his shirt out of his waistband in the process and revealed to one-and-all his hair-covered barrel gut. It wasn't a pretty sight for anyone, but the diner's clientele this particular lunchtime was almost all male, and in general, it seems rare that a man takes offence at a sighting of another man's briefly bared immodest torso. The waitresses were for that brief moment out of sight in the kitchen picking up plates, and Bo had tucked himself back into tidiness and was once more before his plate when the first one kicked the door open with her heel. Spinning her way back out on to the floor with the assured movements of a line-dancer, she bellowed like the farm-girl she once was.

"TWO TACOS, EXTRA SALSA, TWO CHILLI SPECIALS EXTRA HOT AND ONE PITCHER!"

Bo raised his eyes towards Lou once more and nodded, gesturing that he should continue.

"You were sayin'," his eyes followed the waitress to check out who on this earth wanted something hotter than the plate of fire-food he was currently battling with.

"I was?" Lou asked, his own eyes leaked tears in the corners and dabbed at them with the chili-contaminated tissue.

"Well, you were sayin' somethin' about a-sayin', or about somebody else sayin' something, if I remember right," Bo raised his eyebrows at the food and pitchers being placed before an elderly couple near the door and lost his thread.

"So I was. So I was, Bo." Lou nodded, shrugged in surprise at his friend's recall, and scooped a spoonful of chilli and rice into his mouth, following it with a dollop of sour cream atop a corn chip, with a swig of water to wash it all down; he chomped for a moment before swallowing, nodding to himself, and then to Bo to acknowledge his patience. Running his tongue around the outside of his teeth, he sipped some more water, took another napkin, and wiped his mouth once more before speaking.

"I was sayin' somethin' about somebody sayin' somethin', that's true, Bo," Lou's mind worked its way back to find where he'd been, or where he was coming from; he didn't want Bo to see he'd part lost his way. It's difficult for a man to make his point if he has no hold on the thread of his own thinking.

"Oh yeah—it was about flies, that's right. I remember now," a moment of clarity cut through Lou's foggy thoughts.

"Flies," Bo's mouth queried his friend's assertion with a confused upside-down smile. "Flies? I don't remember you saying nothin' about flies, Lou. No-no. Nothin' I can recall about flies at all.

"Bo," Lou put down his fork and held up both of his hands to get his friend to quieten and focus a little more on him. "It was about flies … that's what I was going to explain to you. You never got to hear what it was I was trying to say to you. That's why you can't recall nothin' about flies, 'cos I never got to finish my darn sentence, Bo. Now let me finish my sentence, Bo, and maybe you'll get to hear what it is I'm sayin'. Or tryin' to say, if I'm being right picky."

"Are you fellas all right here?" A waitress passed near their table, and sensed the tone. "Can I get you anything else?"

"I'm fine, ma'am," Lou smiled up at her, before casting a look at shy Bo and prompting him to at least show some manners, and respond when spoken to. Bo swallowed what was in his mouth, and a dry corn chip stuck briefly in his throat as he raised his hand to gesture a need, and for the waitress to wait; he coughed and hacked for a couple of moments, causing other diners to look over in concern, and the waitress to smile, and then look a little worried as his hacking continued longer than she'd anticipated. The chip finally found enough moisture to soften it, and no longer feeling as though he'd swallowed a blade, Bo's watery eyes met the waitress's.

"'Some more water if I could please, Miss?'" Bo wiped his sleeve across his brow.

The waitress smiled, and touched Bo's shoulder in relief that he was okay, before going off to fetch some water.

"You're mighty touchy today, Lou," Bo raised a single eyebrow at his friend over his fork of food. "What's up? You ain't fallen out with that mother of yours again, have you?"

"No, Bo, I ain't fallen out with my mother. And I ain't touchy neither," Lou released a long exasperated sigh and shook his head at his friend.

"What?" Bo asked. "Y'ain't touchy, but you're sour as a sore bear with a burr in his ass? Wassup, Lou? You can talk to me. I'm your friend goddammit."

"I ain't touchy, and I ain't sore as no bear, with or without no burr, Bo!" Lou looked to the side, and then back at his friend before looking away again chewin' on his lip. "I don't think you see it, Bo, but you gotta be one of the most frustratin' men in our county to have a proper conversation with sometimes."

"Me, Lou?" Bo's surprise at the assertion caused him to place his cutlery on the table so both of his hands could come to his chest. "How come's that, Lou? I never mean anybody no harm, Lou, you know that. How can you say such a thing about a friend? Frustratin'? Me? All I do is listen to what you're sayin' and ask questions if I feel a need, Lou. That seems all kinds of reasonable to me. How can that be frustratin', Lou?"

Lou looked across at his friend; both of their plates were nearing empty, and since he'd removed his jumper Bo had cooled down some and wasn't looking so uncomfortable. Looking put out, and even a little hurt by Lou's off-hand comment, Lou realised he'd probably been out of line with his friend.

"I'm sorry, Bo," Lou sought to make amends. "Maybe I am a bit touchy today. Maybe I got one of them spots I can't put my finger right on. I sure didn't mean to snap at you like that."

"Oh forget it, Lou, think nothin' of it," a relieved Bo immediately dismissed any concern about himself; his thoughts were for Lou. "I was just a bit concerned like that maybe somethin' was up, and like they always saying on TV, you got no 'outlet'."

"No 'outlet'?" Lou queried.

"Yeah," Bo nodded, and his gaze drifted curiously to watch the old couple who were eating and talking away as though it was a potato pie and not bowls of fire, they had before them, "no 'outlet'. You know: like a tap."

"A tap?" Lou queried, looking at the glass of water in his hand, and back at Bo.

"Yeah, a tap, that's it," Bo confirmed once more, "but for your—for your feelings like. You know?"

"A tap? An outlet-tap to let my feelings flow. Is that what you're sayin', Bo?" Lou checked, speaking the words slowly and clearly in case he wasn't hearing right.

"That's it! That's it exactly, Lou," Bo smiled and nodded his approval of his friend's grasp.

"You sure do watch a lotta horse-shit TV, Bo," Lou shook his head, and both men laughed loudly.

"You're not wrong there, Lou. With that, I have to agree. But that's all there is to watch these days unless I pay for cable," Bo smeared away his laughter tears with the already used napkin; he felt a tingling burn beneath his eyes from the traces of chilli coming off the tissue. Both men finished their bowls using the few remaining corn chips and the ends of their fingers to clear the sour cream too, before pushing everything to the centre of the table as a cue for the waitress. Rubbing his swollen gut, Bo wiped his face some more with the thin napkins. The waitress noticed them no longer eating and made her way over with a tray to clear the table.

"You gentlemen both had 'The Special'," they nodded at her, still wiping away their laughter.

"Would you like coffee with your pie, or after?" She furthered.

"After, please, Ma'am," they spoke in unison. The waitress nodded and ticked her notebook before sticking her pencil back in her hair bun.

"So," Bo said, once the waitress had left them and was out of earshot. "Fishin?"

"Fishin'?" Lou queried.

"You were talkin'—flies and the like, so I'm thinkin' fishin'," Bo clarified his deductive process.

"No!" Lou contradicted him, "I never mentioned anythin' about fishin'. I said somethin' about flies, but that was only because of the original thing you was sayin', and then I was sayin' to you about a sayin' I once heard. That's all, Bo."

"I see," Bo's thoughts bounced backwards and forwards between what they did and didn't say. "Nothin' about fishin' then? I at least know somethin' about fishin'."

"Where did you learn about fishin', Bo? Was it from the fishin' channel?" Lou asked, and both men once more set off with a fit of giggles.

"You gentlemen sure are a bundle of chuckles today," the waitress grinned at them both when she returned to the table with their slices of pecan pie.

Nodding in agreement with her, they avoided looking at each other in case it set them off again. The pie looked like a fine specimen, and it had come with a big scoop of ice-cream, which was welcome after the heat of the chilli.

"Are we really havin' a conversation about flies, Lou?" Bo shook his head at the seeming absurdity of it.

"I don't think we are, Bo," Lou replied. "I don't think we are, no. I was answerin' somethin' you said, and I was going to use the old sayin' I heard because it seemed to fit what we were talkin' about."

"What is this old sayin' you been rattlin' on about here, Lou?" Bo cut to the chase.

"What—the one about flies?" Bo nodded, without interrupting him.

"Well, Bo, it went somethin' like, 'all things from afar, look a mite like flies'," Lou closed his eyes for a moment before he spoke the words.

"That's it?" Lou nodded to the question.

"That don't sound so old, Lou," Bo mused and rubbed the rough stubble of his jaw in confusion. "I mean that sounds American to me, and you know as well as any man that we ain't no old country now."

Lou's eyes lifted to the ceiling fan, and he shook his head.

"I'm obviously paraphrasin' the darn thing, Bo. It was probably in Chinese or Japanese originally, and that's just the translated version that I'm giving you." Lou watched Bo's forehead crease, and eventually raise in acceptance as he brought a spoonful of pie and ice-cream to his mouth, humming his approval of the cold ice-cream.

"All things from afar, look a mite like flies," Bo repeated the phrase once he swallowed his pie and ice-cream; both men mulled over the words as they polished off their plates.

"It's to do with how you look at things. You know. Perspective, Bo? Y'always gotta put things in perspective, Bo," Lou and Bo briefly contemplated the words, and finally looking at each other they nodded in agreement.

"Coffees, gentlemen," the waitress placed a steaming mug before them both with a small jug of milk and a spray can of cream as options.

Still nodding, they smiled their thanks to her, with the distracted looks of two men lost in thought.

"What in hell's name were we talkin' about, Lou, that made you think of that old sayin'?" Bo finally asked.

Lou shook his head and met his friend's eyes.

"No idea, Bo. No idea at all."

The old couple scraped their plates clean with spoons, and the lady finished the last of the salsa with her finger, unaware she was being watched by a disbelieving Bo, who himself was unaware of being listened in on by another diner pretending to be reading the sports pages behind him. The planting season was still some weeks off it seemed; Bo and Lou usually spent the late part of spring panning the rivers and casual-mining for gems until the season began properly. That's routine up here. Once a year they come to Ed and Martha's Diner, and once a year Bo climbs back in his Dodge, and wonders if he'll make it all the way home without soiling himself, or if he'll have to screech over and find himself a tree to back his ass up to. For Bo, there's always more than one edge to eating chilli, as he makes his way back upstate to New Meadows. Lou isn't so afflicted, and hasn't suffered in the same way as Bo over the years, but is happy not to be sharing a truck with his friend for the few hours it'll take to haul themselves back home.

They put cash down for the waitress Martha, and Lou waited as Bo visited the diner's facilities, having already advised his friend to take some back up tissues; he mulled over their conversation while picking at his teeth, mumbling to himself all the while, before finally looking up and seeing his friend return.

"Nope," he spoke quietly to himself as he rose. "Not a clue what we was rattling on about. Not a clue.'

I watched both men leave and slap each other's backs as they made their way to their respective vehicles, parked as they were, right next to each other. They seem content fellows, and their conversation was perhaps a run of the mill exchange between them, and I did omit some of Martha's chit-chat, and her interactions with them both, which may have contributed to them seeming to lose their thread quicker than they did. I stood up and stretched leaving the paper where it was, for it was unlikely my wife would bother moving it; she usually wants to read it herself when her break comes. I stepped out, and meandered to the side of the highway as both men headed north along that long straight undulating stretch. The spring sun was already low, and the light a little blinding after the diner strip lights, but I watched, drawing my finger along my moustache, which has become a habit of late for me. As they came to the second of the higher crests in the road, I squinted a little to watch them, as they rolled along still in tandem, and I could see the truth in Lou's words.

From afar, they did indeed look a mite like flies.

***

Idaho Special Recipe

Idaho is the land of potato dishes, and an American friend once passed this along to me, assuring me it was an Idaho dish. I explained to him that 'Mascarpone Cheese' was in fact Italian, but he explained that potato was American, and the Mascarpone, or lemons for that matter, would obviously be bought in the supermarket in Boise, and the dish, which he ate, was still an Idaho Special, unless we're going to call everything with black pepper in it Indian, and anything with chillies in it South American. Sometimes you just take the recipe, and leave things be. The recipe originally had salmon roe, which I've replaced, and I might say enjoyed immensely, with beluga lentils.

This is a side dish (four people) to accompany more or less anything you might sit potatoes next to, which in Idaho, like Ireland, is anything at all.

Ingredients

12 medium sized potatoes peeled and boiled to soft in lightly salted water
1 tub of mascarpone cheese
1 lemon (juice and grated rind)
1 bunch of spring onions very finely chopped
100g of beluga lentils boiled (al dente) for twelve to fifteen minutes with a mushroom stock cube in about two hundred mils of water

Preparation and Presentation

Mash the potatoes, add the mascarpone, lemon juice and grated rind with the finely chopped spring onions and fork-whisk it all together.

Using a circular shaper, create a disc of potato about an inch-a-half high on each plate.

With the lentils, when most of the moisture has gone, set them aside (normally 12-15mins). You want them to be still moist and a little runny. Once your potato mascarpone discs are prepared scoop and few spoonfuls of lentils on top.

It really is that simple.

***

Heart on Blanket

TANNED MUSCULAR ARMS WRAPPED AROUND her. Held in a longed-for embrace, she drew a deep, deep breath; the arms squeezed her tight and close, and a twisted knot in her chest released.

Darkness.

The arms tighten; the breath lost in her sigh can't be retrieved. Lights flash, and darkness comes again. Still no give, no release; hands slither as though no longer part of the arms: they claw around her neck and throat. Mouth wide, a silent scream deafens all thought.

Darkness once more.

Nothing. A twilight grey of weary emptiness fills her.

Darkness fills with a cold, frozen silence; her name oscillates on the whirling whim of far-flung lonely winds beckoning her to follow and leave behind the sadness of her life, the sorrow that has filled her lonely world.

Connie woke up blinking back the night, and the darkness of her room; removing the sheet she'd become knotted in she climbed out of the bed shivering; an odd sense of a death memory clung to her. The bedding and mattress soaking wet again; her hair stuck flat to her face, and chilled from her dried salty sweat, she sat on the cold plastic toilet seat contemplating her endless bouts of restless nightmare nights. Anger boiled within her.

Too young for the change, Connie hadn't yet reached forty; the consolation of children had passed her by. Her disturbed sleeping pattern had begun four months earlier with the beginning of the new school term. Other than her promotion, nothing about the job had changed, and she was at a loss to explain it; Connie reflected that she didn't drink nearly as much wine as she used to either, which had always been her first medical concern; the only thing she could really say had changed was that she went out less, and never had sex anymore. Not just sex: she didn't have any physical contact with anybody anymore.

Looking for the positives, Connie had convinced herself that she was detoxing her life. Only for the better, had been her mantra.

Sometimes a girl needs a mantra.

Engaged to Gabriel they had a social routine; all the couples she knew tended to have some kind of social routine, so they'd had theirs.

Fridays was early doors in the pub with the other teachers, before they'd head homewards and stop in at their own local for a couple more. Just being neighbourly! That could, and often did, go on into the early hours. Saturday was a lazy morning with newspapers and breakfast; in the afternoon she'd clean the house, or they'd go to a rugby game at The Stoop if Quins were playing. Sunday they took the bus to Richmond or Kingston, depending on what they were after; usually it was Sunday lunch in one of their favourite pubs. That was their favourite part of the weekend. Sunday night was early to bed.

Mondays Connie went back to school, and Gabriel back to the college, as he liked to call the senior school out by the roundabout; whoever got home first started prepping the meal. Evenings they would do a bit of work, and watch some TV just before bed. Gabriel had squash-ladder night on Tuesdays—it kept him in shape. On other evenings he ran for an hour on the cycle path along and back the A316. Connie was never a fan of exercise and was lucky her weight hadn't ever been problematic. Not a waif by any measure, Gabriel always said he liked a full figured woman; he'd also said he wanted a woman to have her own mind and to be challenging intellectually for him.

Gabriel was full of shit.

The lying toe-rag left her for a frizzy blonde bimbo from Sports Direct in Isleworth. An accident, apparently—they used to see each other when they were running and 'something clicked' when they met in the shop. Connie knew what clicked! In her twenties with an hourglass body and huge fake tits—she also had those weird pouting cod lips that made her look like she'd been punched, and punched hard too. Connie had never forgiven Gabriel. She knew she never could.

Disappearing into her work since they'd split she even avoided the early doors gatherings on Fridays to allow time to pass, and their split to be no longer news—an unspoken decency. Gabriel got word she wasn't going anymore and resumed his visits three weeks later. That wasn't the worst of it: bimbo-babe turned up a few weeks after that. Now a regular with him—just to add to the burn. If this had been one of her friends, Connie would have been told her to get a grip and get back in control of the situation, or even dragged her to the pub by the ear. These were 'Connie's' workmates: 'her' friends!

Gabriel's 'colleagues' called themselves lecturers or tutors, rather than teachers, which they would have been up to a few years earlier— a 'lecturer's' job was more distant from the nitty-gritty of pastoral care, with which much of a teacher's time is taken up. It made them more aloof with others in the profession—down the food-chain so to speak; most of them got in their high-powered saloon cars and bolted down the M3 to a Surrey village they'd relocated to once the working day ended and got to their own locals for early doors. On Fridays they were gone before three: assignments to the students, no need to lecture, no need to be in attendance: email a blessing: twilight golf beckoned through summer. Gabriel never quite achieved the same rank, no matter how he pretended—a comp boy, somehow the adjustment and step-up eluded him.

Connie was relieved she hadn't committed fully with Gabriel and bought the Isleworth flat they'd looked at three years earlier. It would have complicated her life like nothing else. Instead, they stayed renting when Gabriel's hours were cut back to twenty, and the take-home cut that accompanied it shunted the flat out of their price bracket. Gabriel started drinking more then, and he'd brimmed with resentment about a 'de facto' demotion; leaving him in the local pub most Fridays, Connie went on home alone—she should have seen then what a twat he'd become.

Connie saved solidly for the two years since they'd split; she threw Gabriel out after bimbo, and rented alone so made some cutbacks in her life.

Initially, savings hadn't been intentional—simple things, she made her own lunch to avoid costs of the staff canteen, and not going out stopped her paying inflated pub prices. Not drinking at home halved her shopping bill, and no longer needing to buy pre-prepared foods saved her more again. It must have been healthier for her; she didn't need a satellite contract to watch endless sport, or old films she'd already seen and demands from broadband didn't involve gaming or any high-speed package. It was win-win. Connie put in more time at work too and got promoted when she passed her fifteen-year service record. That alone bumped her salary more than her rent was costing her.

How had she not noticed? Gabriel had been a dead weight around her neck.

Last she heard he was sharing a dinky flat with bimbo out the arse-end of Whitton, or Hatton, according to Amy, who still went to the pub on Fridays, and kept Connie up to speed with any gossip. Not having been out that way, Amy described it as where outer London ended, and the nothing of nowhere began—a shit-hole perfect for the pair of them. It made her more determined to get enough money together to buy her own place.

§

Unable to face the thought of re-making the bed Connie went into her kitchen and put on the kettle; still well before six, she knew if she spent ten minutes sorting everything out she'd go back to sleep, and then wake after a couple of hours feeling worse than ever. That had been her pattern for the first weeks of her menopausal nightmare. Now, at least, when she got to work she was wide awake, having been up for quarter of a working day, and she had found that she was also ahead of her workload by a distance. Wrapped in her Kullu Shawl, snuggling into the soft warmth of the wool, she lifted her laptop and typed her password 'gabriel' to open the screen. With her tea made, she picked a breakfast biscuit from the Tupperware container to nibble while she watched. On her favourites bar, she clicked the YouTube cooking channel; there was a Thai chef on it she liked who made stuff that was quick and simple and suited the style of cooking she aspired to do; he was also cute to look at and cheered her up with his smiling and shouting. Having shared the past couple of months with him first thing in the morning, Connie had patterned herself a small ritual.

Scrolling down the options, looking for something that might interest her, she eventually settled on 'Heart on Blanket'. It was how she felt; it promised incredibly tasty, unbelievably healthy, and to be virtually fat free, but Connie didn't care for hyperbole. It was the picture that always got her, and when it opened Connie was delighted; the chef promised to cook the whole thing from scratch in twenty minutes and to make enough for four people as an entrée for a special evening.

Not having an evening planned, especially not a special one for four, and thinking of the new flat she'd have within the year, and the new love in her life who just might appear, Connie's mind searched for a couple they both might get on with, and who might like to have long stimulating conversations and dinner parties. No-one sprung immediately to mind, and searching deep in the recesses of her mind Connie found two new friends she met walking across Richmond Bridge on their way to watch a movie. Joining them, at their invite of course, she wasn't 'that' needy, afterwards they went for drink at the bistro on Richmond Hill that Gabriel had thought looked 'up itself'. They chatted afterwards for an hour or so about everything in the world, before Theo, who was such a gent, organised taxis for them. Both he and Athena were delighted when she invited them to dinner at hers the following week.

"Fine chop one tiny red onion. Two garlic cloves. One baby leek. Two small hot red chilies and a tiny-tiny snip of ginger. Put all in hot pan with little bit of oil. Cook them 6 to 8 minutes. You know how! Simple! That's it!" The chef's clippy voice from the video instructed.

Jeremy. That was her lover's name. Connie didn't want a 'partner' or a 'husband'. It took away from her achieving her personal goal, which was important to her. Jeremy was her lover and Connie had always wanted a lover. Always! Lovers had that edge no boyfriend or husband could ever match. Jeremy wasn't always around in London, and he didn't want to disappoint her with a failed commitment; of course, he would have lived in Notting Hill, or Primrose Hill, in truth, or under normal circumstances, but he did so much international travel that until things calmed down in Unicef, it was impossible for him not to be near the airport. That had been so lucky for her. Fate. Telling him during their evening FaceTime chat about Theo and Athena coming to dinner the following Saturday evening, he immediately promised to fly in on the red-eye the night before. Jeremy didn't need much sleep, so he'd be fine.

"Half block of tofu. Two big spoon plain flour. One big egg. One big bunch spring onions, one little bunch basil, one little bunch coriander! Chop chop everybody! Salt. Juice one lime. Put in bowl. Mash mash mash everybody, nice-nice thick pancakey mix. Add stuff from pan and stir stir stir! You nearly ready!" The chef beamed happily to the world.

Heels with her little black number were Connie's choice for dinner that evening; the dress showed her curves, which Jeremy adored, and she knew her boobs looked pert in it. After a trip to the new 'Parlour' in Richmond earlier in the day, laughing at the frivolity of having a flower plaited into her hair, and having someone else do her make-up and nails, Connie was thrilled with the result; she even shelved her previous misgivings and promised to treat herself more often. Her flat looked stunning, and the open plan style she'd chosen for the renovation work set it off beautifully; the builders had told her she was wasted teaching ten-year-olds. The doors leading out into the covered patio garden were slightly ajar and allowed the city sounds to be distantly heard without being invasive; the interior flowed seamlessly through to the exterior because of the innovative use of contemporary and traditional materials, and the fire-pit Jeremy bought for her was alight and casting a lovely warm orange glow, sending out the smoky fragrance of hickory and apple-wood. Hoping it might snow so that they could watch it later by the fire with warming whiskies, Jeremy finished lighting the candles above the fireplace and had just told her how beautiful she was when the doorbell rang.

"Make blanket of leaf on plate. Grate carrot for pillow. Put big pan on heat. Not too hot now. Never too hot! Remember! Never too hot! Oil pan. Use heart mold—heart-shape you like best okydoky! With big spoon fill four hearts. Cook! Allow to seal for four minutes. Move. Do not flip yet. Bring heat down a bit. Cook more slowly. When texture firm and water gone, flip-flip! Heart mold too like this! Cook maybe five minutes, flip-flip again, another minute, flip-flip! Now you feel if it is cooked through. It solid! Take off mold. Put on green blanket. Add sweet chilli dip! Enjoy!" The chef bowed, and his ear-to-ear grin filled the screen for a final close-up.

The doorbell rang again.
> And again.
> And again.
> Connie woke up and looked around her in confusion, surprised that she'd dropped off. She felt better and lighter in her chest. Almost happy. Stretching her stiffening arms above her head, she yawned loudly before looking at her laptop screen which had stopped playing the clip she'd chosen. The doorbell rang, and she stood up instinctively, opening the door to look out into the hallway in confused surprise; she had an odd feeling that it wasn't the first ring.

"CON?" A voice queried from the face shape behind hands, butterflied against the glass of the front door.

"CON?" The query came again. "Please. Con?"

Gabriel.

It was Gabriel.

Her Gabe.

Connie opened the door.

***

Heart on Blanket Recipe

Mix 1
1 small red onion finely chopped
1 small piece of ginger finely chopped
2 small hot red chillies chopped
1 baby leek finely chopped
2 garlic cloves crushed

Once cooked, add the following
1 small bunch of basil leaf, finely chopped
1 small bunch of coriander leaf, finely chopped
Juice of 1 lime

Mix 2
1 block of tofu, 200g
1 large free range eggs
2 heaped tablespoons of plain flour
1/2 tsp salt

For the bed and blanket
1 grated carrot
enough rocket and mixed leaf to create green beds
groundnut oil/rapeseed oil

Making Heart On Blanket
Gently sautée Mix 1 in the given order until it is almost caramelising.
Mash Mix 2, and pour into a mixing bowl.
Add Mix 1 to Mix 2 and mix well.

Using heart shaped molds, on a hot frying pan lightly oiled with groundnut /rapeseed oil and, spoon the thick mixture into the molds. Allow the base of the mix to seal and wait until you see the top drying a bit before trying to flip. You can cheat and grill the tops here to enable an easier flip and depending on how thick you want your hearts to be.

Spread the leaf on a small plate, adding a little grated carrot to one end. Place cooked heart on the leaf blanket and serve with sweet chilli or a peanut satay sauce. Enjoy!

***

A Situation

THE GHOST TERMINAL ALWAYS DREW Geert-Jan Berger's gaze. A hive of activity, day or night, even after being in it, Geert refused to accept that no human beings mingled among the unloading cranes and blinking red-eye vehicles; all of them endlessly shifting and organising the containers into some remotely pre-devised storage plan. His own ship, a fully loaded Samskip container vessel, returning to Rotterdam from a double-stop visit to the south-east coast of Ireland, and guiding itself to docking, was something Geert was long used to; nevertheless, something about the Ghost Terminal always sent a shiver down him. Raising his binoculars, after picking them from the hook beside his chair, he panned across the bustling terminal. No crashes, no accidents, no lost containers, no theft, and with none of the complications that come with humans, Geert understood the appeal of the terminal for the Port Authorities, and their profit margins. Scanning across the bustle of shiny and swift-moving vehicles, he had to concede a grudging admiration for its clinical efficiency; even the cleaning and maintenance were pre-programmed and undertaken without human involvement.

The first day of May and the sky was clear and blue. Geert blinked up at it; his mind tried to keep the happy thoughts of his secret extra days of holiday free from the dread of the soon to be upon him demands of his large children and the ever varied manipulations of his ex-wife. An odd reflection of moving light flashed above the containers; he raised his binoculars to see a man pacing back and forth on a roof-top talking into a phone pressed against his ear. Geert withdrew his gaze and looked at his first mate who still looked worse for wear after drinking too much wine the previous evening. Most of the Bridge crew look similarly dishevelled. Nobody spoke. Nobody was in the mood to speak. Geert suspected the port staff would be as reticent and as disinclined to communicate as his own.

On the last day of April, the Dutch celebrate.

King's Day, or Queen's Day, depending on the monarch, is a bit of an event.

When the sun shines, which it often does at the end of April, the usually reserved Dutch let loose. The whole country goes off the rails; a carnival atmosphere permeates the streets, bars, cafés, and pretty much all the clubs across the country.

It's difficult not to get caught up in it.

"Man, I feel shit!" Turning his head to roll his eyes at Harry Johnson next to him, Clayton Longmire grumbled and rubbed his gut. They both lay flat on their backs on a Rotterdam dockside warehouse roof-top and stared up at the blue sky.

"You went out later again last night?" Harry stifled a yawn; he knew Clayton had, but played the question prompt all the same.

"I never heard-a-this shit," Clayton covered his eyes with his hands as his body quivered a jaded shiver. "It was like the world had gone mad and fuckin' orange, man. They have a Queen here! Like a real thing too! Did you know that? A Dutch Queen? I thought that was just another way of them saying transvestite. Oh Lord-fuckin'-Jesus, I'm dying here."

Covering his mouth with his hand, he grimaced at the sour reflux, and thumped his chest.

"This lot can put it away too, dude. Shit! 'S like a basketball gig out there! The dudes are huge! Big fucking blonde monsters! Oh yeah! I made a dumb-ass mistake of taking a piece of cake from a cute chic in the street before I got to the bar. Y'know? Yeah? I thought it was just a goddamn chocolate cake! I mean, c'mon? You know what I'm saying here? Fucking pig-tails like Heidi—she looked like some school kid in that get-up they used to wear here way back in the day."

Harry chuckled, trying not to make too much noise. His jacket lay beside him and he fidgeted at his tie; he was stifled. All of the men wore the makings of suits, but the jackets were removed and lay neatly folded beside each of them. They all looked and felt overdressed for the surveillance work they were doing.

"I'm getting fuckin' hot up here today," covering his face with his hands, Clay belched quietly into them and winced. Sweating like a horse, he'd looked off from the start of the day. Lugging a bit of weight, which was unusual for the American agents, everything about Clay seemed oversized; he carried himself like a big man but stood only six feet in his socks—two inches smaller than Harry. Harry grunted his agreement and shifted his gaze around the roof-top. Both lying on their backs in the bright

Rotterdam sunshine; two others of their team, Arne and Gus, knelt in position near the edge of the wooden parapet keeping watch on five men on a lower roof-top. Two of these men were also resting on their backs, and two were at the parapet of their roof watching an assortment of shipping containers whizzing to and fro below them nearer the water's edge. The last man paced back and forth along the rear of the roof-top and continuously spoke loudly into his phone. All of them were waiting for the 'Maltese'.

"Any change?" Harry lifted and tilted his head to look across to Arne; he knew there wouldn't be, Arne would've said something. Arne twitched his head, glimpsed backed down, and grimaced a face to indicate that nothing new was going on.

"That Zoran can talk! Fucker hasn't come off that thing for half-an-hour. Barely taken a breath," he sniffed a small disapproval.

Harry nodded, and resumed his former position. Closing his eyes, his stomach rumbled noisily and he covered it with both hands. Long stake-outs were a pet hate for all the agents. Too many to remember in the past two years. Day three of this and nothing of any note had happened. Clay released a long whispering gas fart next to him; both men grimaced as it rose around them.

"Holy Jesus, Clay! That thing's alive," Harry protested.

"Shit, man, I need to eat something," Clayton rubbed his gut vigorously and waved his hand at Harry. "I'm swelling up here, man. I don't think the Heineken here is the same as England. I been like this for two days already. Fuckin' killing me it is! I'm cramping up all over."

Harry nodded, still holding his breath, and reluctantly winced a half-smile. Clay resumed his former flat position; both men looked into the blue of the sky above them once more, shallow breathing until the waft passed.

"What do you fancy?" Harry asked, to pass the time more than anything, but also to take Clay's mind away from how shit he was feeling. 'An agent not in the game is often soon out of it. Keep focused! Keep alive! Keep everybody focused, keep everybody alive!' His mentor's words echoed in his mind.

These were his men now. His team, and that meant his responsibility. In his own mind he was still too young to have that monkey on his back, but the options didn't leave him with too many ways to turn. Run his own team, or go back to London. Once there he'd be run by someone else! That, was not an option he could take. Not now they'd opted out of most of the game and were still trying to disengage with the rest of Europe. Harry knew most of the London staff and he didn't want to be run by any of them. Being sent back there wasn't a hypothetical either. Command had put it straight to him in black and white. Two-and-a-half years spent tracking Zoran and his team of thugs, as they wheeled back and forth across the continent, had seen Harry move up the ranks in his own team. The previous two team leaders moved on to other pastures. Escaped from this grind of hell, Harry felt; he knew them both, and also knew they were now somewhere in Germany trying to get their heads around Russian mind-games. Probably loving it too. Meanwhile, his life of endless phone-taps, apartment bugs, tails, and the drudgery of fruitless stake-outs was trudging on. Too many things, far too many things were still missing; he felt as though they were constantly chasing phantoms. Nearly three years in total and nothing of substance to show, and nothing in the way of answers to explain it either. Every time they got near, something cocked up; Zoran and his lot were costing the agency a small fortune, and Harry his sanity.

This time he'd kept it tight—real tight: only his field team; a closed loop they called it. Today they hoped to finally get something concrete on one end of the chain they'd been fruitlessly yanking.

A week earlier Gus had picked up a word listening in on Zoran. 'Malteski'. That was it! One word. Maltese. The first and only real break they'd had in recent months. Pickings had been so scarce that they were even calling it a break. It was a mere slip. They hoped it was a slip. Zoran, near the end of a long conversation with a London man he called Bobby, about whom nothing else was known, said the word 'Malteski', causing Bobby to growl, and shout the word 'ideet' or 'eejit', before hanging up. The line was poor, and the recording hampered by wind, but either way they decided that despite his accent, Bobby wasn't a native Londoner, despite an East London edge to his voice. If it was 'eejit', that opened up an Irish avenue without any leads to go down; he hadn't sounded Irish. 'Ideet' otherwise sounded like the Serbian word for idiot, and that, coupled with the fact that Zoran was obviously subordinate to him raised the profile of Bobby to a 'must find'. The Serb connection also fitted; however, Bobby never used the same phone twice, hadn't ever been picked up by any of their cameras, and although they had a list of eight 'possibles', he remained an elusive spectral figure.

The main intelligence they were working with was still American and British. Clay was with them now for over a year on a joint-op assignment. It was the talk of 'red switches' that brought the Americans into play; Clay had been a surprise addition the previous Christmas to last. 'Red switches' meant nuclear by all accounts, but nothing else had ever turned up to help any further investigation. Weapons of all sorts had, and drugs too, and the 'red switches' Harry now thought were red-herrings. Once the 'nuclear switch' had been tripped, it wasn't the type of thing they could afford to switch off easily; half the team and half the resources with them had spent three years up dead-end alleys just to box-tick the negatives. To date Clay had been nothing but balls-scathing over the administrative hoops and loops they were all having to jump through to get anywhere. Claiming to be a low ranking CIA man, he had more field experience than Harry's entire Euro-Intel team combined. Clay was also careful and thorough with everything he did. Aware of the nuances of Intelligence promotions, his methods were not those of any low-ranking officer Harry had ever encountered. Better with a gun too than any agent Harry had ever met; Clay brought home the realisation of how little he, or the rest of his team, really knew about dirty work in the field.

"It's gotta be pancakes man. Gotta be. Banana pancakes too, when I feel like this. With ice-cream. No! Chocolate sauce! You hear me? Banana pancakes with the mother of all chocolate sauces. There's medicine in chocolate man!"

Having drifted off into his 'happy-place' memory bank, coming back Clay interrupted Harry's train of thought and brought him back to the rooftop and the conversation Harry himself had begun.

"Not those skinny little fucking things you lot make! I'm talking American here, yeah? Proper American buckwheat pancakes. You know what I'm saying, dude! You hear me? The sort that soaks that mother-fuckin' chocolate up like a sponge! Ooh, that's it! That's what I'm talking."

"I hear you man. I hear you," his mind briefly asserting to him that buckwheat was a Russian thing, Harry shook his head and smiled at the sky; sometimes things stay in your head you just don't need; the urge to comment suppressed, he turned to look at Clay.

"So! Make me some of your big spongy-chocolate-soaked-mother-fuckin'-American pancakes then. Walk me through it!" Harry said, laughing at Clay's confusion. "Show me the American way, buddy!".

Clay grinned, shook his head at Harry, and closed his eyes as he lay back. Harry glimpsed quickly at Arne who raised his eyebrows, shrugged, and glanced disdainfully at the rooftop below. Nothing to report his face said. Arne hated Zoran with a passion. Harry could never get to the bottom of that. There wasn't a history between them, or not that he was aware of—if there were, it would've excluded Arne from the team. He just didn't like feeling useless probably. Harry had to admit, that had been pretty much how the entire crew was feeling for a couple of years.

"Righty," Clay paused, more for his own thoughts than dramatic effect. Harry closed his eyes glad of a break from the bright sky; his shirt felt as though it was getting tighter in the heat, and he muttered a curse about Mountjoy, and having to wear it.

"Yeah! You're not wrong there! That guy's a fuckin' dick! Needs some fuckin' friendly fire up his ass too!" Clay agreed, and opened a couple of buttons on his. "Okay! The pancakes! Are you ready? You really want me to do this? Yeah? Okay then. Shiit."

Harry closed his eyes again and let Clay ramble on about pancakes and his aunt Ethel's old recipe for ten minutes before having his daydream interrupted.

"Zoran's off the phone boss," Gus relayed quietly, and continued his vigil, one ear half-listening to Clay.

Clay kept his eyes closed, ignoring Gus, and carried on about pancakes; his hands mimed the actions and measurements as he did so. Harry looked at Gus, waiting to see if anything else was forthcoming, or if things were changing below. After a few moments, Gus shrugged and Harry left his head fall back once more.

Clay turned on his side towards Harry, this time releasing gas behind him, and wafting it away with his hand to the amusement of Gus. Clay paused to gather his thoughts, and Harry took a moment to check with Arne once more. Gus on the other side watched Harry as he looked about, and twitched a head shake. He was listening to Clay. Arne had zoned the American's voice out and looked as though the previous evening had caught up with him.

"You with me so far?" Clay asked.

Harry and Gus gestured and mumbled affirmatives, more to themselves than the shut-eyed American.

"Uhhuh! I'm putting aside the vanilla," Harry replied. "On you go! On you go!"

"Yeah," Clay chuckled and held his hands up melodramatically. "Now what you do here is you beat all the wet stuff quickly, and real fast and hard too. Full on, I'm saying! Whisk it like a crazy man. You got me?"

"Zoran's back on it," Gus hissed, his butt slipping off the edge as he leaned towards them; he grabbed at the upright strut behind him reflexively and righted himself again. Harry scowled at his carelessness; the strut continued to shake.

"Arne," nodding towards him, he waited for their eyes to meet. "See if they know who he's talking to now. And put some bloody sun-block on. You're getting redder every time I look at you."

Arne picked his handset out and dropped below the parapet to text Harry's query to 'Control'. 'Control' was two other members of their team sitting in a hi-tech van in the car-park of one of the warehouses near the waterfront. The 'Boss', an overbearing bully who normally never left his London office, was with them, and pissed off with them all, as he'd had to track them. Mountjoy was why they were all over-dressed, overheating, and all cranky as caged cockerels. Since arriving the previous evening he'd pissed-off everyone at some stage. More concerned they all looked like agents than with what they were actually doing: sitting in, supervising, he made both men in the van uncomfortable, and overcrowded the space to boot. Advertising them as paint-specialists for the shipping and marine industries, in stained tee-shirts and jeans both men had fitted, and they hadn't raised a blink from anyone in the first couple of days. Harry argued about the absurdity of them wearing suits. To no avail. Harry suspected it was just spite for having to track them down and being left out of the loop.

Arne ignored Harry's instruction on sun-block. Swedish and fair skinned, he'd probably grow a red beard if he left it come. Most of the year his complexion was pale pig-pink, and only after a good bout of sunshine did he ever manage to look healthy—a little reddening was a small price.

"Are we cooking yet?" Looking back at the clear sky before he closed his eyes once more, Harry checked on Clay. Clay continued, once his chuckling abated. Harry's mind drifted over the previous evening and his row with Mountjoy. Never clever to stir the shit above pay-grade; Mountjoy somehow always got to him. Having eased through the ranks with minimum field time, as far as Harry knew, respect for him and his orders were begrudgingly given. About most of the Senior Command stories of one sort or another leaked around the offices. These fragments never gave away much, most of them were probably controlled releases too—morale-boosting titbits, mini-legend-making shit—most of it probably just crap, but it was there; he never heard anything about Mountjoy. Not that he could find out much either, but something, a commendation, or a muttered grumble about him one way or the other on his performances in the field, or before then, something—something, should have reached his ears. Most of what he heard was resentment. Mountjoy didn't make friends.

"Boss," Arne hissed, interrupting them both.

They looked towards him. "They're moving down there? It looks like this 'Maltese' might be here," Arne said. "Zoran is-?"

Gunfire ripped through the parapet where Gus was sitting, and had turned to look at Arne when he spoke. Felled from his crouch, he didn't move again; most of his nose sat beside him, a fine stringy ligament of sorts keeping it connected to him.

Clay swore and rolled sideways towards the parapet, removing his gun as he rolled. Popping his head up and down in a flash, he took in where Zoran stood tracing their parapet with his automatic.

"Where the fuck did that shit come from?" Clay wondered aloud.

The other four men frozen behind Zoran looked as much in shock as Harry and Arne had moments earlier. A burst of gunfire ricocheted where Clay had been. Four quick clean rounds from Harry cut through the air; all three of the team rolled and crawled to different points.

"Got two ... maybe three? I think," Harry panted. "Zoran's front-left."

Primed, ready, and steaming with rage, Clay angled his arm and let two shots off at the lower roof target zone. One hit Zoran in the face stopping any further outbursts from him. Arne and Harry released three more rounds each. His head up again, Clayton nodded to both that all was clear.

Harry counted the five bodies. The Maltese, or a black Mercedes that might have been him, was distantly speeding away between the containers along the length of the wire fence; they'd probably never even stopped.

Somebody tipped somebody here he thought. Looking at the mess beneath them, there wasn't another conclusion he could make. His pocket vibrated against his chest. Harry patted it reflexively to activate his earpiece.

"Johnson?" Mountjoy's voice barked in his ear. Harry pressed his ear to clear the ringing from the bullets.

"Johnson! What's going on up there?" Mountjoy barked again. "We're hearing all kinds of shit here!"

"We've got a-" Harry said, looking about; he grimaced as he took in the mess of Gus properly and realised fully that his friend was gone. "We've got a—a situation here, sir."

He popped the piece from his ear.

The ship gently caressed the rubberised fenders of the docking area as the First Officer of the Watch reversed her to a halt. Word had already come that dockside staff were a few light on their crew and a 'wait' should be anticipated. Without patience, Geert knew a man should never set out to sea. While time and tide wait for no man, Geert always felt a man was destined to spend an unavoidable amount of his life waiting for both. Nodding to the flagging Bridge crew, he laughed at their young, blood-shot gazes.

"Four hours," he remembered his own youth and tapped his watch. "All of you drink water before you sleep, but be back on shift in four hours."

Opening the door, hooking it fixed, he allowed the breeze to drift through the bridge. Land borne noises of beeping forklifts, whirring cranes, and the Doppler shifts of siren wails all washed away the silence of the sea that still clung to the sweaty stale air of the cabin.

***

Perfect Pancakes Recipe

Ingredients

140g buckwheat flour
50g plain flour
2 large free-range eggs
280ml (approx) buttermilk
1 tsp bicarbonate soda
1 tsp baking powder
4 tsp brown sugar
1/2 tsp salt
honey
groundnut oil & butter for cooking

Making Perfect Pancakes

Mix flours, bicarb, baking powder, salt and sugar in a bowl and make a hole in the middle.

Add in the eggs and buttermilk and whisk to a smooth batter. If you want it a bit thinner, add a little more milk or water.

Add a tablespoon of groundnut oil with a dab of butter to a hot small heavy based frying pan.

Once melted and browning add a small ladle of batter to the pan and swirl it to the edges. Leave it cook for a few minutes until bubbles begin to appear on the surface. Feel it slide on the pan a few times before you flip it and repeat the same process on the other side.

Done, slide onto a warm plate and add a small spoon of honey/syrup before placing it in the bottom of a warm oven. Work your way through the rest of the batter and stack the pancakes.

Eat plain, or with chocolate sauce, ice-cream, berries, or even bananas if you're hungover!

***

Boss Hogg and The Duke

THURSDAY NIGHT AT THE DUKE IS AN unpredictable night these days. Back in the day, people were paid on Thursday: crossed cheques, with no bank accounts to stick them in; back then, the bar was like a platform in King's Cross at five: overcrowded, smelly, and dangerously full of drunks. Cash your cheque? They might just do that. Buy a drink won't you? A round is preferred! Just sign the back and put your address on it—we know where you live! Thursday was session night. If lucky, a man went home with most of the cash from that first transaction and parted with the greater portion of that to his wife to keep house and home for the week ahead. A man's luck isn't always in, and that's a truth no matter where you are in the world. Some Fridays, some men woke with nothing and no memory or knowledge of how they came to nothing. Growing up in a hand to mouth world amidst the romance of the 'working class' wasn't without its trials. School, that was a proving ground; the sanctuary of home was often only an extension of the playground war zone. Giving ground was not optional. Wimp or door-mat only depended on the sex; better to take a beating—even if nobody else cared, you had self-respect, and that was better than no respect at all. Nowadays, if people work, and by no means everybody does, the money goes straight to their bank account. Bank accounts are no longer optional even for those scraping a life on scraps: 'The Man' needs to know what you have! Cares little how little: micros add up to macros. The Duke no longer takes cheques. Or promise notes of any sort except the promises on hard cash.

Growing up in that period, a forgettable window between the last big war and the hope of a future, in streets not far from the docks of Swansea, by all accounts, it was rat-rough. Hope, the poor man's dream, has rarely filled a promise: though without it, life lacks the lustre and love for which lackeys live. Poor man's food for the poor to lap in the absence of anything else. Some things and some people are harder to change than others.

Gentrification and shiny waterside developments abound and surround the docks today, and some people even seem happy. A few hardcore nuts still stumble into The Duke, but nobody ever thinks it crowded these days. Tonight, clutching their glasses with gnarly clawed hands and weathered faces, the Duke's regulars half-watch and half-listen to a row that's been noising at the back for a little while. They know it's the same bickering nonsense that's been running for thirty years.

"Don't blight us with your lying shite," Hanley waved his hands in the air.

Clever clogs, he thought he was; he slammed his fat, flat palm loudly on the metal drinks tray and the whole table shook. A glass fell off and smashed. Breaking glass always sent a signal of sorts in The Duke.

Everyone shut up then. Froze. Even the whispers stopped. Some stole brief glimpses at the men shouting. Suspense sends a charge; the regulars braced themselves with subtle shifts on the seats. The telling moment had arrived. Hanley's never been great with attention, or being the centre of things: he sensed the odd stillness, and he's the type of fella who always stuttered when he had to read aloud; any hint of public spotlight paralysed him and showed him as the fool he was; knowing it he reddened like a rutting baboon's arse.

A cuddling couple chuckled in the corner seeing his discomfort. Hanley turned and recognised the woman. Local. The man was a stranger to him; Hanley held his gaze and watched the other fella look away and resume his canoodling with the woman. The Duke held its collective breath.

"I warned you before, Thompson. Tell me the TRUTH, you lying bastard! I've listened to all the bullshit I ever need to hear in this life from your mouth alone. Now did you, or didn't you?" Hanley pressed his demand again.

Thompson looked out the window. Shook his head. Thinking. He didn't like Hanley and never had. They went way back together. With most of it remembered, none of it was memorable: the fat fuck was always a bully; the cops should have never accepted him. Never! Why the fuck should he help him. Tell me the truth! The fat twat. Always fat too: greedy lunch-nicking bastard. Who did he think he was? Coming into his local and taking over his table. Shouting him down and telling two of his neighbours to leave. Private matter! 'Privacy needed', he said! Shout shout shout. Private, my arse! All of Swansea heard him; the whole time hovering up above him, acting like an overlord. To fucking hell, I will! Fuck him and his fat, fucking horse-shit.

"Did I what?" Thompson soughed the question's end with his deep bass tones and forced Hanley to strain to hear him. Not for the first time.

Hanley roared in frustration. All control lost, he lunged.

Overhanging bellies hamper a man's physical stretch, and Hanley underestimated the width of the table or the size of his own gut; he came up a hand's length short of Thompson's throat. Momentum spun him off to the side and onto the floor beside Thompson's chair where he landed heavily on his back. Winded, he grunted. A fat pig grunt. Thompson in for a beating. A frightened mind works at speed. Fuck it! Can't get any worse with this bastard. A brogued foot swung swiftly across Hanley's face and clipped the chin. The arc of Thompson's leg swing continued higher and above the table height. Thompson rose in the movement. Kicked for Penlan into his twenties: strong legs, he thumped a Rugby ball high above the bar from forty plus yards many times. Pretty good in his playing days too. They didn't have a man with a sand bucket then. A man drove his heel into soft giving earth and balanced the ball in the deep cavity.

In the police car, Thompson wondered how far a ball might travel if kicked from the cavity of Hanley's collapsed face. Kicked it over and over again but never managed to see the ball fly. Just the kick. Over and over again.

"You'll be for the high-jump now! I tell you!" The driver cop wheezed at Thompson, as though short of breath, after he'd secured his wrists in cuffs behind his back.

Thompson shrugged indifferently.

"A man's gotta do, what a man's gotta do," Thompson looked away from the cop.

"You'll do serious time for this boy. You can't just go around smashing police heads in, and then expect to walk away from it. No no. That you can't!" The cop's eyes flickered nervously from his rear-view mirror to the scene around him as though waiting for something more to happen.

"I don't," Thompson replied, trying to maintain a laconic indifference; he shifted his gaze upwards to stop being irritated by the cop.

The cop shook his head knowingly and made a constant irritating whistle sound with air in his teeth that grated on Thompson.

"I don't go around smashing cop's heads in. That bastard Hanley should never have been a cop anyway: he makes a boomerang look like a fucking walking stick," Thompson looked over the cop's shoulder and shrugged to himself.

The cop watched him in the mirror; a slight squint wrinkled around the edges of eyes. Thick twat, he didn't know what Thompson meant. Thompson looked back out and tutted at his thoughts. His gaze tilted upwards at a dark sky and he frowned as a pigeon flew across the moon and dropped in a mad spectacular tumbling display. It disappeared into darkness.

"Odd," Thompson mumbled in surprise to himself.

"What's odd?" The cop asked urgently.

"Nothing," Thompson shrugged at the darkness before speaking. "Just odd to see a tumbling pigeon flying at night, that's all. Struck me as odd. Birds don't fly at night."

The cop turned three quarters with his arm on top of the seat and looked at Thompson, using his chin to point at him.

"You're odd! That's what," he jerked his jaw at Thompson and faced back to the front pleased with himself, as though he'd now gained the upper hand. "Birds don't fly at night! What's an owl? Some kind of bat! Answer me that."

Thompson shook his head and wondered if all cops were aggressive morons. Maybe Swansea was just unlucky and the rest of the world was sane; they might even have sane police. Thompson doubted it. Cops were always the first to declare no smoke without fire; he wondered about that: thousands of cop shows with countless bent cops corrupting livings rooms all over the world. Respect the police? Respect the authorities? Respect? Meaningless drivel in a bent-cop world. No smoke without fire: a bonfire of bent cops was needed. Made him think of dirty pork crackling.

Breakfast was a single Weetabix. A large globule of spit sat in the middle. Tasty with petulance. Thompson slid it beneath his bunk out of sight; he was surprised the station cops hadn't worked him over already and had expected it all night. Hungry too, he'd hoped to pick up a burger after beers the previous night. That hadn't happened, and that was fat Hanley's fault. Now no breakfast was more shit on Hanley! He'd made the call though. The brief promised to be early.

The door rattled.

"Bowl!" A voice demanded.

"Other fella already took it," Thompson took a shot. Footsteps went away. Thompson tense. An hour snailed by. The brief finally showed. Eating a sandwich, he swapped it for the Weetabix and took a photo: evidence of something, he mused.

Thompson de-briefed the brief.

§

"You can't leave the house at all?" Jean Thompson's incredulity was evident as she asked her husband the question. He gestured to his ankle and the cumbersome tag locked on.

"If I go beyond the end of the garden, those tossers will be on me like hogs on a shit-pile," Thompson pointed to the fence less than four metres from the window

"What about food? How on this earth are you supposed to feed yourself if you can't go out?" Jean wondered aloud at the logic of the judge's sentence.

Thompson gestured to the laptop and shrugged.

"Everything I need has to be ordered in or brought in. Simple as that Jeanie. Anything else, and the judge wouldn't have agreed to release me until the trial date," he shook his head at the abysmal state of affairs and held his hands wide apart: the system was what it was.

Jean Thompson knew her husband. Helpless could only be an act; he was a wily bugger and she had no intention of hanging around and finding herself running errands for him; she'd left him three years after they married and knew then that she'd dodged a bullet. Always a rogue, the fucker was full of charm too; she fell for that like a fool: two kids popped for him, boys both, now in their teens. They were already chips off the block. Trouble floats close to them. Nothing stuck yet luckily. Like their father, both slippery as shit through a goose. Only a punch or two from some cop for Gavin the eldest so far. Gary, already a superior version of other two: more brains than street guile. Loved his mum too; he made sure Jean had some luxury to enjoy at her home: flat-screen, I-pad, laptop, American fridge-freezer—water and ice door too! That, the priceless envy of a neighbour. A smart conservatory set off her garden. Her pride and joy, Gary. Fifteen. How? She asked a question once. Where? That was all she said; his head moved an inch and his gaze shifted over her shoulder, beyond—a dismissal worthy of a criminal boss. Jean recognised it. The subject was over, and the look said to leave it. Oddly, all that she had, Gary had paid for—Jean had seen the receipts and got to keep them for her warranties. What she didn't know couldn't hurt her. Some things were best left.

"What are you doing?" She returned from her thoughts in surprise at the strange actions of Lee before her.

"I'm cooking some food. What do you think I'm doing?" Thompson sliced an aubergine in four lengths and salted both sides while talking to her.

"Since when do you cook?"

"I've cooked for years!" Thompson looked at her in confusion, "I never cooked for you because you were always in the bloody way woman, and I didn't get a look in. I like to look after myself," as she watched, he sliced a courgette into half-inch pieces and with a small spoon he smeared an amount of crushed garlic paste onto each one, rubbing in it before adding a slice of chilli to the top of each. Satisfied, he lined them on a tray and popped them into the oven.

A sceptical eyebrow raised, she was surprised but something about his deft handling of the food contradicted her assumptions.

"Dainty looking food for a big man," something had to be said.

"What?" Thompson looked at her in confusion as he continued to fuss with bits of food he was preparing.

"Leopards and spots! That's what," Jean replied, unable to come up with anything else. "I'm off. I'll come over later in the week and see what's what. How long do you think before you have to go inside?"

"Who said I'm going inside?" Thompson almost growled at her as he spoke. Shaking his head, for a moment he held up the knife to emphasise his point and met her eyes. His point made by gesture alone, he looked back at the food and sliced twelve plum tomatoes in halves, before seasoning them and scattering them into a lightly oiled Pyrex dish; he gestured to Jean once more with his fancy chef's knife waving it again. "It was self-defence you know, Jean. Self-defence, so it was. That bastard Hanley attacked me. And another thing—he's the one who did over our Gav too. Did you know that?"

"Sharon Evans said he was on the floor when you hit him, Lee. You knew he was a copper too! You don't get away with that, especially if they think it's revenge for what he did to Gavin. That's pre-meditated, Lee—that's even worse, man," Jean shook her head; some of his aggressive teen behaviour had never been left behind.

Thompson shook his head and picked up a peeler. Sliding it expertly along two carrots, he sliced them into quarter-inch pieces and tossed them into a small lightly oiled dish before drizzling honey and a couple of twists of ground black pepper on top.

"Tell Sharon Evans to keep her big mouth shut—and that fella she was with too—unless he wants his wife to get wind of what those two are up to," Thompson nodded at his ex-wife's raised eyebrows but didn't elaborate on the indiscretion further. "It can't be pre-meditated! I didn't know that fat-arse was going to come into The Duke now, did I. So there! He's on the camera too."

"What? He's on the camera? What camera?" Jean drew her head back in confusion. The Duke wasn't the type of establishment anyone would imagine a camera in.

"The camera in the pub, girl. Dai put one in about three years ago to stop the young lads dealing out back where I was. You probably haven't been in The Duke since you left?" Thompson dismissed her incredulity as he poured away warm water from the soaking dried porcinis. Dabbing them dry with kitchen roll, he looked up at Jean quizzically; her head bobbed from side to side and her thoughts went back—she jumped through the years in seconds.

"You're right," she agreed. "I haven't been in there for what ... fourteen years? God, Lee, where has the time gone?"

"I know," Thompson sighed with her and nodded. Uncorking a bottle of wine, he smelt it first and set it on the table to breathe. Her eyes followed it and watched as he wrapped the fork and knife in a square of kitchen roll. Next to it, he placed a single glass. Her eyes followed him as he dried the aubergine and smeared strips with garlic paste too, before he lay them tentatively into a hot frying pan.

"Does that cop know he's on the camera?" The thought popped into her head.

"I think he suspects, but Dai sent the footage to John Hughes already. Hughes'll keep shtum until he needs to; he said something about not giving the other side too much time on anything," Thompson held his hands out as though balancing something in each like a justice scales before tossing the brown onion skin into the composting pot.

Lee had never divorced Jean; he used to hope they'd get back together, but knew now they wouldn't, yet he still had no interest in moving on. New pastures didn't turn up often, and he had all the kids he wanted. For sex, Swansea was easy with money in the pocket. Quays were full from Thursday to Sunday with girls out of their boxes. The pull was a pushover today: none of them was fussy; from sixteen up they'd bang anything for a drink, and they were all bloody skint. Most were skanky as a junk's ball sack. Lee looked at Jean again: imminently leaving since arrived, she was always that way these days.

"According to Hughes, Hanley has history with the courts, and nearly all of it is rotten. If I get one of the judges who knows him, I might even get lucky, he said. Hughes wants me to counter with something too—said he'd sleep on it and let me know," Thompson spoke to the pots as he added onions and stirred them with a wooden spoon, knowing Jean heard him. Not much went by her.

"It's GBH Lee! They're not going to mess around, and let you walk from this one, I tell you," her emphatic tone told him she was sure of her assertion. "If you'd just punched him, maybe—or even kicked him in the guts or his balls. Sharon said you kicked his head in. Right in too! His head, Lee. Even you should know that! 'Sake Lee, you're a grown man."

"Sharon Evans needs to keep her big tarty mouth shut. You tell her I said that—I'll have her if she keeps on," Thompson fumed and shook his head in annoyance at the interference from Evans' gossip. "I had no intentions of doing anything Jean—I swear to you. God's truth. On Mam!" An unbreakable oath for Thompson, its relevance was understood by Jean, but changed little for her. "I was having a couple of drinks with Rod and Philip, and I swear, believe me now, we were talking about the kids and school. That's all we ever talk about these days! Rod's worried about his lad, and wants to switch him over to Willows to get away from a couple of the messers that he's fallen in with. That was it until that Hanley bastard showed up. Telling you straight, I am."

"What did he show up for, Lee?" Jean knew there had to more to it than just the random chance of those two meeting. As she watched he added mushrooms to the onions and stirred the pot and his focus remained fixed on the food. Still a good-looking man, she thought. Rough at the edges perhaps, and definitely not someone to pick a fight with; his teeth gritted, and she remembered the constant threat of anger. Looking at her, he smiled with his hands held wide: a picture of guilty innocence.

"Three times—no, four. Four times he asked," Thompson reflected and paused as he closed his eyes to remember. Picking the bottle up he poured a glass of wine; Jean's eyes followed his glass but he made no offers. "He never said why he was there, Jean," Thompson rubbed his chin in confusion as he spoke again and wondered at his own words. "He just kept asking if I did, or didn't."

"If you did or didn't what?" Jean's eyes followed the wine, even though she tried not to look. Five years now—meetings every Tuesday. Hello everybody, my name is Jean. Why is he swirling it like that? It tastes the same no matter what. All that poncy nonsense. Just drink it. Jean closed her eyes and turned her head away. Never again was never easy, she thought.

"Do it," Thompson's words brought her back. He'd watched her eyes on the glass since the wine went in. He knew that he should've waited. It was unfair on her, he thought, and tsked to himself as he watched her. She'll go now—five-minutes tops. Is she sweating? That quickly.

"What?" Jean's thoughts came back to the kitchen and the echoes of Thompson's last words.

"He asked if I did or didn't do it," Thompson recognised the drop-out, and repeated where they'd got to.

"Do what?"

"That's it, I tell you! Nothing more," Thompson patted his head to demonstrate his confusion with Hanley's action, before holding them apart to seek agreement from Jean about how confusing it was. "He just asked that. Nothing more Jean. I have no idea what it was all about, and he was about to work me over, so it must have been bad. Hanley usually avoids me."

"Hughes should find out what it was all about. It might help," she confirmed her agreement with the confusing state of affairs. "I'm off, Lee. I'll come over tomorrow or the day after. That food looked good by the way. Who'd have guessed you've changed that much and can look after yourself now? Oh, last thing—if you do go in--what will the council do about this flat?"

"I'll see you then," Thompson allowed her to leave by turning away. "It's not like I'm going anywhere … I'm not going anywhere Jean."

Hughes, not the man he thought; the visiting Magistrate, a woman, a much appalled woman: video footage disallowed; they'd left it too late for the other side for it to be fair. Only a small mitigation granted for Hanley's aggression, given the seriousness of assault. It would have been life. Fourteen years, to serve a minimum of ten. Near fifty on release, Lee thought of how few opportunities there would be for him, in a land of ever fewer. Hanley was propped in a hospital chair through the hearing; tubes everywhere, his face was gone, collapsed in on itself, and his career was finished—he showed no reaction to anything the judge said. Pensioned at thirty-nine, his disability condemned him to a life sentence of limitations. Two lives never in agreement. Petty children leading to petty adults. The trigger to set it all on the slippery slope was 'Boss Hogg' being tagged on Hanley's car—an old school name gift from Thompson. Gavin held his guilty head in his hands and couldn't meet his father's eyes.

On small things, the fate of small men turns.

***

Mushroom Risotto Recipe

Ingredients
200g Arborio rice
25g pack of dried porcini mushrooms
(or mixed wild mushrooms)
1 large onion fine chopped
8 garlic cloves crushed and chopped with sea salt to a paste
12 small plum tomatoes
2 aubergines
2 courgettes
2 chillies
salt & pepper
home-grated parmesan
I pint of mushroom stock

This is not the 'wet baby food' style risotto often favoured by restaurants. It's a drier rice dish with accompanying roasted vegetables, and I've found it has been preferred by friends and family to the other style, especially when served as a main. I've always found a full plate of the other style to be too much of one thing, and yet still not a proper meal, and if out with friends and it's been the only choice available for me, I've often felt like flinging it at the wall or at the chef.

Making Mushroom Risotto

Slice the aubergines and courgettes into centimetre thick pieces. Add fine salt to both sides of the aubergines and set aside to allow it to draw the sour moisture out. Do this about half an hour before everything else.

Fine chop the two chilies into rings

Rub some garlic paste on to the courgette pieces and place on a lightly oiled oven tray. Add a couple of bits of chilli to each piece. Place in top shelf of oven at 190 for forty minutes.

Slice the tomatoes in half. Lightly season and place in a Pyrex bowl with the middles facing upwards. Place in oven next to the courgettes but take out after thirty minutes when they're beginning to caramelise on the edges.

Follow instructions on mushroom packets to hydrate and dry them off. If you've got fresh, all the better: wipe them down and carry on.

Add onion to a large flat heavy based pan with some groundnut oil in it. Gently sweat for ten minutes before adding the mushrooms. Allow the heat to steam off the excess water in the mushrooms for six to ten minutes. Add a splash of stock, stir and gradually begin adding the rice. Add more stock, stir, more rice until it's all in. Reduce heat and cover. After about twenty minutes the rice will have absorbed most of the moisture. Remove cover and stir. Cover again and if the moisture is gone remove from the heat and set aside.

While the rice is cooking and absorbing the moisture, rinse the aubergine and dry with kitchen towel. Spread remaining garlic on one or both sides of slices. Add the aubergine to a good size non-stick heavy bottomed pan and fry gently, turning several times until cooked.

Once ready to serve, take a small cereal bowl and scoop spoons of the risotto into it using it as a mold. Place plate on top and invert. Add four or five slow roasted tomato halves to the top and scatter some grated parmesan on top. Add four pieces of courgette and two slices of Aubergine to each plate. Serve with a mixed salad, garlic bread, and a nice red wine.

***

Raymond Thomas Burke's Experience of Innocence

IT WASN'T COMPLETELY UNUSUAL FOR A young lad of thirteen to kneel before me in the dark. Trembling like a dry leaf on a branch tip, his voice shifted from squeaks to deep bass reverbs; informing me of the loss of his faith and belief in our Holy Church, and all her teachings, wasn't an easy task for him.

Don't get me wrong. Such a thing isn't a common occurrence for me, or anyone else, I imagine.

Not here in the Barony especially, where things tend more towards the quiet and tranquil end of the scale. Truth be told, they muster along pretty much as they have without any real changes for more years now than those living can remember back beyond; a bit of change every now and again would do us no harm—there's not much worse than stale people with stale minds.

The hormones get to some of the boys you see—growth spurts jumping them forwards physically—all those dirty thoughts in their heads swelling their trousers and setting them off into endless masturbating cycles. With our youth-obsessed society seeking instant gratification, and projecting to us a world full of fantasies, there's little else we can expect, is there? It's enough, and you can imagine I'm sure, and I think you'll agree, it's enough to throw anyone, man or boy, off the path every now and again.

"Bless me, Father, for I have sinned …"

He began with the usual rote, and that's me, the Father. Father John. I didn't take another name when I was ordained, which is unusual, I suppose, and I dropped the family name. Not unheard of, but a little curious oddity, that. My life I sought to dedicate to the path of our most Holy Father, Saint John the Baptist. He got me young—the story of him hooked me, and I probably wasn't much older than young Barney Boyle on his knees in the dark in front of me, at the other side of the confessional grill. I think it was the mystery of him being there before our Lord, as it were, y'know, the way he turns up suddenly; the story hadn't even kicked off properly, and there was Saint John already baptising people when the whole gang turn up at the river. None of us ever seemed to notice that, or even question it when I grew up. I know there was probably a ritual cleansing of sorts with the Jews, but his seemed different somehow. Didn't our Lord himself go through the process and wasn't he recognised by Saint John, in a moment of revelation, of course. Out here in our little church I've always kept a statue of him—it's an oversized yoke, for the humble rural church that we are, I'll grant you, but I've kept it next to me on the altar, and it's been taking up space there now at least thirty years.

"Pray tell, my son," I replied quietly, keeping my language slightly archaic, as is our way; it keeps a bit of mystery going in the everyday, I always feel. "What troubles your soul?"

"I've lost me faith, Father," Anthony Boyle was always direct and to the point—unlike his father.

277

Barney was a nickname the other kids gave him. Like most nicknames, some stick, some slip off. Barney was sticking a little to Anthony, and although I knew he wasn't overly fond of it, it was better than the other option of 'Boyler' in the long run. I tried to think of him and call him Anthony, his christened name, after Saint Anthony, you understand—ironically too, I know, for Saint Anthony himself is our saint of lost things, and the faithful need only say his prayer to be finding whatever it is they've lost. His prayer—my memory is not what it was. Ah, here it is now for you:

> O blessed Saint Anthony,
> the grace of God has made you a powerful advocate
> in all our needs,
> For restoring of things lost or stolen
> I turn to you today, Saint Anthony
> With childlike love
> And deep confidence
> For you have helped countless children of God
> To find the things they have lost
> Material and more importantly
> Those of the spirit, our faith, our hope and our love
> I come to you, Saint Anthony, with confidence
> Help me in my present need
> I recommend what I have lost to your care
> In the hope that God will restore it to me
> If it be His Holy Will
> Amen

There now, that's the one! It's an old one that too! A good Catholic only need say that prayer for whatever it is they've lost to be returned to them, you see. They used to anyway. I'm thinking today Saint Anthony is probably too busy, and people losing too much, for anyone, saint or otherwise, to have a chance of keeping up with everything.

I mumbled my way quietly through the prayer, on young Anthony's behalf, my mind, on the one hand, trying to stop thinking of him as Barney, and on the other thinking of the irony, whilst also trying to be faithful and sincere in my incantation of the prayer, and of course, listening to young Anthony emptying his heart out at the same time.

"...and then he showed us that the whole thing was a load of nonsense," Boyler pulled me from my thoughts and holy mumbling.

I interrupted him, thinking perhaps it might be best to listen a little closer to his confession, instead of drifting in my own mind, which of late I've found myself over-inclined to do. I asked him to repeat the last segment about whatever it was he'd been talking.

"...from the debating society bit, Father?" he asked, slightly confused, and as I had no recollection of any such moment in his outpouring, I offered my agreement and asked that he recount for me once more, 'from the debating society bit', and I closed my eyes to listen, and concentrate all the better.

"It was at school. Afterwards," his recollection began somewhat confusingly. "At the debating society meeting. We were practising for the competition, like I was saying. You know, the one in town that gets held in the Tower every year?"

I knew of it, I'd say, more than knowing it. Most, no—all of the teenage lads go into the town for secondary school these days. The town, or the city as they like to call it, is only seven or eight miles away, or closer now if you measure from the sprawling suburbs of the last few years. But for me, who rarely travels in there, it could be fifty miles, and I can't honestly say I have my finger on the pulse of what happens there anymore. I'm a bit of a stay-at-home type now, truth be told, and I only venture out if I'm to catch up with a couple of friends, or to take the bike out for a spin around the lanes. The Tower, Anthony mentioned, that's the rectangular box-like hotel in the city behind a row of international flags, and directly opposite Reginald's Tower, the old medieval tower and the city's most famous building. I've often wondered why hotels feel the need to put flags out, but I can't say I ever found a satisfactory reason. I know The Tower Hotel though, and remember in my younger years having to attend an odd occasion in one of their function rooms, so I presumed it was a thing like that to which he was referring.

"What? Pardon me," I stopped him once more, as my mind tried to quickly recount what he'd just said, and I pulled my drifting thoughts from my memories of my own times in The Tower Hotel. "Lawton you said? Was that it? Lawton?"

"Yes Father. Dermot Lawton. You know him?" The young Boyle leaned closer to the grill as though trying to seeing through.

I knew of a Dermot Lawton, in that he was Donald Lawton's son you see, having baptised him—it's one of the perks, or curses of the job, depending on your point of view. Donald is the chair of our Historical Society out this way; he's been that for as long as I can remember too, and I'm an honorary member myself. The subs are something we can't do from the Church, you understand; I allow them usage of the hall for a token fee— peppercorn, you might even say—and the Church, and grounds too, occasionally, if they're on a more intense fund-raiser. Hence the 'honorary' membership. I went to some of their meetings when I thought a topic might grab me. I'm not averse to a bit of history, especially if it's got a local twist to it now, but in honesty, two or three of the older boys are such dusty academics—you know the sort— when they talk, or drone, they refer to the footnotes and the like, and their deliveries are completely lacking in any 'delivery', for lack of a better word. God! Heaven forbid, but the thought of a night with them all is enough to bring me out in hives.

I honed my ears back into Anthony.

"Jerusalem was flattened in the first century, and that pretty much ended the Temple-based religion that Judaism had been up to then. What they have today is very much Torah based, and in many ways a different creature to historical Judaism, Father."

I mumbled away to myself in our mysterious fashion once more, wondering what on earth the little blighter was wittering on about, but I was getting the atmosphere of the confessional back up, as we like to, and I was also trying to stay a little focused on the young tormented soul.

Memories of Donald Lawton introducing one of his coveted guest speakers, and me unconscious on the chair after ten minutes of him speaking flooded my mind; I decided instead to think about what I might have for my tea later in the day. I'd been over to Mary and Tom Fortune's earlier that morning, and

Mary—Mary, being Mary—well, she put something in a parcel for me. Mary's like that. Salt of the earth, so she is, and she never makes a fuss—she just gets on and does what needs to be done when it's needed. Tom's a lucky man, and he knows it too. I thought about the aroma wafting from the parcel earlier, and where I'd tucked it in the vestry before coming out to the box. I couldn't be blamed entirely now, being in the middle of Lent, and fasting as we were, thanks to our ever spouting fountain of ideas—that new young girl of the Cantwell's— thanks to her, we were all on a vegetarian vigil for the duration. I must confess, I was a little bit gassy at first, and I remembered the feeling from earlier in life—it was the same as when I walked El Camino, that's the pilgrim route to Santiago de Compostella. I managed to do it in my early years, with a couple of other lads I'd met in Rome. That was one of my best years. The three of us sharing food and wine, and trumping our way through the nights in the small Spanish hostels are memories I don't think will ever leave me.

'Vegetarian scotch eggs' Mary had said, and she'd winked at me to assure me they were safe to eat within our rules. I don't think I've stopped thinking about them since I took possession of them. I don't think I've stopped thinking about food since our vigil began in fact.

I shook myself once more and listened back into young Boyler who'd inadvertently elbowed the inside of the confessional in the dark, and brought me back to him with the thumping noise. Probably hasn't realised how big he's grown; he's all elbows, knees, and bony arse knuckles now: he'll make a fine footballer if he moves that back-side of his away from the telly and computer, and those games the young lads seem to spend all their time on.

"Emperor Constantine then became, or should I say, made himself the Emperor Pope, even though he wasn't really a Christian or anything, and things really began to change all over the place. I mean like really all over the place! Until then, the Christians were just a small growing sect, or whatever you might call a group of people with the same ideas. There were loads of different sects and cults too, Father, and all of them were nearly the same, according to Dermot—how did he say it? They were all just a mishmash of the Jewish beliefs with some of the new ideas of the time; the main thing seemed to be believing in just one God though, rather than all the 'pantheon' stuff, I think he said? The Christians though—they were nothing and nobodies! They barely warranted a footnote in any of the written histories from the people who were alive and writing at that time. There's nothing about them, Father, at the beginning anyway. It was all made up after. The whole lot of it came after! It's all a load of lies! It's a disgrace, that's what it is. When all the relic stuff suddenly started appearing, and all the places started getting built—the churches, and the places for pilgrims to visit, and all those bits turning up all over the place—suddenly there were loads and loads of them everywhere, and they just kept on growing and growing. That can't be right, Father. You know like? There's nothing for three hundred years. Loads of different religions all going on about the same kind of stuff, and then BANG! Everybody has to become a Christian if they're under the power of Rome. That's just like when the English started persecuting the Catholics because their King got fed up with his wives not giving him male children. The whole thing is a sham. It has to be! I'm sorry Father. I probably didn't explain it very well, and Dermot really did much better. He's going to be our main speaker this year too. I didn't mean to stop believing Father—my heart is heavy with the thought of it too. Us Boyles have always been good Catholics, Father. But the truth is always best, and the only right way! That's what you said in Mass last Sunday. I'll still be good, Father—as good, and as true and truthful as I can and that. I don't want to have to come to Mass and listen to or believe all that stuff anymore. My mam is making me. I think that's wrong too."

It's not often I'm at a loss for words, in truth. Young Anthony floored me with a sucker; he left me feeling as though I were something of a hollow fraud.

In innocent truth, there is a power that side-swipes you and against which there is little defence, other than a coarse denial, or some stroppy condemnation; we've had a bit too much of that in our history. There was no-one else in for Confession, so once Anthony left, with his recommended penance, which I have to say I issued defensively—suggesting as I did that he learn Saint Anthony's prayer, to take with him on his life's journey—I sat and thought for a while, and I munched on one of Mary's scotch eggs.

Good, he'd said. And 'good and true' seemed to be the main concern of the young lad's troubled innocent heart. Truth isn't always good I thought to myself; sometimes it hurts, and sometimes it causes all sorts of strife—if strife can be avoided, by avoiding the truth every now and again, is that not a better course of action I wondered, as I often have. Was my life itself a sham, a larger untruth, I wondered that too, what, with my preaching as I do every week, even if it is fewer times a week now, and every year to fewer than before?

My own faith, I'd long buried beneath the blankets of community activity. Self-protection really, my own ploy to stop me thinking too deeply about all the various arms and legs of it, I guess. In doing so, I've kept it smothered from observation by myself. Not intentionally, you understand—more unconsciously, I'd suspect. The finer aspects of theology I must admit I've avoided throughout my working life, probably knowing that for my own mind the whole thinking deeply about it was likely a bit beyond me. It might just have been the study. I was never a tremendous academic, or theologian, or even a great thinker for that matter. The focus I've always felt to be more importantly zoned onto has always been simple goodness—rather than piety, or all the observances of the rituals, or the knowledge of it all, you know, like being a barrister-priest, able to put down any contestation. That's not to say I don't agree with many of the things we do in the church; I'm of a mind that doing without things every now and again does us no harm, and might serve to remind us to not take things for granted, or appreciate things more, but the world seems to be too busy stocking up for endless rainy-day feasts of indulgence these days. The idea of a little bit of self-denial, or any personal suffering, now seems redundant to our modern minds.

I stopped thinking of myself as Father John that day.

I continue to serve my community in all ways I can, in the spirit of the early Church, or at least that's what I tell myself. They have needs, my parishioners. Real needs too. I can facilitate their needs without disrupting their lives, so, I carry on. Births, baptisms, communions, confirmations, marriages, and all the way through to death, and the remembering of those passed from us—of these, I am still the person and guardian to whom one and all will turn first; if a hand needs holding in a home, or a hug, a squeeze, or a touch from another human is needed, in the lonely years, when they wait, a little lost in our world, ready to go on in the forlorn hope of once again joining their loved ones, I'm here for them: a comforting rock of sorts in rough seas.

What else would a man of my age do?

My love for them all hasn't changed, and I even pray for them so they may find the things they want, and most of all, to find that happiness and ease with life that all of us wish for; habits of a lifetime are not easy things to break.

The Bishop here is old now, and he's comfortable in his palatial home on the top of Saint John's Hill.

I seem to be surrounded by things mocking my thoughts.

If we meet, the Bishop and I, our health is all we query now, for the truth itself, we skirt in our frocks of office. So we sit, and we share a fine cognac, or a malt whiskey, and we mumble our appreciation of the finer things this life has to offer us.

Our eyes rarely meet like they did when we were young fresh men of the cloth, both of us perhaps aware in the passing of our years how much they'd belie to the other, and neither of us wants to expose ourselves, or indeed the other, to any discomfort of that sort.

We continue the charade as we always have.

I kiss his ring. He pats my head. I call him 'Your Eminence'. He calls me, 'My Son'.

He is no longer eminent in any way to me. I suspect, although I can't be entirely sure, that he in no way feels me to be any son of his. After all, how could I be?

My name is, and always has been, Raymond Thomas Burke, and I am nothing but a man. Granted, a man with an odd job, equipped with an odd outfit, and an oddly consenting parish of people, and all I'm doing is trying to do good in our strange and troubled world. If there is a God, an all-powerful deity, an all-seeing deity, an all-knowing deity—if there is such an entity—then I'm sure my indiscretions, my failings, my shortcomings, my lack—I'm sure all and anything to do with me will be oddly irrelevant in the grander scheme of things.

I don't worry about any of these things anymore. I look now to maybe enjoy myself, and I encourage others too, to enjoy themselves a little more in the time we have left in this one short and wonderful life before the earth reclaims our bodies, and our thoughts disperse in the endless, eternal, empty void that awaits to embrace us.

***

Vegetarian Scotch Eggs Recipe

The scotch egg is popular for picnics or as a gastro pub starter, with a bit of fancy work on the side. With the vegetarian version, the sausage meat is obviously not as 'porky' but with an addition of some crushed yellow mustard seeds, or whole grain mustard, combined with a bit of coriander, you can get a good 'authentic sausage' taste going. You can substitute the veggie sausage with veggie chorizo sausage too, and that works. I've made these using the 'dry mixes' for veggie sausage meat, but in honesty, you're much better off using ready-made veggie sausages that you might already even like. Even the non-veg version is better made with proper hand-made sausages, rather than the frightening 'mystery sausage meat'. At least with the veggie option you don't have the same worries about it being cooked properly, that I remember with the meat version. If you like your eggs runny in the middle take them out a little earlier than indicated and cool them quickly. The soft egg needs a bit more care in the handling.

Ingredients
5 large free range eggs
1 pack of veggie sausages (around 400g)
1 small bunch of parsley (leaf only fine chopped)
1 small bunch of coriander (leaf only fine chopped)
1 tbsp of crushed yellow mustard seeds or a tbsp of wholegrain mustard

salt & pepper
plain flour
100g breadcrumbs

Prepping & Cooking

Break and beat one egg into a bowl. Flour a flat plate. Pour bread crumbs into a bowl.

Boil 4 of the eggs for 3-5 minutes … your preference (3 being very soft, 5 being hard). Cool under a running tap or a bowl of water and peel carefully.

Put a litre plus of groundnut oil on the go (you want this hot--150c plus) ready for deep frying—or if you have a regular fryer, use that.

Remove all the veggie sausages and mash them up in a mixing bowl, adding the coriander, parsley, salt, pepper and mustard seeds once most of the mashing is done. A little bit of olive oil in the mix doesn't go astray either, but it does depend on the brand variety you choose. Use your judgement, and if it feels a bit dry or cakey, add a splash. Split the mix into four (equal weights) and roll first into a compact ball before flattening into a hand-sized patty shape. Then, rub the egg on a flour plate and add it, carefully wrapping the sausage meat around it. Once it's all neat, roll it on the flour plate, dip it into the egg bowl, roll it again on the flour plate, again into the egg mix and then roll it in the breadcrumbs.

Repeat three more times and place all four in a wire basket before gently lowering them into the very hot oil for about three and a half minutes. You can dry them off a bit on some kitchen towel. Serve with a couple of slices of Masala Soda Bread (book

1), on a bed of rocket with a good spicy chutney and a nice mustard. A malty ale, stout, or a dark wheat beer is particularly good company for a scotch egg. If you have two, sleep on your own—it's only good manners.

***

The Garden Party

Marge washed away her avocado mask and dried her face with the Egyptian cotton towels she bought in John Lewis over in Watford. Carefully pouring some Shu Uemura face oil onto the fingers of her left hand, she gently massaged the left side of her face. Repeating the ritual with her right hand, and right side of her face, she left the bathroom and walked across the bedroom, enjoying the soft carpet pile beneath her feet. She stopped briefly at the window and looked out into the garden. A light breeze brought goose bumps on her slightly damp breasts, and her nipples hardened against the smooth silk of her kimono; finishing her facial as she stood there looking out, she gently massaged the top of her forehead with both hands as her finale. Stopping mid-motion, she tilted her head in confusion.

"What is that big ape up to?" Marge spoke aloud to the window.

"I'm busy here Marge," humming a ditty to himself behind her, Geoffrey's reply was dismissive. "Surely you can figure it out. You are looking out of the window after all."

Marge tutted, and gave Geoffrey one of her looks. It had no effect, as Geoffrey was massaging his face with a cedar-scented manly cream before the mirror with his eyes closed. Looking back to the garden, she figured out what was going on.

"That idiot is cutting a huge lump out of my lawn to make a fire!"

"Very good, Marge," Geoffrey's patronising tone set her teeth on edge. "It's for the barbecue, I believe. Remember? Doing a sheep, he is—in traditional South African style too. I believe that's what he said."

"A sheep?" Marge's tone mangled the word into a question. "A 'sheep' Geoffrey? Never mind the traditional whatever! A 'sheep' you say. There are only ten of us, you realise? If we wanted sheep, would we not select the better parts, and cook them in the kitchen. On the stove, Geoffrey—traditional English style, might I add, if that's what impresses?"

"Yes yes yes yes," Geoffrey knew where Marge was going and had little desire to get involved. "Indulge him, darling. It seems it's been something he's been 'dying to do' for-?"

"On our lawn Geoffrey? He can bonfire his own house, when he has a house, for all I care! I've paid Carl for seven long years to get this bloody garden right—and it's been hard work! Hard work, Geoffrey," the absence of Geoffrey's input into the usually designated masculine management task of the household was not lost on him.

"I'll sort Carl out this week," Geoffrey assured her. "Piet has assured me that once he rolls the sod back, everything will sort itself out in a week or two-"

"But-?"

"No Marge. Enough darling! We have guests today. Any problems caused by this, I will sort out. That's it. Now leave the matter be, please," Geoffrey used his chairman voice, and Marge, knowing he wouldn't rise further, let it be.

Throughout, her gaze had remained on big Piet. A strapping man, he must be at least six foot six Marge calculated, and from behind, his waist seemed small and exaggerated by the dramatic V-shape of his back, and the considerable width of his shoulders; his back and arms flexed and rippled as he worked the shovel to remove the earth, which he neatly piled high on two plastic gardening mats before dragging them considerately out of sight beneath the thick hedge. Standing upright, he pressed his hands firmly into his lower back and thrust his groin outwards to stretch out his spine. Marge tilted her head as she scrutinised the length of his over-long muscular body.

"I need to get on with the salads," sauntering back into her dressing room to finish her ablutions, she left her preening Geoffrey to himself.

"Very good dear," Geoffrey tilted his head to see better the stray black and grey hairs visible in his nose. Plucking tentatively, he blinked back tears, sniffled loudly, and raked at his eminent proboscis as he did so, now that Marge was gone.

Striding through her kitchen, Marge swung the backdoors open full and drew a deep breath of the morning; she waved at Piet, who half turned at the movement of the doors, looked towards her.

Marge smiled.

Piet waved back uncertainly.

Approaching him slowly along the length of the garden she gathered a basket of oregano stems and rosemary clippings along her meander—it lent her a sense of purpose and proprietorship.

"Is there anything you need, Piet darling?" When close enough to him to speak quietly, Marge released the words in a husky whisper. "Anything I can get, or do for you?"

"Is it? Yah," Piet, confusedly replied. "Morning Marge, eh? What a day huh? Something for me, is it. A cold beer perhaps, eh? Thirsty work in the sun, yah? True, no?"

Piet's words echoed in her mind—she was finally learning to ignore his unusual "Is it?" response to most things, and Marge worked out he'd asked for a beer. Geoffrey had surprised her the previous evening by putting beers in the fridge, but she understood now why he did it; Geoffrey and his golfing colleagues rarely deviated from white wines.

"I'll pop one along. My, you are a big man, Piet! I can't imagine Geoffrey being able to do this."

Contracting her nose, she smiled in a coquettish flirt, before turning to walk back along the garden; her hips swayed and aware that her silhouette was being picked out by the bright sunshine, she slowly bent over in various spots to pick another stem of oregano from the beds where it had become rampant.

In the kitchen, Marge chuckled to herself and filled the kettle. From the cupboard, she removed a bag of couscous, and from the fridge, she took plum tomatoes, red onions and two aubergines.

Tutting, and twitching his head, as though in disapproval, Geoffrey blustered in.

"I need to go to the clubhouse," releasing an exasperated snort, and tutting his disapproval with circumstances loudly, he scanned for his car keys and avoided looking directly at Marge.

"Geoffrey! You promised-!" In the middle of pouring some boiling water over a stock cube,

Marge raised a questioning eyebrow at his reflection in the kitchen window.

"Not to play dear, not to play. Duty calls I'm afraid. Something's come up with the monthly medal, and I need to pop in to see James and sort the blasted mess out. An ugly little episode too, I'm led to believe. I'll be back at most in a couple of hours. Nobody's expected until mid-afternoon, darling. I'll be here by one," Geoffrey's club affairs were off limits for arguments. As Vice-Captain, he took his responsibilities seriously. "You don't need me under your feet anyway, and I'm not getting involved in whatever it is that Piet is doing. Be nice to him darling, please—he is a guest today, after all. Be on your very best for him."

"Piet!" His needs and her offer had been forgotten in her fun strutting across the garden, "I meant to bring him a beer! Oh God, Geoffrey, I'm useless at this kind of thing!"

Marge quickly poured the couscous into the pan and lidded it, admonishing herself for her inability to multi-task.

Geoffrey was absent when she looked up once more. With a napkin-wrapped beer from the fridge, Marge headed back down the garden.

§

Piet watched Marge walk away. His gaze picked out her shape beneath the light summer clothing, and uncertain what to make of it, or her, he resumed his task. Picking up his large mallet, he tested the ground for his intended rotisserie stands. Then, offering up the rotisserie, he judged that it was good and walloped the stands solidly into the rich earth

beneath the lawn. Satisfied, Piet fed the light
kindling to the apple and ash wood mix he'd piled
methodically into the hole, and after a few minutes
of fixing and fiddling with it, he lit it with the help of a
couple of firelighters. Starting in surprise at a noise,
he felt the cool of a shadow before him. Piet tilted
his head and found his gaze level with Marge's
crotch; the prominent black underwear he'd noticed
earlier was gone. Piet's mouth dried; he knew what
to make of that.

"Some refreshment for you, Piet. Eh?" Marge
grinned from ear to ear.

"Is it. Yah, oh? Marge! You're too sweet,"
Piet rose with stiff uncertainty.

Marge stood her ground, and unable to step
back without going into the fire Piet was forced to
come up directly in front of her; his body slid along
hers as he straightened and took the beer from her.

"Cheers, yah?" Piet looked down at Marge
whose chin was almost touching his chest.

"Yah?" Marge mimicked his questioning tone,
"Cheers, Piet. Oooh! You've got it going?"

Piet nodded, not quite able to turn around
without brushing against Marge, and he was aware
that any movement at all was going to cause him
complications.

"I just need to feed it a bit, and I'll come see
Geoff before I go home for a quick clean-up," Piet
looked over Marge's head towards the house.

"Geoffrey, Piet. Geoffrey is at the club, Piet,"
Marge touched his chest with a single finger, as
though about to prod him. "Until about one he said,
but knowing Geoffrey, he'll not show until after two
at least. You can always clean up here Piet—you
shouldn't have to change … I mean, it's a barbecue,

yah, and you'll be back by the fire with the sheep most of the day, I should imagine, eh?"

"Yah, true hah," without thinking it through, the words fell from Piet's lips. "Ah-? I must feed this, and build the heat first though, eh Marge?"

"I'll go back to my salads. Shout if you want me, Piet. It seems, I'm instructed to be at your service," Marge put her hand on his lower chest to help her turn. Feeling him tense beneath her touch, she allowed her hand to caress along his shirt as she turned and made her way back to the house.

Piet watched her as she teased her way slowly across the lawn and stopped to check the flowers; beneath her white summer dress she was a clear naked silhouette in the bright sunshine.

With his glasses atop his head, Geoffrey glanced through the gates of the club as he cruised past in his cryptically personalised Maserati. Set back too far for him to gain anything useful about who might or might not be playing, he couldn't help but look anyway—habit and curiosity are ingrained in all but the psychopath. Geoffrey was not a psychopath—pathological in many ways, but not a psycho. Half a mile or so beyond the club Geoffrey took the sharp right turn to Little Gaddesden, and after a few hundred metres slowed and eased into the long gravel drive of an ivy and wisteria covered house, grandly named, Beech Reach. The sage green regency front door was wide open, and as Geoffrey stepped into the warmth from the air-conditioned cool of his car, an upstairs sash window opened.

"I wasn't expecting you for another half-an-hour or so," a voice full of surprise called down to him.

Dropping his sunglasses to his nose, to offset the sun-glare from the white of the porch, Geoffrey looked up and laughed.

"I had to get out. I think Marge was beginning to have ideas about me helping big Piet build his fire?"

They both laughed and shook their heads at the image.

"Where are you?" Geoffrey asked. "Shall I come up right off?"

"Come up, come up. I only came here to see you arrive once I heard the car approach. I was just finishing. Come right up."

Entering the house and once again admiring the pristine condition of the porch and doors, which he closed, and enjoying the solid clean clicks they made as they came together, Geoffrey took a deep breath; the hallway was lightly scented with fig, and something else Geoffrey couldn't quite place. Turning and slipping off his shoes he bounded the stairs two by two. Wrapped in a fluffy white dressing gown, having recently showered and shaved, and with arms extended wide to greet him, both men came together at the top of the stairs. Geoffrey slid his arms into the welcoming softness of the gown and grabbed an arse cheek firmly, groaning with pleasure as he did so.

"You smell fantastic," locked in their embrace, they backed through the open bedroom door, half-wrestling with each other in an affectionate tangle.

§

Her ingredients lined up, Marge listened for a moment to see if she could hear sounds of Piet. Not hearing anything, she began grating carrots slightly frantically into a large glass bowl and started on her coleslaw.

Finished prepping in minutes, and tumbling it all together, she strained and twitched at the window to see precisely what Piet was up to, and she felt stirrings of annoyance.

"What is that big oaf up to now?" Muttering, she stood on her toes to try and see better where he'd disappeared to.

With the early beer having cut straight through him, Piet slipped behind the large box-hedge that ran across the lower part of the garden, hiding the shed and disused vegetable patches. Relieving himself as quietly as his flow would allow against the stout trunk of a copper beech tree, he didn't trust himself to go to the house—or Geoff's wife for that matter. In search of an excuse, he decided that more wood was needed, and resolved to set about gathering this if he ever stopped peeing.

Enclosed at the back by a large beech copse, with occasional ash and young oak trees scattered here and there, thick hazel hedges boxed the rear garden into an extended private rectangle with open, empty, ragwort-riddled paddocks unused through the summer on either side. Piet decided the copse was his only option, and when his flow finally stopped, he meandered back into it. Selectively picking dead fallen branches of varying sizes, he began to create small piles nearer the garden.

Hot, bothered, and fed up with cooking already, Marge decided to have a glass of wine, irrespective of the early hour, and she uncorked her favourite Pouilly. Geoffrey didn't like it. 'Too grapefruity' he described it. That suited Marge.

Sharing food or drinks with a man was never a great deal for a woman, she'd long discovered. Taking a long slow sup, she allowed the chill to run down her throat before filling her glass once more. Her fan assisted oven on, and with the salt having drawn the sour water from the aubergines, she watched through the window for Piet as she patted them dry with kitchen towel, before setting them aside on a large square shaped plate to air dry some more with the intention of pan-frying them in garlic later.

Her second glass of wine finished, she checked the tomatoes and switched off the oven, leaving them to finish with the residual heat, and set out to investigate Piet's absence.

Piet, long run out of things to do, finally decided to brave the kitchen, and hopefully get through the house to his car out front. As he approached the open doors, Marge appeared pouring the end of a bottle of wine into a glass as she made her way out.

She looked up.

"Piet, darling!" Holding her arms wide, Marge laughed, "I was just coming to do you."

"Ah! Okay Marge," Piet nervously sidestepped her by turning towards the fire. "Yah? I'm here. That fire is blazing now eh! Should be good for cooking in a few hours. I'm sweating like mad."

"Time for a drink then!" Marge grabbed his hand and dragged him towards the house. In the kitchen, she put down her wine after a quick gulp and removed another beer for Piet. Following her in, Piet traced an escape route in his mind towards the front door.

Dangling a cold open beer bottle, with a delightfully tempting beer froth overflowing, the fire and warmth of the day won, and Piet picked it from her and licked his lips involuntarily before he took a long draw. Allowing her hand to fall to his abdomen, Marge pressed it against him and released a small sigh of approval.

"Marge?" Piet spluttered, "Geoff-!"

"Geoffrey hasn't touched me in three years, Piet," Marge held Piet's gaze. "If I don't get something soon I might lose the will to-?"

Trying to gain some control, Piet put his beer on the kitchen island top. Marge took her opportunity and pushed closer before she grabbed his neck and dragged his head and lips down to hers. Kissing and biting at him roughly, Marge fumbled inexpertly at his belt before giving up and yanking his jeans open; she ripped them in the process but got them down to mid-thigh. Piet's hands slipped beneath her summer dress, and he lifted her slight, willing frame effortlessly on to him. Frantic, deprived, and desperate, Marge finished in seconds and was bounced off the fridge, the granite island top, the wall, and the hook on the back of the door before they finally knocked over and smashed the wine bottle. Hollering an end to proceedings there, Piet stood frustrated, guilty, confused, and apologetic all at once.

Mortified, he buttoned himself back up and stared aghast at his ruined jeans

"Shit man! I'm going to have to leave and sort this mess out."

"Okay, Piet. You should go!" Marge agreed and no longer cared if she never laid eyes on him again; she released a long sigh of relief and Piet, not being entirely with events, took it as her dismay over the mess they made.

"Sorry Marge, I got eh—carried away a bit, I think?"

"Don't worry, Piet. It's okay. It's not that. You go. Go, change, wash, and come back later: our little secret, Piet, yah? I'll clear this up in a minute. Really. Go!" Ushering him out, she watched as he scurried his massive frame along the hallway and out the front door.

Returning her gaze once more to the kitchen, Marge laughed aloud. In moments the smashed glass was bagged and hidden in the depths of her bin; the small amount of spilt wine she mopped quickly; her missing knickers, almost forgotten, she removed from her tea-towel drawer and slipped them back on, before removing another bottle from the chill rack. Uncorked, she grinned from ear to ear at her reflection for what felt was the first time in ages. Marge poured another large glass and savoured a long, cooling, thirst-quenching draw.

On a large serving plate from the cupboard, she scattered a bag of mixed salad leaf from the fridge, before knocking back the end of her wine. Planning to prep her cold salad of potatoes, beets, fig, feta, mixed leaf and puy lentils, with a drizzle of lime dressing, Marge instead sat in her kitchen reading-chair and fell asleep—she didn't wake until hearing Geoffrey come through the front door, just before three.

Two of the guests were moments behind, and Piet arrived shortly after with his sheep, apologising for the delay, and his perceived disruption to everyone's day. Taking some three and a half hours to cook, the novelty of a full sheep became the focus, and everyone was sozzled by the time food was served.

Lying in bed that night with his glasses slid along his nose, blankly staring at pictures of the recent boat show, Geoffrey's gaze lifted to Marge's grumbling groans as she dropped her dress to the floor and wearily bent over to pick it up after kicking it forwards.

Two massive dirty hand prints waved at him from her arse cheeks as she angled over.

Looking back at the boats, Geoffrey's nose scrunched in anger. No more garden contracts for that big oaf he thought. No more. Might have to divorce Marge too Geoffrey thought, his mind an indignant drunken swirl.

Bloody bloody women!

Whatever happened to loyalty, Geoffrey wondered.

His magazine slipped from his fingers, and dropped quietly to the floor.

In moments, Geoffrey was asleep.

***

Three Barbecue Salads Recipes

1. Coleslaw Recipe

A simple and easy to make plate filler that always goes down well. Adjust the mayo to your own preferences … five spoons is pretty rich.

Ingredients

2 carrots, coarse grated
1 large pickled beetroot
1/2 small white or red cabbage, sliced and chopped
1/2 fennel thinly sliced
1 medium red onion finely chopped
1 handful of raisins
5 heaped tablespoons of mayonnaise
1 teaspoon of coarse grain mustard
several good splashes of rapeseed oil
salt & cracked pepper

Making the Coleslaw

Grate the carrots and beetroot, coarse chop the cabbage, thinly slice the onion and fennel, mix it all in a large bowl with the raisins, throw the mayonnaise, mustard, oil and seasoning in. Mix it all together for thirty seconds. Done.

2. Feta & Figs Salad Recipe

This is also a simple to make dish that is both tasty and filling. It also presents well and when you're doing a spread that's often half the battle.

Ingredients

100g of washed mixed salad leaf
300g of charlotte/waxy potatoes (boiled, cooled and sliced)
2 large beef tomatoes (sliced)
4 cooked pickled beets (sliced)
1/4 cucumber cubed and salted
100g of puy lentils (washed and boiled for 12 minutes then cooled under a cold tap)
1 pomegranate (pips only)
200g feta cheese cubed
4 fresh figs, topped tailed and quartered

Dressing
A good dollop of olive oil, 1 lime (juice only), tablespoon chilli sauce,
cracked pepper—all mixed together with a fork

Making Feta & Fig Salad
Spread the leaf on a large rectangular serving plate bunching it towards the middle. Surround it with an ellipse of sliced potatoes, sliced beets, tomatoes and cucumbers. Add the chopped figs to the centre with the feta cheese. Scatter the puy lentils and pomegranate pips across the lot.
Drizzle the dressing in a crazy up and down graph fashion.

3. Mediterranean Couscous Recipe

This dish often happens as a time filler for me. Most of the dish comes together whilst you're waiting on other things. The couscous itself is only a simple boiling of the kettle, and everything with the exception of the aubergine just pops into the oven and can be deemed as ready after half an hour, or an hour if you need more time for other things. The aubergine can also be oven baked if you're struggling for space on top. Cover it though, or it dries out a bit. If you're not sure on the numbers you've got turning up, pad it out with more couscous.

Ingredients

150g couscous
2 aubergines (cross sliced and salted before anything else is done)
200g chestnut mushrooms, wiped and quartered.
12 medium plum tomatoes
4 garlic cloves crushed and chopped with salt to a paste
4 garlic cloves peeled and halved
oil and butter

Making Mediterranean Couscous

To prepare the couscous, put about 6-8mm of salted boiling water in a pot (six-inch pot). Pour in couscous making sure that it is just covered by the water. Put a lid on the pot and put it aside to allow the couscous to swell. It's ready after six or seven minutes, but if you allow fifteen and then add a good splash of olive oil or rapeseed oil, it eliminates the chance that some of the water hasn't been absorbed.

Halve the tomatoes and remove the seeds. Open side facing up, place in an oiled Pyrex or suitable oven dish, season with salt and pepper, add four of the half cloves and put in a hot oven for half an hour, middle shelf at 180.

Put all the mushrooms with the remaining four garlic halves in a Pyrex dish with a small blob of butter. Season with oregano. Cover with foil and put in the oven next to the tomatoes for half an hour.

Rinse the salt from the aubergine, and rub the garlic paste onto both sides. Using a heavy based wide pan fry gently. Once browned on both sides, quarter each slice.

Add everything to the couscous pot and stir together before spreading it all on a long serving plate. Scatter fresh torn basil and sprinkle some olive oil across it, and it's ready to tuck into.

***

Motherly Love

MARIA PETRAS WAS NOT A FAN OF THE
morning. Her sleeping pattern changed sometime
shortly after the menopause, and it had never come
right again. Ten years on, Maria felt she was now
always tired, a bit on edge, and a little at odds with
the world at large. Standing in the kitchen of her
narrow terraced house, in the middle of Shepherds
Bush in West London, the midday November sun
glared through her back windows revealing to Maria
the dirt and smudges all over them. It irked her,
and, for no reason Maria could think of, reminded
her of her daughter's new husband who'd
accompanied her on all of her recent visits. He
hadn't done that before they were married, and
she'd always looked forward to seeing her daughter,
and imparting her advice and hard-earned
knowledge to her. That was now stolen from her,
and her daughter's new husband seemed to be on
her mind a lot these days.

It bothered her.

"I really, really don't know what she sees in
him," Maria spoke the words aloud as she stood
beside her kitchen table watching her husband.

Chris wasn't particularly listening and made a
noncommittal sound that Maria had long learned to
recognise.

"CHRIS!" Maria never liked to be ignored and
had found that most men went out of their way to
appease a shouting woman. "Am 'I' to be the only

one in this family who cares about our children and their futures?"

Recognising the tone, and inching slowly on his hands and knees, Chris backed out across the kitchen floor from beneath the sink where he'd been working.

Saying nothing as she watched her husband's skinny legs and behind nudge their way back towards her, Maria folded her arms, and shunted her sleeve ends beyond her elbows in a business-like manner. Tilting her head slightly while waiting, she looked down the length of her long nose to meet his look when he turned.

"I'm fixing the bloody sink, you crazy old bat! You want me to fix this thing? You want me to fix this thing or not?" Chris barked back, as his head slowly emerged and before he looked up; he changed his mind when he met her eyes and saw the folded arms. Clearing his throat, he retreated forward beneath the sink once more—little good ever came out of arguing with a folded-arm, tilted-head, Maria.

"I just said, I really don't know what she sees in him," Maria repeated her thought in a more conversational tone, satisfied she'd be given a hearing.

Chris shook his out of sight head slowly and carefully to avoid the piping beneath the sink.

"So! You really don't know what she sees in him! SO WHAT? You didn't have to marry him! You don't have to live with him! And correct me here! Correct me here, Maria," Chris reversed slowly once more, but stopped before coming into the open. "SHE! Yes? She! More important than you or me. No? SHE! Not a murmur! Two years married and not a—not a dicky bird, as she would say herself?"

"I'm just saying-," having made two efforts to butt in as Chris spoke, Maria got her tuppence worth in and interrupted him.

"Yes!" Chris cut back. "You've been 'JUST' saying it since they got together, ten years ago at University already! The boy has a Masters thing, Maria! A Masters! That earns him some respect from me, no matter what you say. I've told you before, he's the only person I've ever met, never mind being related to, that has one of those. If I'm not wrong, it's no different for you."

Sniffing, Maria tweaked at the end of her nose and took her gaze out of the kitchen window; always surrounded by idiots, she thought—all of them, always men!

Chris continued his twiddling beneath the sink. Trying to turn off the connecting valve to the mains for the outside tap and hosepipe, it had taken forty minutes just to find the valve he was after. Winter had seemed a long way off a couple of weeks back, but sitting in his car the previous morning before setting off for the doctor's, the heating system had failed to remove the thick frost layer, and Chris was forced into his first scraping of the season. Why he hadn't left the gloves in the car, and why he never had any de-icing spray, Chris knew was due to Maria's obsessive tidiness with everything. Heaven forbid he should bring that up.

"Why the hell, Christ," his frustrated grumblings were amplified by the acoustics of the cupboard. "Why do bloody plumbers insist on putting these things in such impossible positions? I mean! I need a two-inch screwdriver, and a bloody rubber wrist to get to this thing."

"CHRIS," swearing of any sort was intolerable, under any circumstances, for Maria. Probably another reason she had such a problem with her son-in-law, Chris thought.

"Ratchet!" In a moment of clarity and remembrance, Chris exclaimed the word aloud triumphantly. "Ratchet!"

"WHAT! WHAT RAT-SHIT? Where? Let me see!" Chris felt a frantic panic-patting on his leg.

"What? Let you see what? Rat-shit? No! I said 'ratchet'." Chris laughed aloud at her fretting as he raised his head.

"Oh my heart," Maria fanned herself with a tea-towel. "That's all we need now. Rats all over the house."

"Oh stop it, you old drama queen," Chris dismissed Maria's nonsense. "I need to get the tool bag again—where? Will you stop putting things away when I'm still using them. What have you done with my tool bag that was on the table?"

"I never touched it," Maria lied, and looked in her cutlery drawer as though she'd been busy at something. "You men leave things lying about everywhere for us to trip over, and break our necks on. You have no consideration."

Shaking his head at her, Chris slid fully out and stood up to go to the hallway; in the cupboard, beneath the stairs, his tool bag was where he'd taken it from an hour earlier. Releasing air between his teeth in a slow sigh, he returned to the kitchen and rummaged in the bag until he found the ratchet and fittings he needed; he said nothing—some men instinctively know when it's not worth commenting.

"What am I supposed to do for tomorrow?" Chris's head had disappeared once more beneath the sink when her words echoed down the plug-hole to him.

Ignoring the question, he concentrated on getting the fitting to slot home, and then his mind tried to figure out anti-clockwise while he lay in a semi-upside down position. In the end it was the only way the valve would go that he turned it, and, satisfied that it was done, he eased out once more and opened the back door to run the tap and double check it was off. Water dripped for a couple of seconds and stopped.

"Job done," Chris nodded to the back garden and went back inside, pleased with himself; unwittingly conditioned in Pavlovian fashion over the decades, he mused what reward he might treat himself with for having successfully completed his task.

With the tool bag in hand, Maria looked about to see if anything needed picking up; she looked at him disdainfully as though he'd left a mess. Ignoring the look, he took the bag from her and replaced the ratchet and screwdrivers he'd removed earlier before returning it to the stair cupboard. When he came back, Maria was looking tentatively beneath the sink; she scrutinised the surface before replacing her bleach bottles and sponges.

"I told you it was 'ratchet' I said, Maria— ratchet, the tool! You're looking in there, and you still have bloody rat-shit on your mind. Yeah?" The tips of his fingers tapped at his temples as he spoke.

"Don't be so ridiculous," Maria dismissed his accusation out-of-hand with a limp flicking gesture.

"And stop swearing at me! I'm just looking to see if you made a mess as usual."

"I'm making myself a cup of tea," Chris tilted his head towards her and waited for an acknowledgement before speaking; he didn't want to spoil his good mood after fixing the valve. "Do you want one?"

"No. I'm going to cook something, so don't make a mess there too," Maria gestured to the area about the kettle and warned him.

Dipping his chocolate digestive into his tea, Chris allowed it to dissolve and collapse into his mouth, as he had when he was a child. Seated opposite at the kitchen table, Maria began chopping a couple of red onions and muttered away to herself. Chris wondered when she'd started doing this so much. His raven-haired beauty, with a mesmerising sway to her hips and pert bosoms; her broad cheeky smile was now buried beneath layers of oversized cardigans and tee-shirts that used to belong to him, and her lovely laughing face was set in an old scowl of permanent disapproval; a faint moustache, just like her mother had, was no longer being so diligently removed, and was gradually becoming a permanent feature on her face. When had it all happened, and how had they not noticed, he wondered. Releasing a sigh, Maria looked up at him and away from her onions.

"What's got into you?" Her enquiry took him by surprise.

Looking at his wife, for a moment he thought about telling her his thoughts, but decided to leave it.

"Nothing," eventually responding, Chris rubbed his eyes to shift the conversation away from any deeper enquiry about his thoughts. "I guess I'm still a bit tired, or something.

"You're always tired," huffing a dismissal at him, Maria shook her head. "You're old. We're old. We're always tired."

"And always a bundle of laughs," Chris countered her comment with the hope of lightening their mood.

"That too!" For a while, they both chuckled, and Maria chopped three cloves of garlic next to the onions as her head continued to bob up and down.

"Do you like him?" Maria probed, using her large knife to create two separate piles as she spoke.

"Oh not that again," Chris moaned and waved both of his hands in a plea to be left alone. "I don't care either way for God's sake! He's a lad, just a boy to me. I mean—he lives in a different world to us for a start. When he does come with Sasha to visit, you can see it in his eyes that he's lost as to what to do; he doesn't know where to put himself. In this little house, there's nowhere for him to hide."

"Why should he hide?" Maria swivelled her hands out and back with her elbows tucked at her sides. "From who-?"

"From you! His mother-in-law! You frighten the life out of the poor fellow. Watching him like a hawk from the moment he sits down … he's not used to that," answering her, Chris realised he was pushing the conversation back onto marshy ground, and an inner voice began to advise him to shut up.

"Not used to being watched," Maria rose and went to the cupboards, tutting and thinking as she tottered across the tiles. "He's in my house. Of course I watch him. Removing two tins of chopped tomatoes, a bag of bulgur wheat and a tube of tomato puree, she turned her look back to her husband. "If I don't watch him, you and Sasha tell me I'm ignoring him?"

"You know what I mean," Chris picked the easy to remove lids from the tomato tins she handed him. "There's watching, and there's 'WATCHING'. You do the kind of 'WATCHING' that would unsettle a blind man, let alone a nervous young lad."

"What's he so nervous about?" Maria tapped her nose. "That's what I'd like to know."

"Oh for crying out loud!" In despair with the nonsense of his wife, Chris rose to get some milk from the fridge to break the flow of their talk.

"Bring me the Haloumi," instructing him quietly, he picked out the bowl of water with the Haloumi block and passed it to her before sitting back down.

Maria's eyes remained on him as he did so and she sucked a nasally sighing breath.

Such a handsome, tall man once, she thought. Broad shoulders, and slim hips, and nobody, nobody had ever danced a more graceful hasapiko that she had ever witnessed. Even now at weddings, friends still remarked after all these years. No longer much taller than her now, those snake hips she used to dream about she hadn't seen for near forty years, covered as they'd been with rolls of fat hanging over his belt, both front and back. The weight had somehow never gone to his backside or legs, other than his calf muscles which had naturally strengthened to carry his bulk around. Even most of that weight was gone now, and sometimes it felt as though her Chris was slowly shrinking, and fading away before her eyes.

Slipping the smaller frying pan on the heat, Maria added a splash of olive oil, removed the block of Haloumi and cut a large chunk; she stirred the sauce too, and her mind drifted over the years they'd been together. Time seemed suspended as she stood there with the wooden spoon in her hand, lost in her thoughts as the sauce reduced; she felt a small tear well in the corner of her eye before smelling the air and thinking something was burning. The Haloumi was browning and putting a lid on the sauce, she turned off the heat and set it aside before flipping the cheese. It must've been a splash of something, she thought.

"Cut us both some bread," she removed two large bowls from the cupboard, knowing Chris heard her and would act upon it. Chris always liked a piece of bread in the middle of the day. "And get some yoghurt from the fridge, and put some in this."

She passed him a small bowl as he shuffled by her.

Instinctively doing as he was asked, Chris put away his cup in the dishwasher but left his side plate for his upcoming Haloumi. Scooping two large dollops of Greek yoghurt into the bowl, he also picked some cutlery for them both, placing it with the bread knife on the wooden board as he came back to his seat. Cutting a couple of thick slices, he buttered them as Maria put the bowls of pourgouri in front of each set place, and slid a few chunks of Haloumi from the pan onto the side plates mumbling to herself all the while as she did so. Picking off a farmer's cut of bread, Chris sat down with a sigh and a smile, and looked at his wife once more before nodding his assent for her frozen form to release whatever it was she wished to say.

"So what do you think 'she' sees in him then?" Maria asked as Chris forked and mixed a squeaking of Haloumi in with the bread he was chewing.

***

Pourgouri Recipe

Ingredients
2 medium red onions, fine chopped
4 large garlic cloves, crushed with some salt
14 medium tomatoes roughly chopped
(or 2 tins of chopped tomatoes)
1 cup of bulgur wheat
3 vermicelli bunches (fides) or about 36 spaghetti
lengths broken into pieces
tomato puree, about four good squirts.
1 cup of water

Pourgouri is a wonderfully simple Cypriot dish that can accompany a meal of meats, cheese, salad and bread, or on its own as just a simple side for an easy lunch. It's one of the simplest dishes to make, and it doesn't seem to matter what age group sits to eat it, nothing ever gets left and the bread ensures the plates are wiped near clean. I don't know why, but this is a dish I seem to prefer with tinned tomatoes and puree. It's the way the Cypriots that I've encountered do it, and there's something homely about it—it's a dish without fuss!

Cooking

Add olive oil and a little butter to a wide and deep heavy bottomed pan. Add the onions once it's hot and sweat them for a few minutes. Add the garlic and stir in. Break the vermicelli fides into the pan and stir this in too. Move the vermicelli around for a couple of minutes and then add the cup of bulgur wheat, giving this a good stir for a minute once more to ensure it absorbs the garlic oil. Now add the tomatoes and press-stir them in with a spoon to encourage them to release their liquid (not necessary if you're using tinned). Allow the heat to build for a couple of minutes. Add the tomato puree (and a few twists of black pepper if there's some handy. If it feels like there's plenty of liquid don't worry too much about adding more, but if it's not runny at this stage add splashes of the water to keep it runny. Cook for about six or seven minutes on a low heat with the lid on the pan. After that, take it off the heat and set it aside for ten minutes to allow the bulgur wheat to swell and absorb most of the moisture.

Always good served with a nice piece of grilled haloumi and a chunky cut of bread. A light bodied and slightly chilled red wine goes down well too, or a Keo beer on a sunny day.

***

The Brief Love of Peter and Amata

Peter Hardy is regarded by many ladies as the best looking man in Dungarvan. He's a tall fellow with slightly sallow skin, which is blemish free and without a visible wrinkle despite him being in his early thirties. That, though young sounding, for us here in Dungarvan, such an absence of skin corrugation is extremely unusual. Tucked on the southern Irish coast with a wide and occasionally tranquil bay, the waters around here reflect and enhance an often low-lying sun and bounce a glare that would enable a masked welder to walk about, confident of his step; most people, of all ages, habitually squint in our over-bright sunlight, and such squinting embeds the wrinkly folds common in most of us. In the sun's absence on a more turbulent day, with the cutting wind off the sea, or the biting rain from the Comeragh hills—and that's on the rare occasions the two don't coincide— people still have to squint, even when wincing, and tend to favour one eye over the other. After twenty odd years, both the bright and the inclement weather have their say on the face we present to the world.

Peter's eyes are also unusually dark. These depthless orbs absorb the bright light without the need for Popeye contortions the rest of us have to gurn to get about—they're also alluringly dark for an area where blue-green or stony-grey is the norm, and this cloaks him with a Heathcliff-like aura— which is perhaps another reason the ladies think him particularly attractive—those mysterious eyes, and maybe the thick shock of jet-black unkempt hair atop his head that seems to have a life of its own, and to change as fashions change, without Peter ever having to do anything different to it—somehow it all seems to come together.

Peter often looks a little forlorn, or like a man lost, and in need of company. Keeping their distance and preferring to look from afar and admire the view, it's rare to see him in conversation, or even in the company of a woman. Some, rumour has it, some suggest that perhaps he is just 'too' good looking, and several of the ladies feel they couldn't trust themselves about him. More perhaps feel that they wouldn't be able to trust others around him, or even the man himself, and they just don't want the hassle that comes with such an attractive mate. Of course, as is the way of things today, a few suggest that he's gay—this, in part, is because of him being a nurse, and a caring sort of man, and the same people still having those ideas about gender roles, but rumours and smoke being what they are, they proceed to posit he may not be drawn to the ladies at all, and ladies being as they are, more sensitive, and better attuned to the subtler aspects of body language have picked up on this, and so, leave him be. Oddly enough, all have left him be, and now in his late twenties, Peter has not yet shared sheets with a Dungarvan lady. It's nonsense about him being gay, as any sane man who knows him could tell you, and even if he were gay, he'd more likely be surrounded by all sorts of women, catching up on events in his world, advising, cajoling, contradicting, managing, or steering his existence into a more sociable and sexually active pattern than is apparent in his life today. Coincidentally, the only ones to suggest his sexual bent to be other than the approved catholic run-of-the-mill norm, are, of course, other straight men competing for scarce resources.

Peter has retained the same slim waist size he had at twenty-one—an annoying in-between size of thirty-one—and other than a broadening of his shoulders, a subtle increase in strength, and an overall solidifying of his not inconsiderable physique, as he's become the young man he now is, not much else has changed about him to look at. If anything, the ladies of Dungarvan regard him as an altogether better specimen than he was back then. Of course, that could be down to the deterioration of his peers—those visual competitors, or alternative eye candy, so to speak—most of whom are now engaged, married, separated, overworked, overweight, unemployed, skint, or gone away altogether, leaving him alone in the young and 'untaken' aisle, except for the usual dregs that get left in all communities. If you don't know who they are in yours, are young, and don't have somebody with you, or any sign of somebody, well, get yourself a looking-glass, a mirror as we now call them, and there you go. Dregs! I'm sorry if you've had to find out this way, but knowledge ultimately is power, and so now, you have the power to do something about it.

Peter has a favoured spot for swimming in the vast bay we enjoy here in Dungarvan, and privacy for most is not a difficult thing to find in an inlet of a few miles in width. With a small population only ever using the water at best, Peter still rarely changes or swims unobserved. After a swim, if the weather is warm enough, and he's not required back at the clinic, he lies on his towel and reads. Over the past few years, it's become a favoured spot for many people to read.

Peter, over his short life thus far, has always found solace in literature; having so much time to himself, and nothing in truth to distract him otherwise, he's worked his way through the Russian greats—you know the ones: Pushkin, Chekhov, Tolstoy, Dostoevsky, Turgenev, the whole way through to wrist-slitting Sholokov and beyond. Most of the American canon also got a peep, and Peter could never decide whether he favoured Twain over Hawthorne, or Maddox Ford over both, or Steinbeck and Hemingway over them all, but he knew he wasn't a great fan of Stein, no matter how smart her endlessly looping sentences were purported to be, and Virginia Woolf left him completely cold and almost turned off with life. He did like Morrison and Carol-Oates, and even Du Bois, so at least he knew he wasn't being misogynistic, or racist, in his thinking, yet he gave up on Baldwin half-way through his first read of him, and went in search of his own mountain. Malamud had him looking at his wrists once more. French existentialists got a couple of winters from his search for meaning or purpose in life, but although he found Camus held him for a while, Sartre put him asleep, even after coffee—an achievement, considering his restless legs problem after caffeine. German and Scandinavian classics, that result in most people giving up the pursuit of knowledge, as the bliss of ignorance suddenly seems so much brighter than the weighty miserable burden of wisdom offered by them, even they made their way on to his shelves. Other than a maxims and nonsense collection from a delirious, but noted German, no others remained there after his last clear out. All that was after he finished with the works closer to home too, and the usual English speaking, or English writing, suspects.

Peter bought himself an e-Reader a short while back, and since then has spent most of his time reading erotic fiction and romance stories; unable to maintain the concentration for the denser books any longer, as he thinks of them, he now likes the frivolous racy nature of the erotic prose, if that was what it was. It makes him smile and dream of a happier world with a place for him in it.

Peter doesn't care about whether or not it is prose, other than a slightly obsessive compulsion to categorise most things, but he knows it's now unlikely he'll ever go back to the dark depths of serious literature again. Realising he's more or less forgotten or fused everything he's read in one way or another, he still senses his head is technically awash with all sorts of wonderful knowledge and information, but his brain seems to have switched off his instant access key, so when he does try to remember something, preferably relevant, or significant—in a lively conversation for example—by the time he does, everything is further along, his point is out of context if he makes it, and he's generally lost as to where things have progressed to.

Peter is hooked on love. Endlessly day-dreaming, romantic fiction has gripped him by his under-used balls; he spends most of his spare time in Ormond's coffee shop, reading and dreaming. He's waiting for her, whoever she might be, waiting for love to arrive and sweep him off his feet with her devastating otherness and her certainty in knowing what she wants when she sees it—even if he isn't in the billionaire's club, and doesn't have stud horses, or yachts—she'll know it's him, only him, she wants. She won't be from Dungarvan, that, he's now certain of, for as far as he can tell nobody here knows anything about love, and none of them is interested in him in any romantic way.

Peter no longer carries his opinions on his sleeve. That isn't the type of fellow he is anymore; he never seeks to lord it over others with his thinking, that just isn't his way either, at least now. Mostly, if he is in company, he's a listener, a bloody good listener too, and aware of how irritating men find advice—knowing most things better as they invariably do—he rarely offers any, anymore. Men don't go out of their way to avoid him as such, but neither do many of them go out of their way to involve him too much in their events, or their occasional forays into the town. A candle looks all the duller if put next to a bonfire, and even a fool playing a percentage game of chance with ladies realises he must seem like the best option if he's to have any chance of a score—next to him, many of the Dungarvan men look as though they have just scraped through the evolutionary process by the hairs on their overlarge knuckles, only to exist in the same time frame. If out on the town for the night to pull, even his closer friends tend to steer clear of Peter Hardy.

§

Amata Fernandez finally decided that she absolutely hated her parents; this wasn't something she said aloud, or to her parents, but more something growled to herself, especially in the mirror, and something she'd furiously written in her ever-expanding diary. They'd made their choice without any consideration for her, her feelings, her life, her ambitions, her desires, her future career, or even the smallest amount of her happiness! They couldn't have considered anything about her. It was evident to her; her opinions, her feelings, or anything about her life meant nothing to them—absolutely nothing too!

 Amata and her family had just arrived in this hell-hole weird nowhere place a week previously, with no phone line, no internet, no television, no Radio Four, no anything 'cultural' that she could see, or even any proper shops she recognised, and neither of her parents seemed in any hurry either to get, or sort out, anything that would make her life easier. Other than telling her to 'shut up moaning', neither of them had spoken much to her at all. They were busy! Busy! With their new jobs, or their new 'busyness', as they called it, and laughed. Hilarious! Idiots! Buying into 'the surgery' as partners, they were in the process of familiarising themselves with the 'nuances of the practice' and the Irish way of doing things, so they had no time for the silly whimperings of a girl who should know better. Typical! Now a 'silly whimpering girl' was she! Deciding to unload Amata opened her laptop to tell her friend Annabelle—she wouldn't be able to send it now of course, but at least she could compose it, and once she was forced to go in to spend some time in this rural backwater village nowhere-place, at least she'd have something to do. Annabelle would understand. She always did, and she always took her friend's side. Only a week, but she missed Annabelle and everything about their former Greenford home.

Amata had no memory of Goa where she was born. Apparently she was back there when five, and again also when she was ten and her grandparents were still alive—or her mother's parents at least (she never met her other grandparents—they disowned her father in that odd way Indians often do after he married her mother, and now they had no contact with them at all), but whatever, Amata had no real memory of anything significant that happened on either of those visits. Sun, colours, animals, noise, dirt, stinky smells, and the long boat-ride from Bombay to Panjim a little bit, but nothing of real substance of when she was there, or anything about the 'beaches'; she must have been too young she always thought.

Amata was English now, having lived in Greenford most of her life. Once, she went to Spain with Annabelle, her only other trip abroad, and that was for her eighteenth birthday. It was major dramas to get permission for that too until they both agreed on a compromise: Annabelle's brother James was 'volunteered' to be their chaperone! To keep 'her' safe. Such humiliation—even then her parents rode roughshod over her feelings! Annabelle was mortified too, and then Annabelle's parents took a leaf from her parents and warned James about looking out for his sister. Solemnly promising to watch over them as though he was

Lancelot Du Lac—what an ugly liar! Boys just can't be trusted. James disappeared almost the moment the plane hit the ground and wasn't even on the courtesy bus to the hotel; he got drunk out of his head every night, and he still came back with a different English or Welsh girl and then proceeded to have loud sex in his room. Loud! Really loud, in a cursing and swearing loud way! You know—Oh F-! Oh F-! Oh F-! It sounded like he was trying to knock down the wall. Every night! It was so gross and so crude! It was all so wrong. Just so wrong! The girls were never there in the morning, and there was never even a sign of them, or that they'd been there, other than the smell of cheap perfume and cigarettes, or some weird stuff. Most of the time it was just a naked, pink and hairy James on the bed sleeping off a hangover when she looked in. Everything was just hanging there. All of it. ALL of it! Amata suspected James wasn't even asleep sometimes. Also, he never went to the beach, not even once! All his energy was saved for the pool, and nights of drinking, and meaningless drunk sex.

Amata quivered at the memory and opened her laptop.

Amata didn't remember being to the beach in Goa, any beach, or any beach party, which is what everyone expected her to remember, and annoyingly always asked her about, before telling her where they'd been, as though she'd memorised the entire place in two visits. She was only ten then too! Her mother came from a little village called Vazem, inland from a town called Margao, which was one of the main towns in Goa, but nobody in England seemed to know it.

Amata remembered banana trees, rows of coconut trees, and a small brown hut-style house her grandparents lived in, oh, and weird little dogs with big heads everywhere, barking all night long too. And monkeys. Monkeys! Amata remembered monkeys; once she'd liked monkeys, but now was frightened of them, and even hated them. Grandmother told her they stole and ate babies if you didn't watch them, but she wasn't sure if that was true; she wasn't sure if it wasn't either, and a vague memory of a red-raw looking large grey-furred monkey at a window being shooed away by her grandmother with a twig broom sometimes woke her at night; she was never entirely sure if that was real, or something her mind conjured from her grandmother's warnings, but whatever, it only re-enforced her dislike and fear of the creatures. Grandfather worked in the bank she was told; her memory of him suggested he wasn't a banker, but just did some job that happened to be in a bank. He wore a 'lungi', which wasn't really anything—it was a bit like a skirt, or a man-sarong thing—just a piece of cloth wrapped around his waist that covered his knees and he had to keep fixing it because there were no buttons or anything. Sometimes, he wore a shirt too, but mostly just a vest. Her mother adored him and always tried to impress upon her how much he'd sacrificed to make sure she would get her education and achieve the things she had. Achieve the things she had! A dentist! I mean, what kind of achievement is that? It's just another job. A dentist, a bank manager, a pilot, a doctor, a vet, an accountant, all of them are just jobs! Why did they make such a big deal out of having jobs in dentistry? Why couldn't they just have jobs like everyone else?

Achievements! That's what they had! Never jobs! No! Always 'achievements'! Annabelle's father was a solicitor, and he never mentioned it. Just a solicitor; she never heard some huge back-story about his struggle against the inhumanity of people, and his decision to save them all by running a practice that dealt mainly with conveyancing or wills. But no! Grandfather's constant sourcing of candles and kerosene, how long he saved so his daughter could go to college, and then her own mother's years in college, where she had to live in a shanty town as there wasn't enough money to live anywhere else—that was always followed by how she'd met her love, Amata's father, their falling hopelessly in love like Romeo and Juliet, and how their love meant the sacrifice of his relationship with his parents! That's what she got. If she ever had to hear it all again, she would burn whatever house they lived in down to the ground!

Amata left the house in a huff that morning, and went to look about the town; she didn't go to explore, but she exited the house in a dramatic fashion to make a point, and left without saying goodbye, or closing the front door, or even telling them of her plans. Her parents had apparently both gone to work after her abrupt departure—there hadn't been a peep from them all day, despite her phone being fully charged, with a signal too, and when they finally did get home after seven o clock her mother was livid that she hadn't prepared some food for all of them. Livid with her, like she was some housemaid for them both. Storming out again, she was back in this nothing town with no idea what to do, no money to do it, and at least two hours to kill if she was to save face, and by then it would probably be dark too!

Amata decided to have a look at the bay again, as at least she wouldn't need money that she didn't have there, and if she walked from one side to the other and back, much of the time she needed to kill would be done by the time she got back.

Amata watched a seagull alight on a bollard a small distance before her; it eyed her in what she felt was an evil and threatening manner. With large black wings, it was much bigger than she imagined seagulls ever to be; her footsteps veered away from it and crossed the road to avoid any nightmarish confrontation. What would she do if a seagull attacked her? What do you do if a seagull suddenly attacks you? Do seagulls attack people? Sure she'd read something somewhere, it rose when she was halfway across, keowed loudly, and seemed to be screaming 'No' loudly too when directly above her head, as though shouting at her. Fearful of being shat upon, Amata stopped in the middle of the road and watched it warily.

Peter Hardy, having left Ormond's coffee shop, with the intention of grabbing some salmon from Helvic Seafood, to go with his pearl barley medley, meandered to Davitt's Quay where he'd earlier locked his bicycle. With no shift or house visits that evening, Peter looked forward to an early night. Rounding the corner, he froze; a vision of beauty that sung of faraway spices, colours, erotic creatures, music, romantic love, and all the things missing from his life, began to cross the road as though utterly unfamiliar with the mundane world of traffic and mortality. Inexplicably she stopped in the middle, and watching on he sensed more than saw

the oncoming blurry van. He screamed 'Nooooooo!'
as his mind took it all in.

Amata stood stock-still, watching the gull.
Michael Flahavan, oblivious to her having halted,
where she had, finished his text and looked up just
in time to see her head wallop against his van's
windscreen. Braking belatedly, bewildered at what
just happened, the colourfully dressed limp body
continued its journey a further fifteen feet from his
van before it slapped and scraped off the road
surface, coming to a stop in a crumpled broken-
marionette heap.

Peter, at her side in seconds as she moved to
somehow straighten her crumbled body, believed at
first she was dead for sure; he heard her squeak
and felt her wince in pain as his hands held her
gently to steady and stop her movements, and he
whispered to her all the while as he tried to comfort
her and keep her calm.

Amata, in her shock and pain, having broken
her leg, wrist, and her collarbone, as well as a
monstrous bruise swelling rapidly across her entire
face and forehead felt cold all over and trembled;
she sought what tiny comfort she could and allowed
herself to be held in the comforting arms and
reassured by the soft whispering voice. Amata
opened her spinning eyes to gaze up at the most
beautiful man she had ever seen or dreamt of. For
the briefest of moments, their eyes beheld each
other.

Amata Fernandez, moments later, passed out
of this world.

***

Recipe for Pearl Barley Medley

Pearl barley, similar in many ways to rice, is used for a North Italian dish much less well known than its southern cousin. Orzotto, as opposed to Risotto, is where the barley replaces the rice, but little else is changed. The dish here is more of a fusion. Similar in idea to an Oriental 'rice and veg', the veg are roasted, rather than flash fried, and when served, the combination is compacted into a bowl style, to accompany a main dish, rather than being the dish itself—although it could easily be. I tend to serve this with a decent tri-colore salad (Mozarella, tomato, basil leaf), the freshness offsets that lovely sticky caramelised garlic.

Ingredients

200g of pearl barley, cook as per pack instructions (normally boil then simmer for 15 mins)

1 red onion, quartered and roasted
1 bulb of garlic, roasted
I red pepper, sliced and roasted before peeling
16 small cherry tomatoes roasted, or two vines with about 8 small tomatoes on each
1 courgette, cubed, and roasted
100g mushroom, sliced and sautéed to reduce liquid
Parmigiano shavings

Prepping

The dish is self-explanatory from above. The garlic bulb will be ready after half an hour in a medium oven. Remove the papery outer layer and pop in a bowl. Add the peeled roasted pepper, courgette and mushrooms, and then add the cooked pearl barley. Mix.

Using a circular shaper or a bowl, create the shape on the plate on top of a bed of rocket, and add two quarters of onion to the side of each. Add the tomatoes to the top.

Liberally sprinkle with sea-salt and coarse black pepper.

Shave 5 or 6 pieces from a block of Parmigiano on top, dress with a splash of olive oil and a light touch of balsamic vinegar.

***

The Show Must Go On

"One-two, one-two, one-two, one-two, one-two …
C'MON PICK IT UP!" Oscar urged the class through
the speakers as everybody struggled through the
last routine.

A combination of Spin, Pilates, Boxercise,
Aerobics and a bit of Yoga stretching, for the
participants it was exhausting and a bit beyond most
of them. Several failed to raise themselves from the
mats for the last set of star jumps and were lying
with cheeks to the floor with their eyes closed, in a
position Oscar had named 'lie and die'. Even the
warm down was tough in Oscar's class. When he
finally called time after a frantic minute, the
remaining jumpers also collapsed to the floor, filling
the air with groans, wheezing, and massive sighs of
relief now that the whole tortuous session was over.

"That's it everybody," Oscar's amplified voice
boomed across the room. "Everybody lie and die for
a few minutes."

Everyone complied. Oscar watched them and
the room clock for two minutes.

"Hug your knees gently and … hold for three
slow deep breaths," the room once more obeyed.
"Release, put your arms above your head and stick
your legs out to make a star shape—let it all
collapse and ... relax," Oscar checked his phone
and removed his wrap around wireless mic.

Scrolling the menu, he mentally visualised the
remaining classes and clients he had for the day.

After an early start, his afternoon was virtually free; he'd need to get a run in before going home, he thought decisively, otherwise, he'd be a fidget-arse and would struggle to stay still at this dinner thing tonight.

His girlfriend had arranged an evening for them. She worked a straight nine to five. Uncomplicated shit. Oscar didn't. Two evening appointments cancelled because of this! New clients too! Oscar wasn't over-pleased with her laying it on the line the way she had. They didn't see anyone anymore since they'd moved to Osterley, she complained, and had reminded him that the move had been his idea; reluctantly, he agreed to go out, but not before a couple of hours of shouting at each other.

§

Philip Winston undid his tie-knot and slid it from his neck; he removed his blue Hugo Boss shirt, and his cufflinks from Tyler and Tyler, and carefully hung his suit trousers from Ted Baker on a wooden hanger before lying them on the bed. Satisfied the creases were aligned, he then peeled off his Paul Smith socks, groaning with the effort of reaching his feet; shirt, tie, and trousers all went in the wardrobe—he lay both socks in the colour section of his laundry basket, and the cufflinks he dropped into the man-tray Jane had given him for his birthday. Catching himself in the mirror, he raised a sceptical eyebrow—that's what Jane called it, and he was trying to avoid adopting the phrase; indulging her with one of his warm smiles when he'd unwrapped it, with hand on heart, he had pretended to love it;

he liked the idea, but just not in the colour, shape, or brand, Jane had chosen. Shuddering at the thought of Jane's taste furnishing all of his accessories, he winked at himself, and half-turned.

"So what's he like? Or what are they like, should I say?" Jane's loud footsteps came into the room behind him.

Catching her partner posing in the middle of the room in his boxers, having put everything away, Jane put a hand on her hip and stopped.

"Nice look, honey," she suggested, gesturing a nod at the novelty shorts his mother had given him for Christmas again—four pairs that made it now— he only wore them when they were under pressure and weren't keeping on top of things like laundry. A suitcase and a separate toiletries bag, packed by him for the week ahead, sat on the floor in the middle of the bedroom.

"I don't know-?" Jane thought about his question. "I told you already I've never met 'him'. Lauren is desperate for an evening out, and he doesn't do the pub or the cinema. He likes sport, I know that, and Lauren has hinted that he's pretty fit. I just hope he's not one of those football types—you know? But that's all I know. You remember Lauren? She doesn't say much. I've only had her for a year, but I thought I should do something? You know what it's like."

"Not really, darling. I only met her once when I picked you up, that I can remember," Philip made a face at her in the mirror. "This doesn't sound like one of your better ideas—what, a pugilist thug and a mouse come to tea … what'll I make? A cheese salad with a can of Stella on the side? Something for everyone!"

"Don't!" Jane forced a laugh. "You did shop yesterday, yeah?"

"I shopped for us … or just for you this week," Philip hesitated before answering. "I was waiting for a few more pointers, but I got busy at work and, yeah-yeah-yeah! I know. But, in truth, I forgot you said about them coming over. It's not like they're exactly on our radar. Did they mention anything about food? Any likes or even dislikes, maybe?" Philip twizzled his wrists searching for some direction from Jane on her guests.

"Philip … I have no idea! I should have spoken to Lauren today, but you know what it's like when things kick off at my place," Jane scowled as she applied a new liner to her eyes that she hadn't used before—it was an office Christmas present, but from whom, she couldn't remember or care less— she knew she didn't need all these questions just for a simple dinner. Philip was the cook of their relationship, and the kitchen was a control zone for him. Having relinquished control everywhere else, he had to have something to do in the relationship; the furniture, the wall colours, the bedding, the lights, the carpet, and every knick-knack, picture, or candle anywhere in their flat had been chosen by Jane, despite Philip being able to buy them all at trade prices.

"I've got to get myself ready, Philip," Jane held his gaze with her slightly crazed half-lined eyeballs, and he backed down from his sniping remarks to turn away from her and make his way to the kitchen

"Great," Philip muttered to himself as he walked the four steps from the bedroom.

Through the reflection of the mirror, Jane watched him leave from the corner of her eye;

feeling extremely irritable after her day, she was also sore from her Friday morning session with one of the new new personal trainers, Darren, in the company's basement gym. His workout had been tough, and most of the afters had gone as she'd expected, but he took over too much for her in the end; recommended by her former colleague Sandra before the Frankfurt Office headhunted her, Jane was going to have to have words with him before any future sessions. Faced with the novelty of an unannounced Brazilian, she'd given it a shot, even though this was only their second time: the after-burn had left her uncomfortable all day. Also, he'd been way too rough and had bruised her back, pummelling her the way he did against the shower lever.

Working in the Human Resources department of a large recruitment firm, based in London's square mile known as 'The City', Jane had joined them some six years back; at the time she'd been content to piddle away anonymously at lower middle management. The company's designated mentor system worked on her—really worked on her—and at a late spring conference three years earlier something in her changed. Jane found ambition. She hadn't found talent yet, or achieved the salary to match her ambition, but she was now halfway to a proper career path.

With Philip for two years since her epiphany, they'd just bought the flat they now lived in—a one-bedroom affair, at the North Circular Road end of Chiswick, in West London, just beyond the station of Gunnersbury Park. Standing in the cube of space near the front door, which the estate agent creatively called the hallway, it was possible to reach a limb into every room in the flat without too much strain. After a year, the novelty and excitement of owning her own place had worn a bit thin for Jane, but not for Philip. Having decorated it for a second time, Jane was planning on trying to cash in on the latest property shunt; she'd lined up estate agents for valuations when Philip left for work the following day, knowing he'd be away for five days. She didn't work Saturdays or Sundays, but West London estate agents did.

It was 'showtime' for Philip, as he liked to call it. This was not anything particularly glamorous— 'showtime' was the Spring Fair at the National Exhibition Centre in Birmingham, where Philip would do a week's work as an agent for one of the exhibitors he'd been working with for some eight years. Working generally as an agent for several different companies, all of whom were exhibiting at the retail show, caveats in his own recruitment contracts allowed him to continue to solely represent his oldest client at the big shows. On these occasions he was granted a reasonable expenses allowance and stayed at a large hotel on site; this enabled him to eat, drink, and be merry, in the company of like-minded people. Doing about six shows of this calibre every year, as well as his travelling sales work, the two in Birmingham were the longest he was away from home.

He loved it. He loved them! He even loved Birmingham!

Jane, never having been to the shows, or Birmingham, or seen what it was all about for Philip, assumed it to be a longer version of her conference weekends, which provided her with similar expense benefits, and housed her in large corporate style hotels, also with people from the same industry, for the three or four days the events ran. Most of the time the conferences tended towards excruciatingly dull for her, with various power figures poorly delivering inspirational style speeches about mundane topics, all cleverly phrased in corporate speak, and there was often compulsory clapping to boot. Jane didn't mind the evenings though. Fidelity had never been her thing. Philip's demands on her were light, so any mishaps or passion blemishes could be hidden in the blankets of work-induced exhaustion when she returned to their bed.

Nothing planned, or jumping to mind yet, Philip went to the fridge knowing he'd find something that would work. Unhappy with Jane dumping on him like this, as there'd been no real discussion, or any proper request from her, Philip decided to do something he liked and not to worry about any peculiarities of Jane's friends. Removing a block of Haloumi cheese from the bowl, he also picked out a cucumber, some beets, a couple of figs, some potatoes he'd already cooked and sliced, a couple of carrots, and some seeds and lentils; these so-called fitness freaks didn't know healthy until it kicked them in the face, he thought to himself.

Having missed them at the Autumn Fair, he hadn't seen most of the NEC crowd since the earlier Harrogate Show, the previous July. Jane had been a bridesmaid for an old school-friend of hers in Montana, of all places—a school friend at thirty! Who keeps real school friends outside of FaceBook? Montana too! What a place that was! Libby, they called the town. Town! It was a village, no—a drive through housing estate! With a diner, of course, a grocery 'store' too, and a bar behind a petrol, no—a 'gas' station! You could still smell the 'gasoline' in the bar; it was like drinking in a garage pit. Why or how would anybody name a place Libby? Libby—wasn't that a girl's pet name? It took forever to get there too. There must have been at least three, no four—four plane changes! Then the car-hire, and the hotel on top. The whole thing had cost a fortune, as well as costing him his commission from his most lucrative show. And that, that wasn't all of it. Philip shook his head and quivered at the memories.

Creating four triangles of Haloumi, his thoughts mulled angrily over his forced visit to Libby. That was it! Asbestos! Asbestos—how could he have forgotten about the asbestos in Libby! The place was awash with the stuff apparently—it was all everybody spoke about there—even at the wedding! Oh, the wedding! Philip really didn't want to go there. No way José, he was not going to go there again, not even in his head! Not if they begged him! Some memories just have to be left disappear and die!

From the bedroom Jane's muffled swearing reached his ears; lying back on the bed she tried to put on a pair of jeggings she'd picked up in H&M the previous week—the size was what she wore, but the 'end of sale' queue at the fitting room had verged on being ridiculous, so Jane took the risk—and as she tugged upwards and tried to squeeze downwards at the same time the area around the zip gave. It took her another minute to get them off, by which time she was sweating, livid with the jeans and herself, and not really in the mood for anything. Throwing on an older dress from her wardrobe, she stomped into it, before making her way into the kitchen to find

Philip fussing with a new gadget and peeling ginger as though it were slithers of gold and he a cooking version of Rumplestiltskin.

"What do we have to drink?" A sharpness edged her tone as her hands fiddled with the reluctant zip behind her back; the dress felt as though it had shrunk slightly.

"Pinot ... and-?" Philip unwittingly opened to the fridge to list the options to Jane.

"Pinot," he concluded finally and turned to her. "Are you okay? You look a little red. Have you been bouncing on the bed in there?"

"What?" Jane's mood wasn't accommodating of frivolity. "No other options? Just Pinot!"

"It looks like it," Philip's reply came off a little defensively, and his emphasis was subtle. "Did 'you' pick up anything for 'your' friends?" Jane had changed and was now wearing a small, tight-fitting, vintage cocktail dress from Mary Quant. This was something Philip bought her a few years earlier, when they were pottering around Portobello Market one Friday—he couldn't help but think that it had fitted her better before she'd started her five o clock in the morning gym routine a year back and started muscling up.

The front door slammed loudly on her way out to the Off-Licence.

Shaking his head at the closed door, Philip returned to the fridge and tapped the top of the door as he looked in. With long thin piano playing fingers, shiny nails, and perfect sickle-moon filed cuticles Philip was also endowed with a prominent pointy nose he thought Romanesque. Thin lips too, and no earlobes on the bottom of his small ears, above which his hair graduated from a close shave to a longer, lightly highlighted floppy-locks look, that was parted a little off the left side; Philip spent a large portion of his life pushing it back in what he felt was an attractive, enigmatic fashion. Most people upon meeting him seemed to think he was a weight-conscious gay man. Aware of this, Philip believed that it was merely down to his grooming, and stylish clothing, with a tinge of envy, spicing their assumptions. Boasting to be still a size thirty waist, of which he was immensely proud, Philip wore his trousers a little too low for his age. Thirty-two, despite the primping, he looked every day of it. Philip never exercised. When any weight came, it came only on as a bump on his gut and flopped over his belt. Rather than exercising, Philip chose to avoid carbohydrates. Narrow shoulders, and pencil legs, coupled with the way he rubbed his palms together when talking, especially when pitching products to clients, put one in mind of a praying mantis. Preened, handsome was beyond his reach, and when naked, even Jane often thought of him as an unattractive option. An over-large mortgage and the misery of shared or bedsit accommodation as singles kept many London couples bound together more securely than most religious doctrines could ever hope to achieve.

Philip prepped his centrepiece ingredients, slicing everything meticulously, and switched on the oven.

A beep from his phone interrupted his thoughts, and he picked it up—a selfie from two of the gang already in Birmingham propping themselves at the Holliday Inn Bar! A shiver of excitement ran through him as his fingers tapped expertly. 'Can't wait ... b in at 11!'.

Salting a pan, he boiled a kettle and put the potatoes in. Twelve quail eggs went into his egg-steamer—picked up at the last trade show—he poured the measure of water in and set it to hard boil. He adored the egg-steamer. Philip was a fan of gadgets generally, but especially kitchen gadgets. The phone beeped again. This time a close up of somebody's cleavage filled the screen, and he snorted with laughter. 'I c angela has arrivd' he replied, a smiley face with goggle-eyes finished the line.

Tailing the asparagus spears, once he rinsed them, Philip put a small amount of water in a pot, he dropped in his 'everypot lotus leaf steamer' before putting the twelve spears in. Taking four rectangular dinner plates from the cupboard he scattered a small handful of rocket leaves onto the middle of each plate and tidied each of them to a tighter circular bed before surrounding them with layers of his prepped vegetables.

Another beep. Angela responded with, 'If you recognise my puppies that quickly you must have been watching them more than I thought!'. Philip shook with laughter. Flipping back to the previous picture, he expanded it and noticed a small mole on the left side of her right breast: 'The little moley on ur right titty gave the game away darling!' he sent back, knowing it would send Angela flying to a mirror to check. Pleased with his improvised response, his shoulders minced proudly as he walked across the kitchen.

The dressing made and cooled, he sliced the asparagus before dipping the stalks in it to leave them soak.

Jane struggled through the door and into the kitchen with three bottles of Sancerre and three bottles of Argentinian Malbec; she bashed the bottles noisily off everything possible as far as Philip could work out.

"What if he's a beer drinker?" Philip asked when she dumped the two bags up next to him. Just on fire tonight, he thought. Wickedly witty Winston. On fire!

"Oh sod off Philip," Jane's mood hadn't lightened; she wasn't in any mood for Philip's pernickety smart-arse comments, alongside his obsessive food primping.

"If he doesn't drink wine he can drink something soft. He'll probably bring his own beer. Men always do—especially that type darling," she tried to recover the situation a little: Philip's face had twitched in the way she'd come to recognise as an imminent onset of the sulks with her. "I'm sorry. I didn't mean to snap earlier," Philip's sulks could go on for hours, and that wouldn't do for an evening with guests, and one of those her own underling from work. "Going to the offy in my heels, and dressed like this on top of it wasn't part of my evening's plan. I'm frozen."

Philip half-smiled at her, and she knew she'd recovered it.

"Get the place ready while I finish this," his eyes gestured to the flat. "That'll warm you up."

"Are you doing starters and dessert?" Jane put the question in a way that implied she'd forgotten to put in the 'what' and 'for'.

Freezing for a moment, Philip glanced across the kitchen before nodding. "I'll add some chopped tomatoes to last night's dahl with some of the deli-bread? That'll warm them up after the walk from the station, and it'll taste like it's taken hours to cook. I got a lemon flan of sorts the other day, and I can drizzle some raspberry coulis over that later on. But hey! Don't worry about what I'm doing," Philip gestured with flapping wrists for her to pick up the pace and get the flat sorted out. Just like in America he thought, 'everything left to him!'. He could've screamed. Should've screamed then!

Jane carried on once she opened the wine and poured herself a large glass of Sancerre; with the other two in the fridge, she poured Philip a large Malbec and decanted another bottle with the first into an unusual carafe he'd found at the last London Olympia Show. Bashing the cushions, she tidied various things that she felt had gone astray, lit some scented candles, put a couple of tall tapered ones on the fireplace mantle in front of the large mirror to improve the ambient light, turned off the overhead lights as the timers had kicked in, and all the lower side lamps were now on, and looked about; she looked at Philip.

"The table?" Looking back his face pretending a light-heartedness. "Are you planning to eat off our trays on our laps?" 'Bloody hell woman!', his mind screamed, but Philip maintained his decorum.

To eat at the table required the moving of an armchair into their bedroom, removing two table-seats from the bedroom, and then fiddling about with opening out a small double-leaf Ikea table, that acted as a pot stand by the window. Jane also needed to find and throw a cloth over it, to hide the unsightly circular plant stain; he'd warned her about that, but did she listen? It took her a few minutes before everything was wiped and the table was finally set.

Topping up their wines, their eyes avoided the others.

Just like Montana! Her friend, Emily: Emily from Brighton, with a weird American accent, and a deep voice like a man. Well, she was a card! It's lovely here, she'd told them. Summer! Not like England, 'We get a proper summer here in Montana'; eight days they stayed: eight days of rain, and it was freezing once the night came. Freezing! Ice and everything on the car! In September! They should've known. One of the airports had the word 'glacier' in its name! That should have been a hint at least. But no! Her friend, Emily, bloody Bagpuss's sidekick, she knew best! Of course she did! Allowing himself a long draw from his Malbec, he sucked a deep breath through his long thin nose.

With the olives back in the fridge after deciding they didn't fit, he removed the roasted cherry tomatoes from the oven, put them to one side, and placed two non-stick frying pans and one tiny steel pan with an inch groundnut oil on the oven top. The oil pan he put heat under and once it was scorching he added the garlic and ginger wafers in separate small bunches until they crisped up; he scooped them out with a frying mesh gadget from the now defunct 'Reject Shop' drying the oil off with a kitchen towel and put them aside. Carefully placing three tomatoes in the middle of each of the rocket bundles with a little chopped onion on top, it now made a colourful circle in the middle of the plate. Three quail eggs to each rocket nest, as he thought of them, finished the presentation.

"Very pretty," Jane smiled as she passed by on her way to the bin. The wine had hit home.

His phone beeped again. Another selfie, with two more people now having joined the first three. A small squeak of laughter escaped from Philip. Jane peeped over his shoulder to look.

"Who's she?" She asked.

"Which one?"

"The pretty one, of course. What's her name?" Jane didn't care, but idle curiosity prompted her questions, and she knew Philip loved to talk about his colleagues.

"Oh, that's Melanie. She reps for the German Jewellery group—you remember them? The ones with all the pearls, and ribbon work. I showed you their catalogue. Mel does really well," unwitting admiration crept into his response.

"Is she married?" Jane scanned the room to see if anything was amiss.

"God no!" Philip huffed his response and shook his head. "She's an absolute tart! She'll spend the whole show man-hunting!"

"I see," Jane raised her eyes, now more curious than she'd been.

"You see?" Philip laughed at her knowing tone. "She'd eat someone like me alive, and spit me out before she even started on her main!"

Jane smiled and continued straightening the cushions on their sofa. That doesn't say a lot for me, she thought, and she looked back at Philip who'd turned, obsessively fiddling at his plates again.

Another text arrived. Jane having drifted nearby once more peeked over his shoulder to see it with him. A close up of two more cleavages with the message 'recognise these loverly?'. Snorting, Philip felt Jane go still beside him.

"It's not what you think!" Philip defensively scrolled back through the timeline and grovelled about the previous texts. He showed her his bright idea on Angela's and explained this to be just an extension of that joke.

"Didn't realise you were all so physically intimate," Jane shook her head in slight bewilderment; she knew Philip wouldn't be messing around—he just didn't have it in him, or at least not from what she'd ever seen.

"We need to finish everything," she suddenly remembered leaving various bits of clothing lying around on the bedroom floor. It wasn't unusual for someone to want to have a look about, and she didn't want to come off as a slob. "We can discuss your booby friends later."

Philip popped the bread in the oven to lift it. The soup was hot and ready, so he turned the heat off. Everything was ready or just needing a final touch before serving. They only required the guests to arrive, chit-chat introductions, a couple of settling compliments all round, everyone take a pew by the table, drinks for all, cheers all round, and a big well done for Philip. With any luck, they might even have a nice evening. For a change.

The doorbell sounded. Smiling at Philip, after a quick glance around, Jane pressed the entrance buzzer to release the outer door from the latch, before a final swift, nervous sweep of the room.

"Did we forget anything?"

Philip shook his head; he couldn't see anything amiss. Footsteps on the hallway tiles neared, and a polite double tap sounded at the same time as the outer door was pushed to, a little harder than necessary.

Lauren stuck her head in and smiled widely.

Jane greeted her with a hug, taking her into the living space to enable her partner behind to actually get inside too.

The door pushed in, and the towering figure of a man stuck his head in.

"DARREN?" Jane spoke before she could stop herself.

"Jane!" A wide-eyed Darren responded more quietly, but also without thinking.

"WHAT?" Lauren roared, quicker than Jane would have ever thought to have given her credit for; her head swivelled between them. "YOU BASTARD! YOU TOLD ME THOSE TEXTS WEREN'T FOR YOU! YOU SAID THEY WERE FOR YOUR MATE 'DAZ'!"

Pausing in thought, she looked directly at Jane and froze in shock, and a look of disgust filled her expression.

"YOU? You're the 'JANE' who couldn't wait to suck 'DARREN'S' soapy shower cock!" Lauren pointed at Jane before being cut off.

"STOP!" Jane was all too aware that Philip had moved into the side of them and was now listening.

Philip turned his Haloumi steaks on the plate over, and they were now ready for the pan. Initially he hadn't been listening as Lauren entered; he liked to imagine the flat bigger than it was and had found it comforting to do so. His pale features drained of what little colour they'd managed to muster in the cooking process and as he turned, he digested everything being said. Deep in his gut the resentment of Jane's domination of him and the utter humiliation he was facing exploded. Philip Winston did something he'd never done before, and thought he'd never do—he lashed out with his fist in rage, and Jane turning towards him took it full on the chin to be sent stumbling across the room. Oscar, a traditionalist man's man, reflexively reacted; his larger manly fist connected with Philip's jaw sending him stumbling after her with the words "Don't ever hit a woman!" spurting out.

The swiftly swigged glasses of wine, the shortness of breath from their surprise and shock, and with the solid wallops both received; Philip and Jane were out cold.

Oscar and Lauren looked at them both sprawled on the floor like crime scene victims; their eyes went backwards and forwards between the bodies before Oscar finally leaned over and checked Philip's neck.

"He's breathing," he sighed with relief. "He's just out cold. I might have hit him a bit too hard— he's a bit skinnier than I thought."

Lauren did likewise with Jane, glaring at him as she did so. Nodding that Jane was doing the same, she was still too livid to speak.

"Her? HER!" She growled, through gritted teeth but couldn't bring herself to look at Oscar. "You had to fucking pick her?"

"I didn't know it was 'Her!'," Oscar shook his head to explain. "You said she was an uptight cow—that wasn't wha-," Oscar shut up. A slight flaring of her nostrils warned him he needed to stop.

Lauren rose and looked at the door.

"I'm going home," she walked out, less than five minutes after she'd walked in.

Oscar looked at the two unconscious bodies. 'I didn't want to come here anyway', he thought. Following her, he pulled the door to, gently. Beckoning Lauren not to slam the front door when she turned to yank it, she waited, snuffling angrily, and gritting her teeth. Once outside she heaved it to with a force almost enough to take it off the hinges; her glare dared Oscar to comment.

They headed for home. The four hundred metre walk to Gunnersbury Park Station was silent. Along the way, Lauren decided against the awkward tube journey, and the two train changes it involved. The taxi ride was short. Silent too. The row that went on until the early hours was long and loud; their neighbour above was eventually forced to bang on the floor with a shoe, as he roared at them to shut up.

Waking the following morning to the usual sounds of aeroplanes their Osterley flight-path-flat lay in, and they just couldn't get used to, they met at the bathroom door. Oscar cramped up several times on the two-seater sofa, and missed his 'early bird' class; Lauren cried herself to sleep, and her eyes were circled in red, inflamed skin where her tears had reacted badly with the cheap liner she'd bought a batch of for the secret Santa office presents before Christmas.

Apologies and promises of all sorts were made by Oscar over coffee. Nobody left. There was nowhere for them to go.

§

Coming to, shortly after Lauren and 'Darren' had slipped out, and seeing Philip unconscious, Jane roused him with a damp cold cloth while holding him and sobbing her apologies. They both cried. Philip more than Jane. They eventually drank themselves to sleep. Jane slept poorly; she fidgeted most of the night with uncomfortable groin burn and stinging eyes and hoped 'Darren' hadn't given her something. Finally waking in the morning alone in the bed, feeling hungover, and as though she'd been in a car accident, she rose reluctantly.

The four circles of food on the plates still looked pretty, if a little dried out, as Jane lifted and scraped two plates into the bin when clearing up. She kept two back for herself over the weekend and foil-covered them—the expensive Haloumi she put in a small Tupperware container, deeming it better to save the food, than waste money on take-outs.

The estate agents were coming, and her mind was still working away at the limited options in her life.

Even if they made a quick hundred thousand from the flat, it only left her with fifty, plus some savings, and a three or four times salary mortgage—maximum four—if she went solo. That would probably allow her a crap studio somewhere so far out in the western suburbs of London that she might as well be commuting in from Wales. Philip was good with numbers. He'd come to the same conclusion, she thought; he had a car though and wasn't so dependent on London in his work. Planning how she might make things up to him, she thought to convince him that a new start in a new bigger flat, might just be best for them both.

Philip rose early and went straight to Birmingham. Taking some of Jane's foundation to cover his bruised jaw, he knew that it would be a talking point later that night.

Philip was a professional agent.

It was after all 'showtime', and whatever else, Philip knew and believed that the show must go on.

***

Haloumi Steaks Recipe

This is essentially a 'warm salad' dish. The Haloumi can be replaced by or shared with tofu, and cut in the same fashion. It makes a great main course, particularly when you're planning to have a starter and dessert, as it's quite light.

Ingredients
1 block of Haloumi, around 400g
8 med/small charlotte/waxy potatoes, boiled, cooled and then sliced thinly
4 beets (pickled and good sized)
1/3 of an organic cucumber thinly sliced
2 carrots (peeled and grated)
100g rocket or mixed leaf
12 quail eggs
12 asparagus spears, lightly steamed, halved lengthways
2-inch piece of ginger
4 garlic cloves
1 chilli very finely chopped

Dressing
3 tablespoons of mayonnaise
1 tablespoon of coarse-grain mustard
3 generous splashes of rapeseed oil
1/2 red chilli very finely chopped
(or a good splash of Thai sweet chilli sauce)
1 lime, juice only.

Mix all the dressing ingredients together with a fork, and briefly dip the asparagus spears in it after cooling them. Cook all the warm salad ingredients that need it.

Boil the charlotte potatoes in their skin as it keeps them firmer. Once cooked, run them under a cold tap and set them aside to cool a bit (warm is still fine). The quail eggs should be boiled and peeled. Thinly slice/shave the ginger and garlic and prepare a small pot with some ground nut oil in the bottom. Once the oil is piping hot quickly flash fry the thin slices into crisps and set aside on some kitchen roll.

Stand the Haloumi block on its side and slice lengthways through the middle to create two rectangular blocks half the depth of the original. Slice the rectangles along the hypotenuse to create four evenly sized triangles. Cook gently, turning every four or five minutes and allowing the edges of the Haloumi to slowly brown.

On the plate, place a bunch of salad leaves in the middle and surround them with grated carrot. Surround the carrot with the waxy potato slices, then beetroot and then (salted) cucumber slices. Create six wagon wheel spokes with the asparagus spear halves. Place the quail eggs in the leaf nest. Scatter the ginger and garlic crisps on top also.

With the remainder of the dressing draw a spiral over the salad nest. Add the Haloumi to the top. Very nice with a chilled Sancerre, or a glass of iced elderflower with a touch of mint.

**

Three Dead Dogs

"No! I don't miss having a psychopathic, mental, metal-head for a neighbour—if that's what you're asking me," Tom Fortune's reply to his wife's question carried a rare element of anger.

Where Tom had taken the conversation with his response wasn't addressing what Mary, his wife, was asking, but she understood where he was coming from, and his fuddled frustrated response.

"It's not, and you know it's not," Mary worked the butter into the flour without looking at the bowl. "I merely said, 'I wonder where he's gone'. That's all! I didn't like the man any more than you did! His dogs too! To up sticks and disappear like that. Nothing! Not a word! And, before you say it, I know he didn't speak to anyone here, or in the village, and you've never crossed swords with him at all, but that said, Tom, it's still a mystery alright. A mystery. Even Sergeant Halpin says it has him stumped, and the sergeant, as you well know, is a clever man when he wants to be."

"Aaah I know, Mary, I know what you're saying. Halpin's only been to college, girl—and that was only a college for the gards. Weren't they talking of little else in Jack Meade's and The Saratoga all last year. I'm sick to death of hearing about that fella," Tom wiped his mouth with the rough palm of his hand. "The man was a bad egg in every way, and I can only say it's good riddance and all that. He can strike me down if he has to, but that's how I feel."

From the freezer, Mary took a glass of water she'd put in half an hour earlier and splashed a tablespoon into the flour-butter mixture; she caressed the mixture slowly with the butter knife and her mind worried with thoughts over their missing neighbour.

"What do you think happened the dogs, Tom?" She hoped the question about the dogs would be less sensitive to Tom than questions over the man himself, but suspected that he'd react poorly now that his blood was up.

"The dogs?" Tom exclaimed and threw his hands in the air. "The dogs? How on earth would-? That bast-, that fella could've done anything with the dogs! I mean, he could've passed them along to the tinkers easy enough, couldn't he? It's not like they were strangers to him! Those bloody things never shut up, and they were used to being tied up all bloody day too. Perfect for the Tinkers. Perfect! That article could've sold the damned things as trained!"

"Now there's no need for language, Tom Fortune," Mary jabbed her butter knife towards him and shook her head in further admonishment. "I was merely speculating, that's all. It must be said, and I'm saying it, Tom. It's all a bit odd. That's all. No need to be going off like that—no need at all, now."

She returned her knife to the bowl and her caressing of the pastry mix.

"I'm sorry, Mary," a contrite Tom lowered his chin and looked over towards his wife. "I can't help it when I think of that fella, girl—and all the stuff he put us through. I just get a bit hot."

The pastry completed, Mary rolled it into a ball, wrapped it in cling-film, and put it in a bowl in the fridge before flicking the kettle on as she passed it.

"Would you like a bit of cake with a cup-a-tea Tom?" Mary decided to move their chat elsewhere.

"Aye, Mary," Tom licked his lips and tapped his teeth together in his mouth at the thought of food. "Aye, that I would. That'd be grand now."

"Are you going to go pick them goosegogs for me anytime soon?" Mary gestured to the garden with her head as she dry-dabbed her hands on the tea-towel. "I know 'tis warm out there, but it's likely to rain within the hour—I'll do the tea and cake, and you go do the picking—them new bushes are much thornier than the old ones your man next door ruined on us."

Reluctantly rising from his chair and the newspaper he was half-reading, Tom nodded to himself and made his way towards the door with a bowl that Mary handed him.

"Aye, true is that Mary—true is that," Tom muttered the words to himself as he made his way out the back door.

Early morning, late July sunshine flooded the back garden; at the end of his concrete and gravel patio in his shirt sleeves Tom leaned forward and stretched his back. Having expanded over the last few years, his gut now overhung his belt on the front and sides; a stiffness in his broad shoulders seemed to show up on a Saturday morning when he stayed in bed—this morning, the two conspired to awaken him to a body full of aches. Tom Fortune was an ox of a man. Originally from farming stock, he now ran his own groundworks company, and in a working life he'd never been shy of a shovel or a pick if the need called for it; it was machines that now did the work, and Tom cradled his gut wondering if he'd still have it if he'd laboured on the farm as his father had. His eyes fell on the goosegog bushes as he shook his head and stirred himself to movement. The earth beneath them had flattened once more, and after three years there were no signs of him having replanted the whole fifteen-feet run. Other than they hadn't yet managed to become a proper hedge, like the forty-year-old plants he'd dug out, there was nothing there to draw an eye. For that, Tom was mightily relieved.

In his family for six generations, the house he and Mary lived in was initially a single storey cottage with one window either side of the front and back door and was two rooms deep. A hundred odd years back one of his family had been more enthusiastic about breeding than was normal for the Fortunes; to accommodate the nine children, he'd added the second floor. Following this particular proliferation of the family, the work and income from the farm had sustained three separate Fortune families at the same time, which later resulted in an extension to one side. That ultimately became its own house. This hadn't ever been a problem when in the ownership of his ancestors. The extended family worked the land and the three outbuildings for forty years before things went into decline. Agricultural practises changed. Fortune families went back to being smaller, and some of the family chose migration to the bigger cities, Fortunes in search of fortunes—America, Australia, and England

took others and ultimately this left just one family—
Tom's father's—to run things. Over time, the rest of
the family lost interest in the farm, and Tom's father
sold the extension as a separate house. He also
sold a considerable amount of land, and for the
Fortunes, it meant they were no longer full-time
farmers—also, for the first time in many generations,
they had neighbours. This in itself wasn't a problem;
Tom's father Eamonn had sold the extension to a
former labourer on the farm called Benjy Breen,
known by his friends, and Eamonn too, as Brenner.
Brenner and his wife Nora lived happily next to the
Fortunes for fifteen years before an accident, while
fixing machinery in the Jute Factory on a nixer, took
Brenner's life. Nora lived on for a while as their
neighbour before also dying quite young at fifty-
eight; she kept her cancer quiet and had declined
the various treatments offered her. Empty for a few
years after that, for a while an elderly Eamonn
Fortune sought to buy it back. But, as often
happens in untimely death, it was intestate, and until
things were resolved, there was little he could do.
Eamonn passed away a couple of years after his
wife died, and Tom was left alone. By then, a grown
man of near forty-five years, Mary and he had been
an item for some years, and after a small time
passed they got married with a modest ceremony in
the church over in Faithlegg, where they had a
dinner and dance for their friends and family in the
Faithlegg Golf Club Hotel. Staying for just the one
night, they walked the half mile home with their
cases the following morning after breakfast.

Six years later, Paul Breen, also known as
Brenner, walked into their lives, and the house next
door.

Peeled, quartered, cored, and then fine-chopped, Mary scooped the skins from two Bramley cooking apples and watched Tom as he finally began to reach in and pick some goosegogs. Keeping an eyes on him, she flipped her pig-bin open and dropped the skins in. She shouldn't have mentioned that Paul Breen. Mary knew that the mere mention of his name was enough to set Tom off in a sweat.

She still remembered the day Breen arrived into their lives.

Tom was at work over the other side of the river; going across to Arthurstown on the first ferry just before six each morning, he'd been in the same routine for nearly a year, so it was a well-set pattern for them. Mary sat, at nine o clock, as she usually did, to listen to a few minutes of local radio with her cup of tea once Tom had left when a crashing bang against the inside of the house announced that there was someone next door. It nearly spooked the life out of her.

From the front room, she peered out through her net curtains to assess what was going on. A large white van sat half-reversed into the driveway next door. Unable to contain her curiosity, she wandered out to have a look; a man of about forty came out carrying a table and shouting at a younger man to pick up something. Giving out and swearing about something they'd obviously broken, the younger man laughed and replied. Hearing a tinker's voice, Mary decided to poke her curiosity stick a little firmer.

"Hello?" She greeted them both with a friendly questioning lilt to her voice. "Hello? What might be going on here then?"

Both men stopped. They looked over at her and said nothing; the tinker looked to the older man to deal with her.

"This is my place now," the older man said. "I'm Paul Breen, and my uncle used to own this before he died. This is mine now, so fuck off and mind your own business."

The tinker snorted with laughter, and both men continued loading the table and a box as though nothing had happened.

Mary Fortune was no shrinking violet; reared in a rural community, she was used to bluntness, ignorance, and even coarser manners if they came. This was different though—this fellow had a mean, menacing edge to him; his words carried a threatening air. Deciding to say nothing she went back indoors. An hour or so later both men got back in the van and left.

Later, she told Tom and was relieved that the men hadn't stayed or come back that night. Tom fumed and growled and stomped about the house huffing and clenching whatever muscle his mind imagined walloping or choking Breen with when he heard her story. Calming him over the weeks, by the time Tom finally did encounter Paul Breen, he hadn't forgotten, but he heeded Mary's advice to say nothing. Breen brought his three dogs to the house, where he left them tied them to stakes in the back garden. For a month they barked relentlessly, and Tom, at wit's end, invited a Garda friend over to witness the racket. Some quiet words in Breen's ear and the dogs came and went over the next few months. When summer arrived, Breen and his various oddball friends that showed up would often light a fire in the garden and loll about drinking and playing loud rock music into the early hours. Tom's contract work outside Arthurstown continued, and as the weeks went on the lack of sleep gnawed at him, causing Mary to worry that he'd make himself ill.

The back door opened. Tom stepped in with a large bowl of mainly reddish goosegogs.

"That should do the job, Mary," he nodded his satisfied agreement with his suggestion.

The bowl ready with water, she agreed and measured five hundred grams of them into a pot and let them sit in it to wash.

For a while, they sat together listening to the local news on the radio and supped their tea, accompanied by a small slice of Mary's fruitcake.

"That was a grand cake, Mary," Tom pushed his cup away and released a relaxed, contented sigh. "I'm going to prune a few of the stragglers back out there. Off-shoots are going off in every direction."

Rummaging around in the tool cupboard, he appeared moments later with a pair of secateurs.

Spreading butter around a Pyrex pie dish, Mary left him to it, and he wandered back outside. With her fingers in the water, she caressed the goosegogs, before topping, tailing, and slicing each one in half, before then placing them in the pot with the slices of apple.

Stopped before the goosegog bushes, Tom's eyes tracked across them; he struggled to see the vagrant shoots he'd noticed earlier which had drawn him back out to tend to them. They were young bushes yet, and needed early care and regular pruning if they were to thrive over the years. Tom Fortune knew his goosegog. It was the goosegogs that finally broke the camel's back for Tom, with

Breen, and as he stood before them in the warmth of the day, his mind wandered.

Breen had been entertaining a Tinker friend, and a notorious layabout from Passage East too, one Friday night in August three years back; the dogs slouched about, tied to the stakes, and Breen, after getting blind-drunk started shouting at one of them. One of the other rogues, Tom didn't know which, but suspected it was the layabout from Passage, well, he tried to appease him, but in their stupor, he ended up tripping them both, and Breen ended up in the goosegog hedge that Tom's grandfather had put in. Scratched and lacerated by the abundant thorns, after forty-odd years the bush didn't collapse to break his fall but instead almost embraced him; getting out of it was as painful as falling into it, and Breen looked as though he'd been dragged through the proverbial nightmare hedge when he finally stood upright once more. Having watched it happen, Mary told Tom about it before she went away that weekend to visit her sister in Dungarvan. They had a chortle together over breakfast.

Upstairs alone an hour later—Mary having gone off in her own car—Tom happened to glance out the window. In his garden with a pump weed-spray, Breen was aggressively spraying the length of the goosegog hedge; he looked as though he was still drunk. Shouting out the window at him, Breen ignored him. Stomping through the house, and around to Breen's front door—there was no bell, just a knocker—Tom slammed it six or seven times. Breen ignored it. Familiar with the door, Tom kicked the bottom left corner, and it swung in; he met Breen just as he re-entered the kitchen. Tom Fortune was not a man who got angry often; there hadn't been a need for Tom to develop, or nurture an inner mechanism for anger management. He swung once at Breen and connected with a haymaker that would knock out any ordinary man. Breen wasn't exactly an ordinary man, but physically he was no different; his head smashed into the side of the kitchen door, before it rebounded, bounced, and cracked off the stone kitchen floor. Breen never moved again of his own accord.

Tapping on the window as she watched Tom stand frozen before the bushes—he was doing that more and more these days, Mary thought, only a young man too, but she hoped it wasn't a sign of something—she opened the kitchen door.

"Is everything all right out there?"

Tom shook himself from his stupor.

"Ahh—no-no—I'm grand Mary," Tom lied, and smiled away her concern shaking his head. "I can't quite see all the bloody stragglers I was looking at earlier ... that's all."

Nodding, she scrunched her nose a little at Tom's unnecessary language flourish, and went back to her fridge.

Tom clipped at a couple of stragglers his eyes managed to trace, and he found himself on his knees as he reached in to remove them as far down as possible; with his hand on the cold earth, his thoughts sent a shiver through him.

Tom Fortune was no 'killer'. Not in any planned way. Justice can be fickle when deciding such things, and Tom suspected that "being a massive pain in the arse" and "killed my goosegog hedge!" were never going to be particularly successful in swaying a jury's sympathies. In truth, he had no idea, but thirty years of occasionally watching crime dramas suggested it was unlikely to hold much water. Looking at Breen lying on the floor, he noticed there was no blood. Needing time to gather his thoughts, he picked Breen up and slumped him over his shoulder; an unwashed slob, Breen stunk strangely of beer and rotten bananas. Outside the back door, all the dogs barked frenziedly at him; he walked down the garden until near the end, where the hazel hedge thinned, to where Tom himself had removed a couple of stray ash trees a few years earlier. Stepping back over into his own property, he struggled into the second and driest of his outbuildings which he used for his cement, sand, and lime storage and dumped Breen onto the floor. Back outside, Tom found his hands trembling, and beyond his control. The dogs were still going berserk. Sweating like a cart-horse, he could sense panic rising in him. With one of his larger heavy shovels in hand, it was the first thing that vaguely fitted what he needed, he went back next door and smashed the skulls of the three dogs. In the following quiet, Tom could finally think; there was a little bit of blood on the grass, but not much, and not particularly noticeable. Finally, going back through the house he closed the front door. On his way through the kitchen Tom picked up the ropes that Breen used as leads, and over the next ten minutes carried the ropes and the dogs to the building he'd dumped Breen in.

 That afternoon Tom went back across the river to Arthurstown in his open-backed van; he followed the back road to New Ross where he picked up two eighty-gallon plastic barrels, and twenty gallons of sulphuric acid. When he got back home he managed to get all three dogs into one barrel, and Breen into the other. Unsure what to do with the acid Tom left it to one side, but he got as much lime in with them as could fit. At least that would keep the smell down while he figured it out, he reckoned. Tom Fortune wasn't a slow man. Deliberate, and thoughtful, which to some seemed slow, Tom rarely made mistakes. He took his time at most things he did, Tom. The barrels he rolled in mud to blend innocuously with the rest of his equipment, and then went in and out of the building a few times to see if they jumped out at him in any way; still seeming too new, Tom muddied them more and threw cement bits on to them as naturally as he could. Following this, he went back to the other end, near the kitchen, ran his garden hose through the goosegog hedge, and washed down the grass areas the dogs had been tied-up in. Changing, he washed his own clothes and put them through the dryer. Later when they were dry, he changed once more and put them back on again, so Mary wouldn't think anything was off. After that, he had a cup of tea, spent an hour trying to calm himself, gave up, and took a spin over to Jack Meade's bar a couple of miles away, where he supped half a dozen pints of Guinness in the old bar, before driving home again. This was something he hadn't done for twenty years. Later in bed, he slept fitfully and fidgeted, worrying like a woman with nettles in her knickers all the following day until Mary finally came home.

Over the following weeks, Mary commented a couple of times over the fact that Breen wasn't using his house much, or even at all, as she hadn't heard him; he was a noisy so-and-so, after all. The goosegog hedge also died back, and they were both livid. Occasionally, Tom stomped around and hammered on Breen's door to have words with him, if Mary thought she heard something. As October came on, Tom put forward the idea that he needed to put in a new hedge if they wanted one, and also advised Mary that he'd need to bring the digger from the site over. Anything to do with diggers was a messy business, but a goosegog hedge had always been there for them, and they both wanted it back. Mary visited her sister in Dungarvan to avoid the dirt. Over that weekend Tom excavated a fifteen-foot long trench about seven feet deep. Into it went Breen and the three dead dogs, and he covered them a mixture of lime and sand. Unsure what else to do with it, the sulphuric acid went into the barrels, and Tom took those to the Arthurstown site when dropping the digger back; he shook them about before pouring the acid down the industrial drains. Scattering the extra soil beneath the hazel hedge, he also seeded the muddied area. Managing to plant the new goosegog bushes before Mary came back, Tom swiftly erected a concrete post and wooden slat fence behind them. Delighted with the new look, and extra privacy, should Breen and his cronies plan to do the same nonsense the following summer, Mary rewarded him with a lift to The Saratoga over in Woodstown, where he supped a few pints and had a game of cards with some friends.

§

Removing the pie from the oven, Mary stood it on her cooling tray for another fifteen minutes. After that she cut it into thirds, and halved a third onto a plate each, calling to Tom in the garden, knowing he'd take a while to finish up. To contrast the sharpness of the goosegogs, Mary put a scoop of chocolate ice-cream on the side of both. Looking out at her big, gentle man, she smiled as she watched him scurrying about like a lad home from school, trying to tidy up quickly so he could come and have his pie and ice-cream. You really wouldn't want to get between Tom Fortune and his goosegog pie, she thought.

Once or twice one of Breen's cronies knocked on his door. They never bothered Mary or Tom.

Sergeant Halpin came over a couple of times over the years, but mainly for a cup of tea and a slice of Mary's fruitcake. If Tom wasn't about, Mary asked the sergeant about Breen, but he always admitted to not knowing anything more, and to not really having any motivation regarding it. The investigation died in the starting blocks, and nobody cared if it went onwards, or nowhere at all. But, without fail, the sergeant noted one thing on every visit.

Mary Fortune made the best fruitcake in all of County Waterford.

***

Goosegog and Apple Pie Recipe

Ingredients
The Pastry
200g sieved spelt white flour (or plain flour)
80g wholemeal flour
1 tsp salt
1 tsp caster sugar
100g butter
Several splashes of very cold water.

Wet Mix
2 small cooking apples, peeled, cored, quartered and sliced
500g goosegogs (gooseberries), washed, topped tailed and halved.
100g brown sugar
100g caster sugar
3 tablespoons of honey
5 torn mint leaves

Making Goosegog & Apple Pie
To make the pastry (a couple of hours beforehand is best but even half an hour is okay)

Put all the flours, salt and sugar into a mixing bowl. Add the butter and rub with your fingers until there is a nice breadcrumb texture to the mix. Once this is done, take a glass of chilled water and dipping your fingers in it, splash some into the mix and caress the mix with a flat butter knife. Continue to caress and add an odd splash to bring the mix together into a pastry lump. Take it out of the bowl and make a ball. Wrap it in cling film and leave it in the fridge for whatever time you deem expedient to your needs (within 24 hours).

Once you remove the pastry ball, flatten it into something resembling a rectangle or square. Cut approximately one third from it for a lid and put it to one side. Roll the two thirds out to double its size without flouring the surface. Butter it lightly and fold it in half. Flour a board and roll out to a size large enough to fill and overhang an 8-10" Pyrex or quiche dish. Roll out the lid using the same technique and keep it on the roller. Fill the dish with the wet mix and add the cover, folding the over-hang base and lid into each other to create a nice crust. Three fork prongs, brush with a little milk and place in a hot oven on the middle shelf at 180 for about forty minutes...keep an eye after about 35, and leave to stand for at least half an hour before serving. Ice cream, cream, custard - the sharpness of the goosegogs ensure that almost anything sweet works with them.

***

Barry Jacques

Born in Waterford, Ireland; after meandering about for a
while, Barry has now settled in England, and spends most
of his time writing, teaching, or wandering about in the
Chiltern Hills with his wife and dog.

OTHER TITLES AVAILABLE FROM THIS AUTHOR

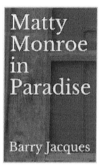

@barryjacques6   barryjacques@wordpress.com

Printed in Poland
by Amazon Fulfillment
Poland Sp. z o.o., Wrocław